MORE PRAISE FOR
ORGANIZED MONEY

"Money is leverage and power. In this striking book, both wide-ranging and fast-paced, Keith Mestrich and Mark Pinsky show that if progressives organize our money as well as our people and our ideas, we can build the muscle to make profound and lasting change. Now is the time for a progressive financial network."
      —Felicia Wong, president and CEO, Roosevelt Institute

"At a time of unprecedented and accelerating wealth inequality, *Organized Money* offers a breathtakingly bold vision to help level our country's economic playing field. . . . Mestrich and Pinsky, both pioneers in developing progressive financial system innovations, outline a strategy that cannot be ignored, even by those entrenched in the status quo."
      —Janet Murguía, president and CEO, UnidosUS

"*Organized Money* lifts up the new inclusive economy we are building and explains that it cannot succeed without a financial system that moves beyond shareholder primacy."
      —Jay Coen Gilbert, co-founder, B Lab
      and the B Corp movement

"I have long held that the 'three Bs' necessary for transforming our communities are the ballot, the book, and the buck. Utilizing their perspectives as seasoned activists and entrepreneurs, Mark Pinsky and Keith Mestrich succinctly lay out the case for 'the buck,' clarifying a sometimes unnecessarily complex conversation."
      —Marc Morial, president and CEO, National Urban League

"In this provocative and must-read book, Mestrich and Pinsky argue that the financial system is ultimately a public good, created by and for the public. And it should be governed as such. *Organized Money* provides a vision for a democratized financial system that serves, rather than exploits, we the people."

—K. Sabeel Rahman, president, Demos, and author,
Democracy Against Domination

"*Organized Money* is a compelling business plan for how we can bank and invest with truly progressive institutions, so each of us play a larger role in changing the world for the better."

—John Hickenlooper, former governor of Colorado

"*Organized Money* gives us a road map of how our nation's business, tax, and regulatory policies simply make the rich richer and everyone else poorer. . . . Mestrich and Pinsky go on to show us the solutions that progressives are exploring to use their capital to express their values, and how you can join them and fight back too."

—Morris Pearl, chairperson, Patriotic Millionaires

"*Organized Money* highlights the need to restructure and redirect the vectors of power and influence in the financial services industry. Mestrich and Pinsky provide us with provocative and unique perspectives and actionable ideas to move us off of the traditional path toward an alignment of capital flows, leadership, and values required to create the good society that works for all of us."

—Chris Varelas, co-founder, Aspen Institute's Finance Leaders Fellowship Program, and co-author,
How Money Became Dangerous

ORGANIZED
M❖NEY

HOW PROGRESSIVES CAN
LEVERAGE THE FINANCIAL
SYSTEM TO WORK FOR THEM,
NOT AGAINST THEM

KEITH MESTRICH AND
MARK A. PINSKY

THE
NEW
PRESS

NEW YORK
LONDON

Requests for permission to reproduce selections from this book should be made through our website: https://thenewpress.com/contact.

Published in the United States by The New Press, New York, 2019
Distributed by Two Rivers Distribution

ISBN 978-1-62097-505-3 (ebook)

Library of Congress Cataloging-in-Publication Data

Names: Mestrich, Keith, author. | Pinsky, Mark A., author.
Title: Organized money : how progressives can leverage the financial system
    to work for them, not against them / Keith Mestrich and Mark A. Pinsky.
Description: New York : The New Press, [2019] | Includes bibliographical
    references and index.
Identifiers: LCCN 2019018325 | ISBN 9781620975046 (hc : alk. paper)
Subjects: LCSH: Finance–United States. | United States–Economic
    conditions–2009- | Progressivism (United States politics)
Classification: LCC HG181 .M477 2019 | DDC 332.0973–dc23 LC record available at
    https://lccn.loc.gov/2019018325

The New Press publishes books that promote and enrich public discussion and understanding of the issues vital to our democracy and to a more equitable world. These books are made possible by the enthusiasm of our readers; the support of a committed group of donors, large and small; the collaboration of our many partners in the independent media and the not-for-profit sector; booksellers, who often hand-sell New Press books; librarians; and above all by our authors.

www.thenewpress.com

Book design and composition by Bookbright Media
This book was set in Minion, Euclid, and Frutiger

Printed in the United States of America

10 9 8 7 6 5 4 3 2 1

To Tilney, the kids, Shorty, and all the employees, clients, and
customers of Amalgamated Bank
—Keith

To Jennifer, Clara, and Nate
—Mark

Give me a place to stand and with a lever I will move the whole world.

—Archimedes

CONTENTS

PREFACE: THE PROBLEM

It's a "heads they win, tails you lose" game. What are your odds?

In 2008, the financial system broke, causing trillions of dollars of damage throughout the economy.[1] Many things changed in the riptide of the Great Recession, including personal financial habits, business practices, and presidents. People lost their jobs and struggled, lost their homes and moved, lost their savings and started over. Towns and cities grappled with economic volatility. Businesses slowed down, afraid to hire, and then cautiously grew. Foreign businesses took American market share. Inequality returned sharply to public awareness, while racial, gender, ethnic, and other forms of injustice made headlines, often bad news.

One thing that did not change, remarkably, is the financial system. The system that needed to change most did not change much at all because many of the people who knew it best and organized it had the most power and influence to shield it from change. They kept control of the institutions and the rules that governed them and made sure the future of finance worked an awful lot like its past—but more profitably. Leading up to 2008, the financial system worked to maximize private profits by accepting federal government subsidy

in the form of a safety net—the safety net that caught it when it col-
lapsed. A decade later, it is largely the same.

It is a system of private gains and socialized losses.

On the campaign trail in 2008, Barack Obama drew a bright line
around the financial services industry. "Let me be perfectly clear,"
Obama said in Reno, Nevada, on September 30, "The fact that we
are in this mess is an outrage. It's an outrage because we did not get
here by accident. This was not a normal part of the business cycle.
This was not the actions of a few bad apples."²

Obama laid it out plainly. "This financial crisis is a direct result
of the greed and irresponsibility that has dominated Washington
and Wall Street for years. It's the result of speculators who gamed
the system, regulators who looked the other way, and lobbyists who
bought their way into our government. It's the result of an economic philosophy that says we should give more and more to those with
the most and hope that prosperity trickles down to everyone else;
a philosophy that views even the most common-sense regulations
as unwise and unnecessary. And this economic catastrophe is the
final verdict on this failed philosophy—*a philosophy that we cannot
afford to continue*" (emphasis added).³

Candidate Obama sounded firm. If elected, he was promising
far-reaching structural change—equitable change. He sounded as
if he would take prisoners, including speculators, regulators, and
lobbyists. To his progressive backers, it sounded like a call for progressive financial policy change rooted in a direct assault on conservative ideology, known as market fundamentalism. It seemed to
be a call to action against the market fundamentalists. It sounded
like a demand that private gains carry public responsibilities and
deliver public benefits. It sounded as though an Obama administration would be ready to write that into law.

When Obama took the oath of office as president of the United
States on January 20, 2009, nothing was more important or more

urgent than fixing the financial system. His team—led by Secretary of the Treasury Timothy Geithner and National Economic Advisor Larry Summers, working hand-in-hand with Federal Reserve Board of Governors Chairman Ben Bernanke—went to work.

Waiting for Obama in the Oval Office was a new report from a special panel convened by Congress to study the collapse of 2008 and recommend policy changes. "As financial markets grew and globalized [over decades leading to the financial crisis], often with breathtaking speed," the Congressional Oversight Panel's Special Report on Regulatory Reform lamented, "the U.S. regulatory system could have benefited from smart changes. But deregulation and the growth of unregulated, parallel shadow markets were accompanied by the nearly unrestricted marketing of increasingly complex consumer financial products that multiplied risk at every stratum of the economy, from the family level to the global level. The result proved disastrous."[4]

There was bipartisan consensus on that point.

The financial crisis was the product of "the spectacular excesses and catastrophic failures of the past decade," the *Wall Street Journal* editorialized, echoing candidate Obama and the congressional panel. In public, at least, the *Journal* was pointing fingers at the financial system, if not more directly at specific individuals or institutions.

By early 2009, most progressives hoped far-reaching, fundamental financial reforms would produce a system of private and broad societal gains supported by a public safety net. For a few months—from President Barack Obama's inauguration until the Obama economic team unveiled his financial reform plan in late March—progressives envisioned a new financial era and the corresponding policy changes that would bring. Like the New Deal but better.

In late March 2009, Geithner and Summers put the Obama plan in motion.

The venue for the rollout was an elite gathering of financial titans selected by the *Wall Street Journal*. It was called, immodestly, the Future of Finance, and the participants were, according to the *Journal*, "100 of the brightest minds in finance."[5]

"The two-day conference will include a group of financial luminaries," the *Journal* promised, "including Goldman Sachs co-president Gary Cohn, Blackstone Group co-founder Steven Schwarzman, BlackRock co-head of fixed income Peter Fisher, Kynikos Associates founder James Chanos, star analyst Meredith Whitney, and TIAA-CREF CEO Roger Ferguson Jr."[6]

The participant list sparkled with the wealthy, powerful, and famous.[7] Libertarians, conservatives, moderates, progressives, and liberals, they were the keepers of the financial system. It also included a few outsiders, including one of the co-authors (Pinsky), who had a ringside seat throughout the discussions.

"Their goal," the *Journal* laid out: "Nothing too intimidating. Just fix everything." They were there "to discuss not just how to restart the global financial system, but how to reconstruct it, so both the spectacular excesses and catastrophic failures of the past decade can be avoided."[8]

In fact they were hand-selected by *Wall Street Journal* editors to defend the world they had helped create. No surprise, then, that the convening was a war council for continuity. Events since have proved they were effective beyond expectations: a decade later, the 2017 tax cuts produced record 2018 earnings and profits across the board for many of the same financial institutions.

For conservatives and financial executives, the story line from 2008 through the Obama era is a narrative of affirmation. For progressives and financial reformers, it is an instructive cautionary tale of money muscle, the power and influence that comes from organizing other people's money.

In his opening comments to the financial titans, Geithner echoed the challenging tone of President Obama. "People across the country are angry and frustrated, as they should be, that this economy, the United States of America, got itself in the position where enormous damage has been done as a consequence of a long period of excess risk-taking without meaningful adult supervision."[9] Geithner's tough talk had a bark, but would it have a bite?

"We have a much more complicated financial system than just a system that relies on banks, and banks can't compensate for the broader dysfunction," he said ominously, as if preparing to hold the whole lot jointly accountable. In other words, it's complicated and the financial system did not have the ability, at least at that time, to get itself out of the trouble it was in. "So, to address that," Geithner reasoned, "we believe we have to provide very substantial forms of financing to help get those markets going again."

The whole financial system is to blame, so we need to invest "very substantial" capital into those same systems? Come again? The progressive new president was doubling down . . . on the old model?

"And we're going to have to do this with the rest of the world, because unless we move with the world and bring the world to higher standards, prudential standards," Geithner explained, "the effectiveness of what we do in the U.S. is going to be eroded again."[10]

The same American system, practices, and standards that led the financial system to implode is the solution? The money titans listening to Geithner that night knew then that they had won even before the Obama proposal saw the light of day.

When you make yourself indispensable, you are powerful. When your government cannot fix a problem without you, you are politically powerful. When supply and demand will not meet without you, you are economically powerful and socially essential. When global financial markets would stop unless someone keeps you going, you are systemically important—and remarkably powerful.

It was not their money or their ways of life that they came to defend; it was their life's work—the financial system that maximized private gains by socializing risks. To be in that room, to hear what got discussed and what got ignored, was to witness a revolt of the haves.

When the odds and public opinion are against you, even when you are among the wealthiest people on earth, you need to remind yourself that you have power. Lots of it. So you flex your muscles. Inside the Future of Finance gathering, the spirited indignation of the titans defined the mood.

"I think we're really caught up right now in a political frenzy and it's denying any intelligent analysis," Steven Schwarzman of the Blackstone Group snarled with the force of the multi-trillion dollar private equity balance sheet he oversaw, "and we're risking throwing sand in the gears of a market system" that he inaccurately claimed had kept running smoothly when the global economy seized up in 2008.[11]

There were a lot of angry, bitter people throughout the nation in March 2009—people who had lost their homes, their retirement money, their jobs, their businesses. Main Street wanted justice and compensation, and many elected officials in Congress felt pressure to rein in the too-powerful forces of finance that had broken the housing market and the global economy.

Arthur Levitt, the soft-spoken and highly regarded former chairman of the Securities and Exchange Commission (SEC), which oversees large swaths of the financial securities industry, told a *Journal* reporter, "We're now shifting to the left pretty far in terms of business bashing, and it's reached the extremes of incivility that just are intolerable."[12]

Gary Cohn of Goldman Sachs (later national economic advisor to President Donald Trump) prescribed a return to business as usual. "I think the need for the goods and services that we provide and we facilitate is higher today than it ever has been," Cohn reasoned.[13]

Progressive finance experts saw Obama's proposal for what it was—a conservative policy coup on top of an economic subsidy rooted in a financial deception. Within a few days, Nobel Prize–winning progressive economist Joseph Stiglitz objected to Geithner's scheme. "The Obama Administration's $500 billion or more proposal to deal with America's ailing banks has been described by some in the financial markets as a win-win-win proposal. Actually, it is a win-win-lose proposal: the banks win, the investors win—and taxpayers lose."[14]

He described the Obama administration's proposal as "a 'partnership' in which one partner robs the other. And such partnerships—with the private sector in control—have perverse incentives, worse even than the ones that got us into the mess."

The particular incentive at the heart of the financial system is a complex system of rewards and subsidies to encourage risk-taking and profits in support of public policy goals including, but not limited to, economic growth and employment. The system comprises government spending, tax incentives, a legal framework, and public persuasion. It boils down to private gains made possible by socialized losses—that is, a taxpayer safety net. And it carries with it the potential to incent too much risk, and that is called "moral hazard." Moral hazard is the risk that you will make a different—and riskier—decision if someone else is paying your bill or picking up the pieces after you, that is, if you do not bear the consequences of your actions. It's how you might act if, for example, the government protected you from the impact of your lending products and practices by providing a safety net. Or—to witness theory in practice—it's how many mainstream financial institutions acted during the predatory mortgage lending debacle that culminated in the Great Recession.

"The trouble with Wall Street isn't that too many bankers get rich in the booms," explains conservative Wall Street pundit James Grant, editor of *Grant's Interest Rate Observer*.[15] Grant's views go so hard to the right that they seem to come around to the progressive left. "The trouble, rather, is that too few get poor—really, suitably poor—in the busts. To the titans of finance go the upside. To we, the people, nowadays, goes the downside. How much better it would be if the bankers took the losses just as they do the profits." [16]

Preventing that—not holding financial titans and their investors accountable for their actions—is why so many titans participated in the Future of Finance strategy session. They came together to preserve their financial franchise.[17]

Nomi Prins has studied the intimate interdependent relationships among powerful politicians and powerful financial titans. She believes the economic and financial bonds among them are more influential now than ever: "Since America's latest elected leader [Obama] pressed the pretense of financial reform instead of actually pushing for real reform, bankers can do greater damage than ever before," she wrote in *All the President's Bankers: The Hidden Alliances That Drive American Power*. "It no longer matters who sits in the White House. Presidents no longer even try to garner banker support for population-friendly policies, and bankers operate oblivious to the needs of national economies."[18]

Wall Street Journal editor Alan Murray wrote in his wrap-up summary of the March 2009 Future of Finance gathering that bringing one hundred of the brightest minds in finance together for a few days to fix "the spectacular excesses and catastrophic failures of the past decade" was itself a failure. "The participants were challenged to set aside, as much as possible, their self-interest, and consider changes that were good for the financial system and society overall. But inevitably, self-interest reared its head."[19]

Some things never change, it seems.

Secretary Geithner's career after he left government and joined Wall Street is a case in point. Geithner became president of Warburg Pincus, a legendary New York investment firm that owned, among other companies, Mariner Finance. A 2018 investigation of Mariner by the *Washington Post* found a series of predatory lending practices, one worse than the other. The *Post* titled the article, "'A Way of Monetizing Poor People.'" The article compared Mariner's practices to Geithner's rhetoric, quoting from the former secretary's book on the financial crisis: "Many borrowers, especially in subprime markets, bit off more than they could chew because they didn't understand the absurdly complex and opaque terms of their financial arrangements or were actively channeled into the riskiest deals." Geithner did not talk to the *Post* for its story.

In late 2018, Robert Kuttner of the *American Prospect* and a noted progressive economic historian looked at the missed opportunities of March 2009 with a wider view and a generalized sense of failure: "In the United States, the bipartisan financial elite escaped largely unscathed," he wrote in late 2018 in the *New York Review of Books*. "Barack Obama, whose campaign benefited from the timing of the collapse, hired the architects of the Clinton-era deregulation who had created the conditions that led to the crisis. Far from breaking up the big banks or removing their executives, Obama's team bailed them out. None of the leading bankers whose fraudulent products caused the crash went to jail; criminal prosecution took a back seat to the stability of the system. . . . But the economic security of most Americans dwindled, and the legitimacy of the system was called into question. One consequence has been the rise of the far right; another is Donald Trump."[20]

Kuttner concludes that the financial collapse and the absence of meaningful progress is an example of a turn in history that "failed to turn." He writes, "Instead, the old order reasserted itself, and with calamitous consequences."[21]

Let's don't do that again.

In this book, we propose a strategy to organize the power of money so that the progressive movement can make the most of a seismic shift we see building throughout finance and business. Our purpose is to influence the mainstream financial system and the policy makers that shape it by demonstrating the value and urgency of progressive approaches to money.

To that end, we envision a market-scale, full-service progressive financial network (PFN) to organize at least $1 trillion of the considerable wealth that progressive people and enterprises hold today. That network will include banks, insurance companies, credit unions, investment banks, venture capital and private equity firms, impact investors, community development financial institutions (CDFIs), socially responsible investment managers, and individuals. It will be profitable so that it can be sustainable, with the understanding that profit is not the same thing as greed. There are countless ways for financial institutions to make profits at different levels over time that make it possible—often more likely—for them to prosper economically as well as socially.

That infrastructure will rest on the principle our nation's financial system was founded on—that public gains need to balance private ones. That principle has been undermined by conservative and libertarian pursuit of self-interest beyond reason to greed shaped by an ideology we call market fundamentalism. Our strategy rejects market fundamentalism in favor of progressive finance—allowing for private gains while expecting inclusive and sustainable social, economic, environmental, and political outcomes as well.

In contrast to conservative finance—a system of private gains leveraged off public risk sharing—progressive finance is a balance of public and private gains based on public and private risk sharing.

To implement a progressive finance strategy, the left is going to have to face up to some shortcomings of its own. Progressives undervalue and underutilize organized money, the management, structure, systems, and control of our financial lives and our financial world. Instead they rely heavily on organized people and organized government action, often with incomplete and frustrating results. Making things worse for themselves, progressives give control of their money to conservatives.

Organized money holds immense power and influence, which we call money muscle. The U.S. financial sector is the dominant economic, policy, political, social, and cultural force in the world. It largely determines who in the private and public sectors gets to do what with the extraordinary amount of money in play. And it is deeply and proudly conservative. The U.S. government is powerful in other ways, but it is in fact dependent on and shaped in significant and substantial ways by the financial sector.

The important question is not whether our world revolves around organized money (it does) or whether it is organized by government or markets (they are inseparable and interdependent). The key is who controls how money is organized and what they do with it.

The evidence is compelling that corporate CEOs, including financial CEOs, tend to act in support of conservative outcomes. CEOs in the money business favor Republicans over Democrats by nearly a two-to-one margin, according to a March 2019 study by the Project on Corporate Political Spending of the Harvard Law

School Program on Corporate Governance.[22] The study notes that
the CEOs of the fifteen hundred public companies they examined
have "disproportionate influence over American policymaking
and politics," the authors conclude. They comprise less than one
one-thousandth of U.S. voters and their corporations are six one-
hundredths of all U.S. companies, yet they are responsible for more
than 30 percent of private-sector employment, 40 percent of sales,
and 50 percent of pre-tax profits.

"Most importantly," the authors emphasize, "their positions
enable CEOs to influence policymaking and politics through two
important channels," political spending and "the significant impact
that the expressed views of CEOs have on policy discourse and pol-
icymakers. . . . Because CEOs are (rightly) viewed as individuals
of high standing, authority, and expertise, their expressed policy
positions have long been relatively influential."

Progressive strategies have driven many transformational social,
cultural, economic, environmental, and political changes behind
the principle that society's common good is the responsibility
of each of us individually and all of us together. The progressive
movement today comprises individuals and institutions working for inclusive prosperity; equal racial, gender, ethnic, national,
and sexual justice; social and economic mobility; global economic
interdependence; peaceful resolution of conflicts; and sustainable
climate practices.

Most modern progressive movements in the United States—trust
busting under Teddy Roosevelt, the New Deal of Franklin Roosevelt, Lyndon Johnson's Great Society, the environmental
movement, community development, the Consumer Financial Protection Bureau—were government-centered interventions. That is,
government was or is the driving force. The civil rights, labor, and

women's movements organized people to drive government interventions. Gun control, Black Lives Matter, and other targeted campaigns are political strategies against government inaction; they are built on philanthropic and campaign finance. Together these progressive efforts are a pillar of civil society.

Yet these and other successful progressive gains are incomplete or, worse, are losing ground. Global corporations found creative ways to re-create trusts for a new era. Conservatives doggedly whittled away worker protections, retirement security, and other labor movement gains. The Reagan Revolution blocked the New Deal and dismantled much of the Great Society. Gerrymandering and attacks on voting rights, affirmative action, and other civil rights laws set back political justice. And on and on. Conservatives have organized people to fight progressive organized people and organized government to counter progressive policy gains. Progress takes two steps forward and gets pushed two steps back. Most progressives know that the movement as a whole is falling short and underperforming. And they are tired of it. Something is missing.

Conservatives organize people, government, *and money.* Conservatives hold unimpeded sway over organized money. Money muscle powers conservative strategies for social, cultural, economic, and political change on the principle that pervasive self-interest stirs good social outcomes. That is why our nation has recently moved substantially to the right—on civil rights, labor rights, gender equality, climate change, and racial justice, for example—even as we grew more diverse, more culturally and socially inclusive, and more environmentally active.

Progressives need to do more to organize money if they expect to compete and win. They need financial *systems* literacy—to understand financial power and how it works. Progressives let conservatives organize our money and leverage the power it brings them to suit their values, goals, and priorities. That means our money often works against us. Through the financial system, by the choices we make about how to organize money, progressives are funding our opponents. That is the problem we need to solve.

This book examines the deeply conservative roots, causes, sources, and influence of financial power. More important, it details a set of encouraging trends that are converging to create a gateway to the next progressive era, but they will not come together on their own. Progressives must see the potential to make themselves indispensable in the financial system (and therefore powerful) and take action to achieve that potential.

The solution is equally simple: progressives must organize money—theirs and others'—by increasing progressive ownership of financial institutions. We must form a market-scale network of progressive financial institutions working together.

When progressives stop funding our conservative opponents, put our money to work supporting our own progressive interests, and bulk up money muscle of our own, we will reduce the enormous power and influence that conservatives have in policy, culture, politics, and civic discourse. A progressive financial network will work for us instead of against us. It will give progressives the ability to push back against conservative money muscle in virtually all areas of law and policy, politics and public opinion, culture and society—not to mention money and finance. Organized money is the gateway to the next progressive era, and progressive money muscle is the key.

Progressives have the means—the wealth, the knowledge, and the expertise—to transform the financial system in service to progressive values, for the common good, and away from conservative outcomes. We offer this book to help you understand what we can achieve so that progressives will use our own money muscle in line with our values and goals to make the next progressive era structural, systemic, and enduring.

1

You and Your Money

If you don't know how the financial system works, it probably doesn't work for you.

Everyone organizes money. It's how we get things done. We are all connected through a global finance network that is incredibly complex and useful. Organized money runs like a nervous system through our lives, making the world as we know it work.

"Money has allowed us to develop the vast, intricate, and amazing modern society that we all share, that makes life worth living and money worth earning," explain economist Dan Ariely and his co-author Jeff Kreisler in their eye-opening book *Dollars and Sense*.[1]

We try to organize money—as individuals, nonprofits, businesses, and governments—to make our worlds work for us in ways we want. You do it. Retirees and kids do it. Women and men do it. The smallest enterprises and the biggest businesses in the world do it. Local food trucks, national hardware chains, and global construction companies do it. Nonprofits, churches, and hedge funds do it.

Governments do it. Political parties do it. Heck, even anarchists do it.

As a result, the ways we choose to organize money tell others about us. And we learn about ourselves. Do we buy fancy clothes? Help homeless people? Sell environmentally green products? Advocate for progressive, conservative, or other types of government policies?

How we organize money is also cultural (Do we spend to go to movies? Or to the beach?) and social (Do we focus on racial aspects of income inequality? Or quarterly corporate earnings?). Money is political, too, expressed in campaign contributions and policy lobbying.

We organize our money to live our lives the way we want to if we can. We plan our finances, or we figure everything will work out okay. Sometimes we think that our money is working against us. Most of us worry.

No one organizes money on their own. We depend on our financial institutions, along with financial markets, government policies, families, friends, experience, guile, and luck. The intricate money pathways that link each of us to others are potent channels. Individuals and institutions that own or control those channels are powerful and influential directly within their networks and indirectly because of them.

Mary, a teenager, saves the money she earns walking dogs to buy an iPhone of her own. She organizes her money in a bank with a branch in her neighborhood and tracks the latest technology.

Her neighbor Betty, a retired corporate executive, takes a retirement package in her mid-fifties to invest in her forever house and lives on a strict budget to make her pension last for thirty years or more. She organizes her money in a diversified investment portfolio managed by an independent financial advisor through several independent asset managers, banks, and insurance companies. Betty monitors major stock market indices like the Dow Jones Industrial Average and government reports on business performance.

Ron invests an inheritance of several hundred thousand dollars to start the business he dreamed of owning, while his brother Pete puts an equal amount in a low-risk annuity so that he can take a job that pays less but is close to home. Ron relies on his bank, an attorney, and an accounting firm. He is focused on news about his target market of commercial real estate developers. Pete is organizing with a bank, a pension fund manager, a money manager, and a financial planner. He wants to know what is going to happen with income tax rates so that he can plan for when to withdraw money from his retirement accounts—and so when he can retire.

Alicia buys a new car with cash she scrimped and saved. She does not have to worry about monthly payments or about a used car that might break down. She organizes her money in a credit union at work, where she saved for the car. She wants to know how her employer is doing to be sure her job is secure.

And Zeke juggles bills each month to make ends meet—keeping his home heated and his kids fed, if just barely. Zeke has a bank account, and he sometimes borrows from a payday lender. He organizes his money (a lot of it is money he owes) among the credit departments of utilities, stores, and several credit card companies (that help him skip payments or make minimal payments when he needs to). Zeke is alert for phone calls, emails, and snail mail bringing demands for payment.

The choices we all face are complicated and exhausting.

We open accounts (savings, checking, money market, cash management, investment, direct deposit, stored value) for convenience or for professional guidance. Or we don't. Instead we cash checks at work or at a payday lender. We pay cash or credit or debit. We pay monthly installments or refinance. We invest in fixed-income funds, equities, tax-free bonds, annuities, insurance policies, and money market accounts. We go to a bank or "bank" on our phones. We make a budget and keep to it or don't make one or don't keep to it. We try to understand what the federal, state, and local governments are doing—how *they* are organizing their money (our money, really)—and we respond the best we can.

We *save* money for when we need it by lending it to a bank as a deposit or we *borrow* money in a loan until we have enough of our own. We probably do not think about what our money is being used for or where the money we borrow came from. We *invest* our money so that other people will pay us to use it. We *spend* it on all sorts of things, some essential and some whimsical. We buy insurance in case something happens. Other times we *give* money away so that organizations we believe in—our faith communities, environmental groups, political candidates, social service organizations—can organize it for their own purposes. Sometimes we make contributions for tax reasons even though we are not deeply committed to the organizations we donate to.

Most people and businesses do not understand their choices or the consequences of their decisions. The consequences are personal, social, economic, and political. We make the best decisions we can, however, because we need to function financially to live our lives.

Most businesses face similar challenges and worries. When the world around them changes, they adapt. Reorganizing their money is essential but hard. Many businesses are reactive because they are not focused on or able to shape things in their favor.

A nonprofit women's health organization suspends a project because donations are harder to get due to political noise. It relies on a big bank to organize its money, including funds to meet payroll twice a month, emergency funds in case donations slow more, and its small pool of net worth that it has built over years. The big bank used to contribute a lot of money to the organization, but its giving priorities changed. The organization's board wonders if the bank caved to public pressure, but it's too much work right now for the nonprofit to even consider changing banks.

Even good things can bring difficult money decisions. A local solar installation company nervously adds staff when homeowners and businesses rush to get solar panels for fear that the 30 percent tax credit to encourage solar energy production will get eliminated. The tax credit survives the 2017 conservative tax reform bill only to be shoved aside by President Trump's tariff on imported solar equipment. The company cuts jobs but demand for solar remains high, and the owners are forced to use part-time workers as a hedge against the uncertainty and volatility. Even with strong demand, organizing money is harder than it used to be and the company's investors and lenders—banks, family, friends—are nervous about the future of the business.

Sophisticated small businesses, including small financial institutions, sometimes give way to the harsh financial realities they must organize around. A community development financial institution, or CDFI, tells local, low-income residents that it can no longer complete a long-awaited apartment building for 130 families because the Low Income Housing Tax Credits it plans to use are worth less under the new tax laws. Instead, it says it will pay to fix up a dozen small houses for families in need. It organizes money from faith-based investors, local community banks, a large institutional investor, even a single socially responsible fund manager. It relies on one of the nation's largest banks to keep it all organized because the community banks cannot handle it on their own; they would have to hire the same big bank, and that's expensive for everyone.

Major global companies start with far greater expertise, knowledge, and influence. They work under a financial market microscope and need to answer to many masters. Still, they organize money in many of the same ways but with advantages of wealth. Apple, the computer company, pays $38 billion in a special, one-time federal tax to get more control over its finances and production of its products (and, not coincidentally, to curry political favor that it can "bank" to use later). Many other companies do the same with the surge in profits from the 2017 tax bill, strengthening their ownership positions instead of investing in growth. Apple organizes its money by making the most of every part of the global financial marketplace; in fact, organizing money is a business that Apple is especially good at. But they rely on insurance companies, investment banks, banks, venture capital funds, and many other types of financial institutions.

None of us can organize money without skilled financial professionals and sophisticated financial intermediaries—banks, credit unions, money managers, pension funds, insurance companies, mortgage companies, brokers, dealers, investment advisors, financial planners, accountants, lawyers, and many others. That's one of the inescapable facts of organizing money—it takes a lot of expertise and experience to organize lots of peoples' and organizations' money. Money organizers get paid for their knowledge, experience, capacity, and advice.

Most of us are managing risks and opportunities with limited, often insufficient, understanding of money and the financial services industry. We bundle our trust with our money and hope for the best. And so we depend on financial professionals to tell us how to organize money and to make more money for us. To do that, they organize their money, too, in ways that make money for them. Financial institutions match those who want money with those who have it, and vice versa. This is called financial intermediation.[2] That means that they, too, rely on financial professionals, in the widening concentric circles that connect your savings account to global markets. In each concentric circle, financial institutions need to make money from those in the circle inside it or the system fails.

The U.S. financial sector today is roughly three times as large as it was sixty years ago, according to Thomas Philippon of New York University.[3] That is remarkable growth. It is the largest single sector in our economy—the big dog that wags all tails. Near year-end 2018, it totaled more than $110 trillion. For context, the total wealth in the world is not much more than double that amount.

In that time, Philippon has found, the financial system has not made itself more efficient—that is, it is not any more productive than it was sixty years ago, just larger.[4] That means it has to grow and find new ways of earning money while aggressively containing the cost of its raw material—money. Your money. Look at that another way: it needs to pay you no more than it used to for your money but make more profits using your money. Most of the new ways it has created for earning more money can be classified as derivatives—complicated financial products that are, in essence, bets on other financial products. If construction companies build homes and apparel companies make clothing, financial institutions manufacture financial products.

Using your money. In creative ways.

Many financial companies own or work with brokerages—intermediaries that buy and sell financial products for their customers for a fee. Both Charles Schwab and E-Trade are large brokerages. Customers put money into an account (a brokerage account) to pay for their transactions. When your money is not invested—if you have not made decisions yet what stocks to buy, for example—it is parked in a brokerage account until you are ready to use it. Brokerage accounts are generally safe and pay you modest interest. As far as you are concerned, the money in your brokerage accounts is waiting quietly for you to return.

Just below the placid surface of brokerage accounts is a fascinating and troubling illustration of how money organizers profit from their customers' funds. "The Bottom Line: Brokerages Are Getting Rich on Your Money," explains a 2018 *Wall Street Journal* exposé.[5]

Reporter Jason Zweig investigated brokerages, including Ameriprise Financial, Raymond James Financial, and others. He found that the brokerages bundled customers' idle money for their own use (they could replace it at any moment). They used it in a way that is much more profitable for them than for their customers, and they pocketed the difference. For the brokerages, idle brokerage account balances are a source of "low-cost funding," Zweig explains, because they can borrow it cheaply to use until it is needed again. "You've probably never realized how badly you could be getting stiffed," he concluded.[6]

It is totally legal, though the laws say that brokers must act in the best interests of their customers. Zweig's investigation questions what that means for brokerages. Similar questions surround many other financial products and practices.

"You have the right to change how they handle your cash, and you should," he concludes.

While your financial institution almost certainly organizes your money well and carefully, the question is, to what end? Who benefits most from your money?

Most of the time, you benefit through interest payments, dividends, or other returns. The people and enterprises that ultimately use your money—to buy houses or build factories, to pay for college—all benefit. The financial intermediaries, if they are doing their job well, always get paid. And when they profit from their work, they use some of that money to support the ideas, businesses, politicians, and other things they believe are good for the economy and for them. The choices they make reflect their interests and their priorities.

The key is that financial institutions tend to be successful, beneficial, profitable, powerful, and influential in proportion to how much of the money they organize comes from other people. Liberals and progressives have criticized financial institutions for profiting using "other people's money" for at least the last hundred years. In 1914, future U.S. Supreme Court Justice Louis Brandeis popularized this phrase when he published a series of articles that became a book called *Other People's Money and How the Bankers Use It*, in support of President Woodrow Wilson's New Freedom progressive agenda.[7] Since then many more, similar books with variations of Brandeis's title have joined the bookshelf.

Financial institutions are based on the business model of "leverage." In financial terms, that means making money from other people work for you because you own and control the intermediary that is organizing the money. The ownership share is described as equity, equity capital, or sometimes just capital. The twist here is that owners of financial institutions might actually own as little as 3 or 4 percent of the total worth of the company and leverage the rest. If the financial institution gets in trouble or fails, the equity owners are the first to lose their money, before other investors and lenders. When the enterprise does well, the equity investors do better than those with less responsibility. The basic model is known as risk-reward—the more risk you take, the higher reward you can get. For that reason, owners make the critical decisions about what companies do and how they do it. In publicly traded companies, equity is sold on stock exchanges, so many individuals own shares of stock in financial institutions—either directly or through mutual funds or other products that pool investments. Without significant share ownership, however, they have little effective control over decisions.

Equity owners hold substantial power and influence because of leverage. For each dollar of their own, they organize, manage, and control many dollars more—perhaps $10 or $20 or more—that come in the form of loans, deposits, or investments. Ownership gets you leverage; leverage gets you power; power gets you authority; authority gets you influence; influence gets you control; control gets you the independence and the freedom to act as you see fit.

It is not hard to see how that leverage translates into the business practices that the *Journal* found at brokerages. Owners' first obligation is to the financial interests of the company and its shareholders. After that, they have an obligation to act in the interests of their customers.

Almost all financial intermediaries leverage other people's money. Plainly, mainstream money organizers want to shape the financial system in ways that help them make more money. This may or may not make more money for you; your interests and theirs are not necessarily aligned. Likely, they use your money to do some things you like and some, perhaps many, you don't like. Are your retirement savings helping to finance the gun industry?[8] Is your bank donating to politicians who want to stop federal funding for Planned Parenthood? Is your retirement account manager giving priority to wealthy customers taking lucrative tax breaks that support gentrification of low-income communities?

Financial intermediation today creates distance between financial customers and their values. Unless you are wealthy and politically conservative, it is distancing you and your money from your values and impeding the societal progress that you would like to support. That is called, with a big-money word, disintermediation.

Most of us worry that we're overlooking important information affecting our money. We are. We overlook the fact that financial institutions—our money organizers—thrive by hiding in plain sight. They influence our lives far more than we know. Or care to think about. Our lack of awareness and attention helps them be very influential and powerful in business, culture, politics, policy, and your life. They further and perpetuate their own world views and not necessarily yours.

They want you to keep as much of your money with them as possible because that potentially makes you a more profitable customer, of course. And many provide you with more products because you give them more money to organize, while reducing or eliminating the fees that customers pay. They sell you products using insights from behavioral economics and algorithms based on large data sets that can induce you to use your credit card more, for example if you usually do not pay off the full balance due each month. That means they are earning interest from you each month. And the financial sector as a whole gives more money (some of it earned from you) to Republican politicians than to Democrats and to lobby for policies that favor them but not necessarily you.

The vague organizing call to "move your money" is a familiar progressive response to the belief that financial institutions are working for conservatives and against progressives. But even millions of progressives taking their deposits from one financial institution and depositing them in another would do more to make the progressives feel good than it would to pressure conservative banks to change. The end is clear, but the means is not, and everyone knows it. It's like rearranging your furniture in a home you rent. It might make you feel better, but it won't make you the owner.

Lasting, systemic progressive change in American society and law requires a strategy that targets the core of the conservative world view, the financial system. It demands proven experience building and leading progressive financial institutions. It rests on evidence that old and conservative business approaches are eroding and decaying. It requires achievable policy changes for financial services and in other areas. It requires trillions of dollars. And it needs a central organizing idea.

That idea is organized money. In our view, it is a strategy to disrupt the conservative social influence of the financial sector, the corresponding financial market bias favoring conservative outcomes, and the unrivaled public policy might of the financial industry lobby. By taking control of even a modest but material slice of the financial system, progressives will exert a gravitational pull on finance, federal policy, culture, and so the world we live in.

We envision a network of progressive financial intermediaries of all types (insurance companies as well as banks, and private equity funds as well as credit unions) that are consequential enough individually and together to wield power in financial markets, business practices, and policy. By working in a network, they will be able to overcome their current over-reliance on conservative business partners. By providing a full range of products and services, they will grow and gain market share and increase progressive power over time.

Many ideas in this book will seem unfamiliar because they contradict the market fundamentalism that most people have accepted as fact for too long—the interlocking beliefs that inclusive finance doesn't work, that greed is good, that mainstream financial institutions are apolitical and unbiased, that wealth is (and should be) controlled only by conservatives, and that government has no business asking social responsibility of financial institutions. In fact, our nation has prospered *because* inclusive finance works, *because* we have to some degree rejected greed in favor of a moral contract to care for one another. Public opinion has muted the billions of dollars of political giving by the financial sector. Now, perhaps for the first time, progressive wealth rivals conservative wealth, while new financial networks are channeling capital in increasing amounts to progressive goals through businesses that balance public good with private gain. Moreover, we learned from the crash of 2008 that the financial system could not and would not work without deep federal backing and a government safety net made possible by taxpayers.

The progressive movement stands to pass through the gates of the next progressive era when it organizes its money and puts it to work. It can restore public purpose, social benefits, and responsibility to a financial system that has veered far off the course that our nation's founders intended and that made possible our nation's growth. It can overcome conservative ideology and refocus the American people on core founding principles that bind our political independence to economic equity and our social well-being to inclusive prosperity.

2

Market Fundamentalism

The financial system must be working for someone. Who?

The global financial system is as vital to most people in the United States as the electric power grid that delivers electricity to their homes and workplaces. From early in Franklin Roosevelt's New Deal in the 1930s until the Reagan administration in the 1980s, the role of banks as the backbone of a public-purpose financial infrastructure shaped the behavior of the financial industry, its customers, and American society. It was finance organized around progressive New Deal principles, just as finance today is organized around conservative ideas.

Much as publicly owned electric utilities powered jobs and economic opportunities throughout the nation, public-purpose finance drove the greatest period of sustained economic expansion ever, anywhere in the world. It produced real gains steadily for many millions of people outside the upper echelons of income and wealth—though predominantly for white people, because discriminatory laws and lending practices systematically excluded people of color.

The public-purpose system first cracked in the 1970s, so today we are more than forty years into a conservative finance era that has increased inequality, fueled regressive social policy, divided society, and increased economic volatility. The rise of conservative market approaches aided a broader conservative shift in public policy, civic life, culture, society at large, and individual attitudes about money and life. Today, however, we see promising conditions for restored public purpose, equitable finance, and support for progressive agendas.

In the rough wake of the Great Depression, the New Deal reconstituted the U.S. financial system to safeguard against reckless bank practices, protect small depositors, and expand access to credit for lower-income earners. Unlike 2009, when demand for government action melted facing the heat of market fundamentalism, in 1933 President Franklin Roosevelt led an overhaul of the financial marketplace. It included insurance to protect bank depositors, separation of risky investment banking from more tightly regulated consumer and commercial banking, and the creation of new ways to organize money outside banks, such as mutual funds and what we now call hedge funds. It also led to expanded consumer finance choices, including the thirty-year mortgage, which remains popular today. The New Deal created structures, put insulation between different types of financial risks, and set a framework for future growth, innovation, and regulation. Later on, that framework would embrace state regulation of insurance companies, the expansion of important but riskier product lines such as venture capital and private equity, and strict regulation of banks to ensure their sustainability no matter what happened around them. Those bank regulations put boundaries on how much banks could pay for deposits, for example, what they could lend for and how much they could charge for loans, and other operational facets of everyday finance.

Over decades, Congress added other consumer and civil rights protections such as the Fair Housing Act of 1968, also known as the Civil Rights Act of 1968 (to stop racial discrimination in housing),[1] the Consumer Credit Act of 1968 (to shine sunlight on credit card and other consumer lending),[2] and the Home Mortgage Disclosure Act (HMDA) of 1975 (to require transparency on loan terms and racial disparities in mortgage lending by banks).[3] They were well-meaning and effective measures that reflected the need to stop emerging risks in the finance world.

Laws, rules, and regulations respond to changing social and market conditions, but rarely as quickly as or in ways industries want them to. After forty years of this rigorous and economically advantageous regulatory structure, the financial sector was bursting at the seams. It wanted more. The civil rights movement and the Vietnam War had stirred a sharp rise in domestic social unrest, awareness, and action. By the mid-1970s, the United States financial system was pulsing with change as global forces—particularly the growing economic power of Japan and the rising political clout of oil-producing states organized in the oil cartel, OPEC—rattled the nation. Facing once-in-a-lifetime domestic and global challenges, the financial system bristled at restrictions on banking in particular and finance in general. In addition, its customers had changed. The long economic New Deal run-up through World War II and the record growth through the 1960s had resulted in new, deep pools of wealth in homes and financial instruments. In particular, consumer credit was bustling, spurred by Visa, MasterCard, Diner's Club, and American Express. Wall Street was surprised to learn how wealthy many Americans (particularly white Americans) had become, and its leaders were determined to compete for the right to organize—and profit from—that wealth.

The financial system had its eye on the big prize. In 1976, Merrill, Lynch, Pierce, Fenner & Smith—a complex nonbank financial company that specialized in buying and selling stocks and securities—literally broke the banking system when it introduced the cash management account, or CMA. For wealthy customers only, CMAs provided core "banking" products—savings, payments, investments, and loans—for the first time outside the banking system (but within the expanding financial system). That meant that customers could conduct their money business that they used to do at banks, where they were shielded from most harm by government oversight and an insurance safety net, at what would become a much wider range of types of financial institutions where they assumed greater risks and less protection.

Think of it like this book. Not that long ago, the only place to buy books was at bookstores. Then books started showing up in other types of stores. Perhaps you bought this book at Target. That's like what it meant in 1977 for Merrill Lynch to offer banking products. Then came Amazon. That's more like the financial marketplace today.

Banks were helpless to compete with the CMA.[4] Regulations tied their hands. For instance, the Federal Reserve's Regulation Q capped the rate they could pay for savings deposits.[5] Merrill Lynch, and soon other investment banks and money organizers, took the money in as investments rather than bank deposits and paid more to attract the customers from the banks. The CMA also let Merrill and others lend and invest the money they brought in without the geographic boundaries and tight risk constraints that banks followed under government rules.

Most people outside of finance did not notice the CMA at the time, but it is the most disruptive product in modern American finance.[6] It marks the turning point from bank-centered public-purpose finance to the go-go years of deregulation in the 1980s and 1990s to the Great Recession, then to the largely ineffective financial reforms of 2008–10.

The CMA unleashed the modern financial system. For tens of millions of Americans, it converted a narrow set of banking options into a cornucopia of increasingly complicated investment strategies. So long as the economy continued to grow, the customers did well and the financial institutions did better. But as bank customers migrated to new products, banks lost market share. In the late 1970s, about two-thirds of Americans' long-term investments sat in traditional banks. Today, due to products ranging from CMAs to individual retirement accounts (IRAs) to 401(k) retirement plans to exchange traded funds (ETFs), less than 20 percent is in banks.[7]

The CMA also fed conservative anti-regulatory rhetoric and fueled opposition to a government role in ensuring the public purpose of the financial system. The narrative that overbearing regulations were suffocating banking anchors the pro-business, anti-government conservative argument to this day.

The person who steered Merrill Lynch to create the CMA was Donald Regan, then chairman of Merrill, Lynch, Pierce, Fenner & Smith.[8] In 1981, Regan became President Ronald Reagan's secretary of the U.S. Treasury and later his chief of staff. He was an architect of Reaganomics—the popular conservative economic theory that making rich people richer will benefit the rest of us. In that way, his experience at Merrill Lynch, particularly his success with the CMA, influenced financial and economic policies for several decades. His role in encouraging yield-chasing investors (those who focus on nothing else but maximizing their gains and profits) fueled the expansion of derivative markets created to meet demand for high-yield investment products. Out-of-control derivatives markets led to the frenzied collapse of the mortgage markets in 2008. Most significant, Regan led the effort in Washington, DC, to take public purpose out of the financial system.

President Bill Clinton championed and signed two major laws that completed the transformation. The Riegle-Neal Interstate Banking and Branching Efficiency Act of 1994[9] tore down longstanding geographic boundaries for banks, weakening small community banks and making way for national banks, such NationsBank (later merged with Bank of America), JPMorgan Chase, Wells Fargo, and others. The number of banks has declined sharply from a peak of more than thirteen thousand to about five thousand today, while the average amount of money each bank holds has gone up.

Later, in 1999, Clinton signed the Gramm Leach Bliley Act.[10] It ended the 1933 separation of consumer banking from investment banking, a change that accelerated the forces of predatory mortgage lending and helped bring about the Great Recession.

The last gasp of the public-purpose financial system as we knew it expired in March 2009 with the Obama administration's concessions to the finance sector at the Future of Finance gathering.

The financial system today works for everyone, in theory. The theory is that money organizers are apolitical and unbiased and that they will do what money owners want. The theory is that it does not matter where and how you, other progressive people, progressive investors, and progressive businesses organize our money.

In practice, it does.

Most financial institutions in the United States (and almost all around the world) lean conservative in clear ways: passive government and self-interest before the common good.

Financial institution executives and employees trust that they are working for the common good, if only by ensuring that our financial system is operating smoothly and creating opportunities, and we trust they are. Our world requires that we have ways to keep our money safe, to pay our bills, to exchange labor for housing and food, and they provide it efficiently and conveniently.

Most financial professionals have succeeded financially in a world that is conservative. To be conservative in 2019 can mean many things in the fluid philosophical and political dynamics that span from Donald Trump to the Tea Party to the market fundamentalists. It might mean that you are:

- *Fiscally* conservative. You balance your budgets. You don't like or support deficit spending; you tolerate debt but resist it.
- *Socially* conservative. You oppose a woman's right to decide what is best for her health. You expect traditional heterosexual identities and conventional social choices, such as marriages involving only a cis man and a cis woman.
- *Culturally* conservative. You oppose racial and ethnic integration and civil rights. You oppose nontraditional lifestyles and wish to impose traditional gender roles.
- *Economically* conservative. You trust that wealth trickles down to those who deserve it. You favor lowering taxes, perhaps for everyone but particularly for businesses and high-income earners. You prioritize economic self-interest, nationalism ("America First!"), and protectionist trade policies.

Progressives want the financial professionals to conserve their money by being *fiscally* conservative. But chances are that you want to conserve your money so that you can use it for different things than conservatives want. In fact, most investors and customers are not socially conservative (see chapter 10). You can be fiscally conservative but socially, culturally, and economically progressive; we are. Progressive social, civic, economic, and environmental policies work together well with conservative financial management practices.

Most financial institutions, however, seek socially, culturally, and economically conservative outcomes. They favor ideas, decisions, and people that help, reward, protect, and maintain a world that is socially, culturally, and economically conservative. Their successes depend on helping people with wealth conserve it and get more of it. They are more inclined to finance mainstream things they know about, such as suburban single-family housing, than to fund emerging alternative housing options, such as multi-generation homes. They partner with community organizations that support their outlooks, if not their businesses, conflating the public interest with their self-interest.

Conservative financial institutions adapt and change at measured paces, when they are ready. Even the "greenest" of them—those most committed to reducing the carbon footprint in their holdings and their operations, for example—go green slowly. It has been almost fifty years since the first mass-movement Earth Day and, despite climate-change evidence, green financing is still only "emerging" as an asset.

Conservative institutions promote conservative ideas, ranging from deregulation to trickle-down tax cuts. They favor right-to-work policies, which weaken labor unions, and defined-contribution pensions over defined-benefit plans to pass retirement financial risks from employers to employees. It also benefits them that they sell services and products to help employees manage the increased risks they take on.

They work for conservative finance policies that advance their economic prospects. That is apparent in the Trump era in the financial industry's efforts to get rid of the weak provisions of the Dodd-Frank Wall Street Reform act of 2010.[11] For the same reason, the industry has mounted a sledgehammer attack on the Consumer Financial Protection Bureau (CFPB), the primarily progressive gain in response to the Great Recession. Deregulation is a political goal of conservatives on the ideological principle that markets self-regulate (fix themselves) and the pragmatic principle that it's easier and cheaper to operate without public accountability.

They encourage conservative thinking. As quasi-public figures, bankers and other finance executives use public speaking opportunities to promote "free enterprise" and "free markets." They tell stories that reflect their approach to money, including "bootstrap" entrepreneurs and the American Dream of the self-made man (and sometimes woman). They promote a financial brand that ties economic independence to self-realization in ways that seek to keep you bonded with them by tying your well-being to theirs.

Financial institutions are used to being in control. People who own things expect to control what happens—the laws that affect them, the rules that they operate by, and the way people talk about them. They want to keep what they have and so reject and oppose anything they believe threatens them. In finance today, that means much more than preserving the federal safety net that boosts profits. It also means targeting customers to pair supply and demand—for example, finding investors who want to put their money into coal mining to pair with your client who operates coal mines. It means creating new products to help customers avoid paying taxes without a commensurate public benefit outcome, such as affordable housing or new financing for minority-owned businesses.

And it means fending off rules intended as guardrails to protect customers and taxpayers. Deregulation is not just a plank in the conservative platform; it's a war cry for a libertarian, hands-off business environment without public responsibilities. But regulations protect consumers and the public, on the one hand, *and* the regulated activities or companies, on the other hand. Rules for credit cards, for example, help both sides to untangle a mess of claims and counterclaims and sort out legitimate issues from wishful thinking.

The truth is, we want finance to be *fiscally* conservative because it means being prudent with other people's money. Acting responsibly. We *need* it to be. But unchallenged social, cultural, and economic conservative control over the financial system is dangerous in the same ways that single-party control of policy and narrow-channel media are. We all suffer from the resulting lack of perspective, the shortage of critical analysis and thought, the overabundance of self-satisfaction, the drive to divide insiders (the haves) from outsiders, and the excess of power and influence without reasonable checks and balances.

Most people assume that at their core the U.S. and global financial systems are neutral and unbiased—neither conservative nor progressive. Progressives and conservatives alike act as if the business model benefits everyone equally, that market fundamentalism is normal and optimal, and even that the financial system as we know it the only viable choice.

Progressives by and large have unwittingly internalized the fundamentalist conservative ideology that preaches that money is conservative and therefore no business of the left. Whether that is a product of anti-capitalist reasoning, heavy reliance on government, or trust in the public sector born from positive experiences out of the New Deal or Lyndon Johnson's Great Society, the left has an uneasy relationship with money. Its relationship with wealth is simply dysfunctional.

Far more money is organized by conservatives than by liberals and progressives, but conservatives may not *own* more money—not a lot more, at least—than the rest of us. The aggregate billions of dollars owned by just the top 10 on the 2018 *Forbes* 400 Richest People list seems to lean to the left.[12] While conservatives hold $165.4 billion, progressives and moderates in the top 10 have $458.1 billion. The fact that the progressive list includes controversial figures such as Jeff Bezos of Amazon and Warren Buffett of Berkshire Hathaway reinforces the complications around progressives and money (see chapter 10).

Many progressives assume that financial institutions are not working for progressive causes most of the time. They are tentative or silent in their responses, however. Conservatives embrace wealth. It is celebrated and amplified by conservative culture, and so it permeates our culture and molds our thoughts and actions. The cultural influence of organized money affects every business, nonprofit organization, and person in the United States.

We tend to take for granted, however, how hard financial institutions work to get inside our heads—to win our business and our affections, and to influence us, through broad channels (marketing, branding, reputation building, and politics) and narrow ones (products, services, transactions, interactions, and policy). They want us to like them, to trust them, to hear them—in part because they know that they are not liked, trusted, or heard. At the same time, they like to sell.

To that end, they:

- Invest their power and influence in economic opportunities that generate financial returns and growing customer bases;
- Support diversified political causes that build public support for financial products and services;
- Back profitable policy strategies that produce new business opportunities through policy change as local as zoning decisions and as global as tariffs and subsidies;

- Sponsor civic spotlights that add glow to their brands and market visibility by affiliations;
- Burnish their public reputations through good deeds; and
- Donate funds in exchange for social capital, encircling themselves with respected and revered nonprofits, hospitals, and houses of worship.

As a matter of course, successful financial institutions are very good at most, if not all, of these things. They *are* inside our heads and our lives. We experience and describe our world much of the time using financial metrics, looking through their lens—wealth, income, sales price, assets, liabilities, salaries ("keeping up with the Joneses"). We agree or disagree most often using dollars and cents ("Let's split it fifty-fifty"). We compare and contrast each other in financial terms ("a First World problem" suggests wealth, status, and education). We fantasize, some of the time, in dollars (think Powerball and Mega Millions) and worry in assets ("We could lose the house!").

We view one another against financial standards. We used to say someone comes "from a good home" to suggest they were raised with good ethics; now we take that phrase to mean they grew up with wealth. "How many times have I been in conversations where people presume that if you're wealthy you're virtuous?" asks Sister Corinne Florek, an Adrian Dominican investment fund manager who is an expert on money and morality.[13]

Financial institutions reinforce the idea of the "virtue" of wealth, as their desire for wealthy customers for business reasons (they are more profitable) skews their business lines to favor customers in proportion to the scale of their financial relationship with them. That outlook can lead to bad outcomes.

The mainstream financial system is organized around scale.

It favors efficiency and dislikes costs it can avoid or push onto others—other financial companies, government, or customers. It seeks to acquire customers as cheaply as possible (for example, signing up new college students at first-year orientation), to maximize customer relationships (by cross-selling products to existing customers of other products), and to keep customers as long as possible (for instance, by making online bill paying services as "sticky" as possible). It likes to help you increase your financial assets so that it can manage them for you. It's a win-win, sort of.

A depositor with a lot of money in an account routinely earns a higher return on that money because it costs the financial institution less to get those funds—a single relationship that brings in, say, $250,000 in deposits instead of one hundred relationships that bring in $2,500 each. Wealthy people tend to get more personalized attention, more products to choose from, lower fees, and free benefits. As a rule, not often stated out loud, big banks seek customers who have $100,000 or more to work with, and Wall Street firms and institutional money managers use higher thresholds for many of their businesses.

At the same time, at the other end of the income and wealth continuums, "it is very expensive to be poor," warns Mehrsa Baradaran in *How the Other Half Banks: Exclusion, Exploitation, and the Threat to Democracy*.[14] "One of the great ironies in modern America is that the less money you have, the more you pay to use it," she writes.

"The American banking industry has stopped serving those who are too poor to bank," according to Baradaran, a professor of law at the University of Georgia. This is not just a problem of extreme poverty. According to Baradaran, about 90 percent of Americans consider themselves middle-class, but 20–40 percent of Americans are underbanked or unbanked.[15]

"Instead of bank wars or even bank skirmishes, politicians

pushed laws favoring bank profitability and efficiency over public needs," Baradaran explains. "Any suggestion that banks should be forced to lend to less profitable borrowers was seen as a government intrusion into a private market."[16]

It seems rational and reasonable for financial institutions driven only by profit to select profitable customers and avoid less profitable ones; it is not necessarily ideological or biased. Financial institutions want to treat money well so their customers will keep it with them. It sounds reasonable until you think about its unintended as well as the intended complications. Money and finance have another, moral, dimension because it is the means by which we take care of one another, the basis for public-purpose finance.

If you believe that people without money are less deserving of care and respect than people with lots of money, this imbalance might be acceptable. If, however, you believe that people with only a little money are as deserving as people with more of it, you stumble on a moral quandary. If access to the financial system is necessary to get things done, why do profit-maximizing businesses get to decide who gets access?

This question leads to a slippery slope. It's not just a question of assets. Wealth correlates unevenly with race, gender, ethnicity, and other factors of discrimination. Wealth in the United States is dramatically male and white (see page 45). Most moderates and progressives see a problem in a system that succeeds by perpetuating inequities, as a financial system geared to reward wealth does.

According to the Urban Institute, "Families of color will soon make up a majority of the population, but most continue to fall behind whites in building wealth. In 1963, the average wealth of white families was $121,000 higher than the average wealth of nonwhite families. By 2016, the average wealth of white families

Average Family Wealth by Race/Ethnicity, 1963–2016

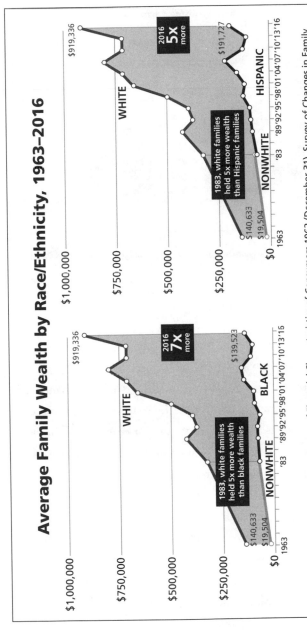

Urban Institute calculations from Survey of Financial Characteristics of Consumers 1962 (December 31), Survey of Changes in Family Finances 1963, and Survey of Consumer Finances 1983–2016.

Notes: 2016 dollars. No comparable data are available between 1963 and 1983. Black/Hispanic distinction within nonwhite population available only in 1983 and later.

Source: Serena Lei, Fiona Blackshaw, and Melissa Favreault, "Nine Charts About Wealth Inequality in America," no. 3, Racial and Ethnic Wealth Disparities Persist, Urban Institute, Washington, DC, October 24, 2017.

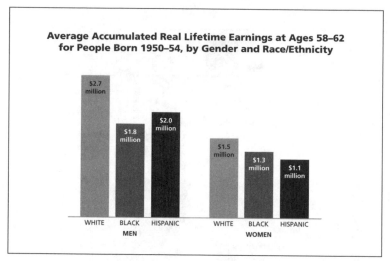

Average Accumulated Real Lifetime Earnings at Ages 58–62 for People Born 1950–54, by Gender and Race/Ethnicity

Source: Serena Lei, Fiona Blackshaw, and Melissa Favreault, "Nine Charts About Wealth Inequality in America," no. 5, Differences in Earnings Add Up over a Lifetime and Widen the Racial and Ethnic Wealth Gap, Urban Institute, Washington, DC, October 24, 2017.

Notes: 2015 dollars. These people are ages 58–62 in 2012. Excludes people outside the US for more than 10 years of adulthood; this is especially important for Hispanics, who are more likely foreign born. Earnings are accumulated using assumed interest rates from the OASDI trustees report.

($919,000) was over $700,000 higher than the average wealth of black families ($140,000) and of Hispanic families ($192,000)."

Research from the Urban Institute and other sources has focused on the racial and ethnic wealth disparities that result from income inequalities. Income is an entry point into our consumer economy, offering social mobility and status; income sufficient to accumulate wealth confers financial health and stability.

Financial institution culture as a place of employment and a customer-facing business is a substantially white, male environment. The National Women's Law Center found that women working in financial services lose approximately $430,000 over their careers compared to men, on average, assuming a forty-year tenure. One possible reason is that, even though women make up half the workforce in the financial service sector, very few play a senior leadership role. They comprise just 14 percent of C-suite executives.[17] (C suite refers to corporate senior management including chief executive officers, chief financial officers, chief operating officers, and other top-level executives.) In other words, women are not promoted to senior levels in finance at the same rate as men, with a consequent negative impact on employment and pay conditions for women more generally.

A study of racial diversity in financial services firms in Chicago produced corresponding results. The Financial Services Pipeline Initiative, started by an array of Chicago-based financial institutions to increase black and Latino employment in the sector, found that "the industry has mostly hired minorities for low-level jobs and kept them there, which left them especially exposed to layoffs and general attrition," according to reporting on the research in *The Atlantic*.[18]

According to *The Atlantic*'s Melvin Backman, the research—done in collaboration with the Federal Reserve Bank of Chicago—found, "some (sadly) unsurprising findings about the ways black and Hispanic folks in finance interact with their field":

- Like women, black and Hispanic finance workers (a group that includes women, of course) tend to see fewer opportunities to advance to the top.
- They tend to spend less time at the top once they get there.
- They're more skeptical than their white peers of their companies' commitments to diversity and inclusion.[19]

Inequity and injustices along racial, ethnic, gender, and other lines are also expressed in business strategies, products, and practices. Discrimination is both unintentional and intentional. It is both culturally embedded, often unconscious, but sometimes, sadly, it is conscious and malicious, meant to favor white people over people of color, men over women, and straight people over queer people.

A 2019 study of diversity in company ownership in the asset management sector (including private equity, mutual funds, hedge funds, and real estate) found that diverse-owned firms make up less than 10 percent of all asset management firms despite comparable financial performance. The report concludes that "within conventional statistical confidence levels, funds managed by diverse-owned firms typically perform as well as non-diverse funds, after controlling for relevant firm- and fund-level characteristics (firm size, fund size, geography, investment focus, etc.)." Yet "modest" increases in the percentage of all firms that are diverse-owned mask inconsistent gains in diverse ownership.[20]

Karen Firestone, president and CEO of Aureus Asset Management, suggests that corporate culture and practices impede women in pursuit of leadership roles in the field. "The ranks of women investors dwindle as you go up the career ladder," she writes in *Harvard Business Review* online. "Something obviously happens between the enthusiastic arrival into an MBA program or job acceptance at a major investment institution and when peers would be offered funds, partnerships, or even launch their own firms." In support of gender diversity in investment fields, she urges more flexibility in working conditions, expanded mentoring programs for women, and management focus on bias.[21]

The financial sector's bias in favor of wealth also affects employment practices, products, services, business partners, suppliers, policy priorities, and other aspects that influence whom they help and whom they do not.

The wealth factor also limits basic access to essential financial products and services in retail, or consumer, banking, the entry point to the financial system for most people. According to the

National Community Reinvestment Coalition (NCRC), the leading advocate for bank services in low-income and low-wealth communities, including communities of color, banks closed branches
from 2008 through 2016 in patterns that had a far greater impact
on low-income communities.[22] The NCRC reported that the clo-
sure of 6,008 branches in that period resulted in eighty-six new
banking deserts—"service gaps in which there were no banks within ten miles of populated areas."

This loss of access to financial services "disproportionally
increased the reliance on expensive alternative financial services by
low-income working families and minorities," the NCRC researchers found. "Additionally, the loss of branch banking access impedes
small business lending, hampering capital availability to the primary engine of U.S. economic growth."[23]

The impact of these patterns is often racially disparate.

Racial differences are well documented in lending products
ranging from home mortgages to business loans to personal loans,
including car loans and credit cards. In 2018, the Center for Investigative Reporting (CIR) found that "the gap in homeownership
between African Americans and whites is now wider than it was
during the Jim Crow era," the period between the Civil War and the
civil rights movement. Based on 31 million mortgage records, the
CIR determined that "people of color were more likely than whites
to be denied a conventional home loan in 61 metro areas."[24]

Racial discrimination in mortgage lending was legal for more
than forty years, starting in the 1930s and ending, in law but not in
practice, with passage of the Community Reinvestment Act in 1977
(see chapter 9). The social, cultural, economic, and financial impact
is multigenerational, however, and far from over.

Richard Rothstein of the Economic Policy Institute researched
the impact of racial discrimination in mortgage lending for his

book *The Color of Law*.[25] He charges the federal government with intentionally segregating scores of American cities and countless other places, starting with New Deal housing programs, which endorsed discrimination in multiple ways:

> Racial segregation in housing was not merely a project of southerners in the former slaveholding Confederacy. It was a nationwide project of the federal government in the twentieth century, designed and implemented by its most liberal leaders. Our system of official segregation was not the result of a single law that consigned African Americans to designated neighborhoods. Rather, scores of racially explicit laws, regulations, and government practices combined to create a nationwide system of urban ghettos, surrounded by white suburbs. Private discrimination also played a role, but it would have been considerably less effective had it not been embraced and reinforced by government.[26]

The fact that discrimination was written into the law under Franklin Roosevelt and left on the books by presidents Harry Truman, Dwight Eisenhower, John Kennedy, Lyndon Johnson, and Richard Nixon before it was overridden under President Jimmy Carter reflects the enduring nature of bigotry. While there were protests by public officials, lenders, homeowners, and civil rights organizations over that time, the multigenerational damage to families of color is inexcusable. The fact is that discrimination and racial bias remain pervasive in the financial sector today. Addressing them is a priority of any progressive financial system.

Racial and other forms of injustice stir up a complex mix of deep emotions in people about financial institutions: cold-blooded self-interest, deep suspicions, blind faith, and a willing suspension of disbelief. Many people are ambivalent about the sector.

As a nation, we are becoming culturally and socially more progressive, yet our system for organizing money today is conservative, and it anchors a conservative economic world view. Reconciling the public purposes and private objectives of the financial system is difficult. In truth, we need them both, no matter how paradoxical that seems. They are hard to balance.

We project onto our money organizers our confusion and anger about their actions, particularly since the Great Recession, even as we fill them with our grandest expectations and hopes. The language we use—that the financial sector encourages us to use—to talk about financial institutions is revealing. It reveals that, at least subconsciously, we understand that we are dependent on people and institutions we distrust. We use soft-edged, double-entendre language that reassures us. We like the sweet talk.

We feel safe with banks because they have "safes" and "safe deposit boxes." We trust financial institutions that offer "trusts." We invest in financial "securities." We feel a personal connection to companies that issue "bonds" and those that "insure" us against harm to our lives, homes, and cars. We like to work with companies that "extend credit" more than with those that "lend" you money, because we earned that credit. Perhaps you earned a "personal" loan because you are an upstanding citizen who came from a good home. On some level, don't you assume that your "individual" retirement account is customized for you? And it would be almost unpatriotic to dislike U.S. Treasury Bonds, which put the "full faith and credit of the United States" in your hands!

There is an extra dose of confidence in financial institutions backed by the government—whether explicitly (such as congressionally appropriated federal bailout funding during the Great Recession), implicitly (a deposit insurance pool funded by participating banks but created and operated by the federal government), guaranteed (many small business loans), or conditional (many defined-benefit pensions that the government guarantees in case the company cannot afford to pay). Government is our ultimate backstop. The financial system knows you depend on that, because it does, too.

The next era of public-purpose, progressive finance has to answer this question: why do so many progressive people and institutions hand control of their money—many trillions of dollars—to people working against their interests and values?

In a world where the priority is on getting rich or richer, financial institutions treat money well when they maximize its financial return. Progressives have bought into that model.

But in a world where values matter, money is well treated when it works in line with the values of the people who own it. For conservatives, the status quo is aligned with their values because it is built on, promotes, and rewards them. Progressives, on the other hand, take the financial system for granted. In exchange, it takes them for granted.

Some progressives make values-informed choices about what they do with their money, as best they can based on what they know, what options they have, and what effort it takes. They live and work within a financial system so big it's hard to work with, so usually we choose convenience, habit, or familiarity. Fewer people, businesses, nonprofits, and governments think about the *consequences* of their choices involving financial institutions. We know money is power, but we almost never question the choices we have made to date.

Not thinking about organized money means accepting what we are told and letting others decide what to do with our money. It makes us complicit in the choices others make for us, the values they promulgate, and the policies they lobby for. Imagine a world where your decisions about organizing money align with your preferences for society, your hopes for the environment, your expectations for the economy, your belief in political justice, and your aspirations for your kids. Most people imagine that they *do* align, but they are more wrong than right.

There's urgent need and real opportunity for improvement. The discussion heading into the 2020 election cycle about the future of capitalism is a turning point as important as March 2009, but this time progressives are on defense. The turning point rests on a provision slipped into President Trump's 2017 tax cuts that is raising defining strategic choices for the current network of progressive financial institutions, heightened the core issues of organized money, and poses a threat to a wide range of progressive policies for decades to come. Either we will double down on the market fundamentalist status quo or start building a new, inclusive and sustainable, financial system.

It is a case study in Opportunity Zones, and it will play out in real time in 2019, 2020, and beyond.

3

Missing the Opportunity

If you want to see how far off track we are, follow the money going to Opportunity Zones.

On December 22, 2017, Republican President Donald J. Trump signed into law a deeply conservative program that could become the biggest, most far-reaching federal program in our nation's history for financing development in low-income communities. (Yes, you read that right.) Under the Investing in Opportunity Act (IOA), Opportunity Zones (OZs) have the potential to stimulate trillions of dollars of new investments in a few years for economic development in almost nine thousand low-income places throughout all fifty states.[1]

Republican senator Tim Scott of South Carolina proposed and sponsored the law with broad bipartisan support. In a time of partisan chasms, that in itself should get your attention. Many Democrats backed it—including popular progressives like New Jersey senator Cory Booker, Ohio senator Sherrod Brown, and former Texas congressman Beto O'Rourke. It won approval as part of the Tax Cuts and Jobs Act, the big 2017 Trump tax reform package passed by the Republican-dominated 115th Congress.

Republicans pushing unprecedented new investments in low-income communities with progressive and bipartisan support?

Opportunity Zones raise two questions: First, what's not to like? It seems too good to be true. Second, what's the catch? Someone must be getting played here.

At first glance, there's a lot to like about Opportunity Zones. The sheer scale of the model is exciting the attention of new and powerful investors. A new way to organize money is sprouting in the financial system to pump investments into communities that progressives have long focused on.

Who is getting played? Progressives.

Opportunity Zones are a case study of bluewashing—selling conservative Republican policy using progressive Democratic language. It is hard to imagine a more clear-cut example. Opportunity Zones are a tool for securing conservative influence over social and economic policy for decades to come, and the fact that leading progressives are eager to promote it is not a good sign. It deserves a wary look, because it exposes the long-term risks progressives face if they let conservatives control financial strategies and do not push back with progressive alternatives.

The Opportunity Zone law rests on a pure profit motive rather than a public purpose; it uses profit maximization to attract investments while reducing taxes on rich people. It is a screen to meet social problems at a safe arm's length using classical conservative and increasingly suspect economic assumptions. It works by immobilizing federal involvement, expanding state control, and trusting blindly that market forces will solve problems in time.

Hold that up against the conservative policy pillars:

- Conservatives favor tax-centric policies that reduce money available for federal spending reduce resources for discretionary social welfare programs. At least as far back as Ronald Reagan, conservatives have sought to shrink the federal government down to "the size where I can drag it into the bathroom and drown it in the bathtub," in the words of Grover Norquist Jr., founder of Americans for Tax Reform.

- Conservatives prefer state-level decision making because it decreases federal authority to impose national standards.
- Conservatives want to limit federal influence on most things, particularly social, cultural, and environmental matters, except when they can use that influence to advance conservative principles or benefit conservative people.
- Conservatives favor trickle-down policies that rely on wealth holders to pass on a few drops to everyone else.
- Conservatives prefer financial solutions because they define problems in narrowly economic ways that exclude and discredit externalities like race, climate change, education, and other factors.
- Finally, conservatives embrace the "efficient market" hypothesis, which assumes against evidence that markets always make the "right" decisions for society, based on the assumption that all participants have the knowledge, means, and opportunity to make informed choices.

Here's how the Opportunity Zones program is set up: The law rewards investors in easily designated Opportunity Funds that channel investments to Opportunity Zones. The Trump administration gave governors unscreened discretion to select the OZs in their states, as long as the zones are made up of census tracts that qualify as low-income.[2] In policy decisions, census-tract income levels are a necessary but imprecise baseline measure.

Investors get substantial relief from taxes on their capital gains, the profit on certain investments made most commonly by wealthy individuals and large companies. The first benefit to investors is that taxes are deferred on capital gains invested in Opportunity Funds at least until they are withdrawn from the funds. If they stay in the funds for five years or longer, only 90 percent of the deferred amount would be taxed, lowering the tax bill; seven years reduces the expense further. Investors who stay in for ten years or longer get an adjustment that could eliminate or sharply reduce their capital gains tax bill from ten years earlier. One benefit of deferring taxes is that cost is going to be less in five, seven, and ten years than it is today because of inflation, so paying $10,000 five years from now is cheaper than paying it now.

As additional incentive, the Trump administration okayed investors putting money in Opportunity Funds in 2018 (assuming they have capital gains they don't want to pay taxes on) and claim the tax breaks even though the program is not set up yet. In other words, investors could claim tax savings before their money is put to work. That will result in tax benefits before there are economic benefits, if any, to low-income communities.

It's not the sort of tax scheme most people engage in, so, the Trump administration made it simple to use—so simple that there is very little compliance required and there are no limits on who can set up an Opportunity Fund. The administration made clear that it will not attempt to influence who benefits or who is authorized to set up and manage Opportunity Funds. All you need is access to investors with capital gains they don't want to pay taxes on—pretty much everyone with capital gains. As a matter of fact, you can declare yourself an Opportunity Fund if you want.[3]

The money organizers most likely to set up Opportunity Funds—and those certain to organize most of the money in them by far—are large investment banks, hedge funds, and other financial institutions that serve wealthy investors. A program this size rewards money organizers who can manage at market scale.

Progressive financial intermediaries (which we discuss in detail in chapters 7 and 8) are trying to get in the game too, but they will be picking up the scraps. While they would be more likely to use Opportunity Funds to help low-income residents and to work for equitable, inclusive development, they lack the scale to meet investor demand. They will be competing for investments against larger and more powerful institutions that will enable the tax breaks with little or no expectation about social benefits or public purpose. As a result, progressive financial institutions risk getting lured off mission to satisfy investors.

It will all be worth it, supporters say, if and when investors pour hundreds of billions of dollars or more into businesses that create family-wage jobs in high-unemployment areas, community facilities for quality health care and education, and new commercial buildings designed to high climate-sensitive standards.

That *could* happen.

More likely, what *will* happen under the loose terms of the law is that investors will pour money into luxury hotels and office buildings that produce a few low-paying, limited-benefit jobs for local residents, storage facilities that produce almost no jobs but generate sweet earnings, and nonunion factories. They could finance upscale market-rate housing, because gentrification needs all the help it can get. They could even invest in payday lending operations that prey on low-income people in the Zones.

Congress created Opportunity Zones to make rich people richer, not to help low-income people move into the middle class. The law makes it easy for an investor to get a big tax break that gets better over time. President Trump has called the breaks "massive incentives."[4] What end do the giveaways actually serve? There is nothing in the law or in the proposed regulations that encourages, let alone requires, that investments benefit local residents or low-income people. In fact, one of the likely big beneficiaries, for example, is Jared Kushner, President Trump's son-in-law,[5] because his family is one of the biggest investors in high-end condominiums and apartments in OZs in Jersey City, New Jersey, Detroit, Michigan, and other locations.

This is organized money, Trump style.

Opportunity Zones already are causing investors to focus on rich returns that can be extracted from low-income and low-wealth communities using government subsidies. This borders on abusive finance. We have lived through it before. It started in the 1990s with overpromotion of home ownership, especially to people of color. That opened the door to predatory lending, using deceptive marketing, hazardous financial products, and aggressive sales strategies to lure eager people into risky financial decisions. It targeted low-income people without partisan regard, and it led to the Great Recession.

Greedy investors spurred race-to-the-bottom mortgage product innovation—practices that harmed low-income people, particularly African Americans. Millions of homeowners lost the equity they had built up in their homes and damaged their financial status for decades to come; close to 9 million people lost the jobs that would have made it possible for them to fight for their economic lives.[6]

In the early 2000s, as the Great Recession was starting to take form, many investors bet against reason on the "opportunity zones" of that era—working-class homeowners. Countrywide Financial was one of the most egregious predatory lenders. A senior executive at Countrywide callously told one of us that Countrywide's strategy was based on one insight: "We can make a shitload of money off of poor people." That strategy ruined the company, the lives of millions of people who trusted it, and millions more lives pulled under by Countrywide's economic undertow. Countrywide and others caused a widespread loss of confidence in both the financial system and the government that failed to stop the crisis as it spread globally.

Because the Opportunity Zones model gives outsize control to investors, money organizers will stoop to please them, as money organizers did with yield-chasing investors in the years leading up to 2008. Opportunity Zone investors are looking to increase their gains and will push to constantly maximize their profits. This, in turn, squeezes the projects being financed and forces out the low-income people in the Zones. Unless and until the Investing in Opportunity Act is amended to include requirements in support of progressive outcomes, with rules about who can manage Opportunity Funds and what the proceeds must be used for, Opportunity Zones will be a win for most investors and their financial institutions but a lost opportunity for most low-income communities. It is a framework for financial disappointment for everyone except the recipients of the rich tax breaks.

Progressive financial institutions are attempting to salvage Opportunity Zones. They're trying, with little success, to get Trump administration officials to adapt the program's rules to support inclusive investing, but their greater potential is to show in practice what is possible. Jeremy Nowak, a widely regarded expert on finance and urban development, first said, "Implementation is policy." Keeping a hand directly in running a program both authorizes implementers to craft policy by the decisions they make day-to-day in their work and positions them to influence policy makers by the experience they gain from their practice. Working in the middle of supply and demand gives implementers leverage on both sides. That's why it's so important that progressive intermediaries gain greater control of and influence in Opportunity Zones and in financial markets in general.

Taxes—and ways to not pay them—are powerful policy levers. "It's arguably the most significant tax break in decades," Ben Miller, co-founder and chief executive of Fundrise, a real estate crowdfunding site, told the *New York Times*.[7]

According to the *Times*, "The funds are spurring interest among investors as a way of deferring and reducing capital gains. But whether they will substantially help needy communities is another question."[8] Timothy Weaver, a professor of political science at the University of Albany, has an answer: "There's no question that the primary beneficiaries of the program are the investors," he told the paper.[9]

If they were redesigned, Opportunity Zones could be a breakthrough in the use of financial policy to benefit society. Implemented to serve progressive ends, Opportunity Zones might bring unprecedented investments to benefit under-resourced communities in line with resident interests, to support environmental sustainability, to stimulate inclusive economic growth, and to change the power dynamics of organized money.

As it is, however, the Investing in Opportunity Act looks to become one of the most significant community development policy changes in years, if not decades. It is a fork in the road for public purpose finance that, so far, is going down a conservative path, increasing the role of large financial institutions to privatize a widening circle of public policies. It's a new version of a longstanding conservative strategy made all the better for conservatives because it co-opts progressives by pretending to address problems they care about. No doubt it will be a subject of debate in the 2020 election cycle and beyond.

Worst of all, the IOA is slyly subversive of government and supportive of markets because of a single provision that is *not* in the law. There is no limit, no cap, on the program, unlike virtually all other tax breaks. None. There's no constraint at all on the total amount of potential tax revenue it might hand to investors for Opportunity Zone investments and thus keep from use for other public purposes. In a tax bill that experts estimate will cost the federal government more than 2 trillion dollars over ten years,[10] Opportunity Zones add the possibility that it will cost considerably more. How much more? No one can calculate how much more.

The open-ended loophole leads to two troubling possibilities.

It will spur a new generation of investment products to produce capital gains. The capital gains tax rate is higher for people with the highest incomes, so the tax relief is worth more to them. And the more ways investors have to avoid paying taxes on their capital gains, the more they'll seek investments that produce them. Opportunity Zones are likely to increase demand for such products. In that way, Opportunity Zones will grow the market for investments that generate profits that investors can avoid paying taxes on. No gains, no tax breaks. It's already happening.

More consequential, the Opportunity Zones law is a road map to privatize government in many and almost all areas. Markets are highly skilled at "monetizing" (making financial products out of) anything that involves finance, and everything governments do involves finance. This new tax break scheme—with generous incentives to wealth holders and no limit to the generosity of federal tax breaks—is a smooth way to hand public interest decision-making authority over to private financial institutions in service to wealthy investors.

It is possible that Opportunity Zones could result in substantial and sustainable benefits for people living in them. We can hope, and we do.

The outcome will depend on how high a return investors demand. Will they give up some return because they are making it up in tax savings? Or will they want both a high return *and* the tax benefits? Will they offer generous and flexible financing terms to improve working conditions, ensure good environmental results, and create career pathways for women? Or will they want only the highest possible profits?

It depends.

What it depends on most of all is who is in control of the investment decisions. Wealthy investors or local community organizations? Wall Street investment banks or nonprofit financial intermediaries? Hedge fund managers or low-income credit unions? Private equity funds or local economic development groups? Global banks or community banks? Employers or employees? Chambers of Commerce or union pension trusts? Real estate investment trusts (REITs) or CDFIs?

They all organize money. They all seek to profit. They are not all the same, however, and they are not all equal. Some are more powerful than others.

4

What Is Money Muscle?

When you make yourself indispensable, you're powerful.

When you organize money, you accumulate power and influence. Power is what you generate to get things done in the world; influence is the gravitational pull you exert on the world around you. In this chapter, we describe how organized money results in organized power that is so pervasive that we tend to look past it. "The average American, with other things to worry about, had little inkling of the financial sector's gargantuan size and clout,"[1] explained Kevin Philips, a well-regarded conservative observer of the financial services industry.

Most money organizers use their power primarily to accumulate more money to organize and so more power and influence to use. We call this money muscle. They exert their money muscle to advance practices, values, policies, and people that are in line with their world views and good for their business.

In principle, there's nothing wrong with money muscle. The problem is that the overwhelming majority of financial institutions work for conservative policies, practices, and values—things that preserve business as usual, use wealth to increase wealth, and result in exclusive prosperity. By and large in the United States, financial professionals and financial institutions lean conservative in support of strategies that conserve historically prevailing products, services, and world views.

The progressive financial system we are working to organize skews toward a more inclusive prosperity. Like a progressive tax system, progressive finance weights its benefits toward low- and middle-income and middle-wealth people and communities. In addition, it supports nonprofit organizations and small businesses working to increase social and economic mobility; social, economic, and political equity; environmental preservation and justice; and racial, ethnic, gender, and sexual inclusion and justice.

We believe the financial system today is unbalanced in ways that harm most Americans and sorely needs a counterweight of progressive financial money muscle organized to serve both public purposes and private gains—both and, not either or. As the world faces current and future financial challenges, crises, and opportunities, there needs to be a progressive voice at the most important economic, financial, and policy tables to speak for and about progressive ideas.

Most of the time the financial industry's power and influence spreads unseen, like a root system, connecting people, communities, towns, cities, states, and nations. It links us to our food, our culture, our homes and workplaces, our nonprofits, our houses of worship, our businesses, our schools, our transportation, our energy. That system connects the many parts to one another: our money behaviors to our voting decisions, our private decisions to buy and sell things to our public policies, and our everyday decisions to our culture. It works through economic leverage, social norms, civic thought, political access, policy change, and technological transformations.

Power and influence are big responsibilities that money organizers use as best they can to shape the world as they want it. This is
important: influence and power are necessary, though they can be,
and sometimes are, exploited and overused, particularly when one
side holds lots of both and the other does not. Power and influence
are not illegal, untoward, or inappropriate. Because they are a product of organized money, money organizers wield a lot. But because
money organizers are conservative, the balance of power and influence in the money business is conservative out of all proportion to
the amount of money owned and controlled by the rest of us.

The history of the financial system, federal policy, and American
society over the decade 2009–19, from the Future of Finance gathering in March 2009 described in the preface to recent headlines,
offers a remarkable lesson in money muscle and how much it shapes
our lives—and will continue to shape them unless we do something
about it.

The wake of the Great Recession of 2008 was an extraordinary
time. We were in the riptide of a devastating once-in-a-lifetime
financial storm that caused trillions of dollars of damage. The U.S.
economy shed more than 8 million jobs from 2007 to 2010, disproportionately harming low- and middle-income people.[2] About
170,000 small businesses failed, exacting a lasting toll on entrepreneurs and their families, particularly those without deep financial
reserves.[3] Some 7 million families lost homes, many millions of
others could not afford to pay rent, and some 5 percent of banks
went belly-up along with many other financial companies.[4] American homeowners lost $16.4 trillion, or about 20 percent of the total
wealth in the world at the time. Stocks lost $7.4 trillion in value,
according to a 2010 analysis by Pew Charitable Trusts, hurting people in the short term and undermining retirement plans for almost
everyone with an individual retirement account (IRA), a 401(k) or

403(b) workplace retirement plan, or long-term savings.[5] It is not so easy to quantify—or to ignore—the social and psychological trauma, political turmoil, and global economic riptide, yet their ripples affect us even today. An entire generation of young people experienced the Great Recession, much as their grandparents experienced the Great Depression, renewing skepticism about capitalism and distrust of the government, which did too little to help or shield them.

Mistakes metastasized into a crisis, and the crisis overran the money organizers, the financial system, businesses here and in every nation with U.S. business (pretty much every nation), the U.S. government, the media, and nearly everyone in the United States. When a Republican congressman challenged Federal Reserve chairman Ben Bernanke in 2008 to explain the need for congressional action when, according to the congressman, in his community, "We're not seeing any problems," Bernanke famously told him, "You will."

"And he did," Bernanke told National Public Radio's *Marketplace* ten years later.[6]

Of course the damage was not evenly distributed. The losses fell hardest on people of color and low-income, low-wealth communities, as documented by the Social Science Research Council and the American Civil Liberties Union. Research by Sarah Burd-Sharps and Rebecca Rasch found that financial institutions' targeting people of color with predatory products caused a reversal in previously positive trend lines:

> Coming out of the Great Recession, one of the most pressing economic problems is the widening racial wealth gap. In the lead-up to the financial crisis, economic opportunity remained deeply unequal across racial lines, but economic trends suggested that

America was on a path toward narrowing the yawning wealth disparities between white and black families. Deeply rooted economic inequality, however, fueled some of the most harmful lending practices, allowing financial institutions to engage in discriminatory and predatory lending that accelerated the financial collapse.[7]

The authors identify the prolonged impact of the harm for homeowners of color despite stabilizing conditions for white homeowners.

From 2007 to 2009, household wealth, with and without home equity, dropped sharply for black and white families, But during the crucial recovery period of 2009 to 2011, black and white families had very different experiences. In that period, white wealth levels, excluding home equity, began to show signs of recovery: median white household wealth exhibited zero loss. During that same time period, however, black households continued to experience severe declines, with the typical black household losing 40 percent of non-home-equity wealth. Similarly, black and white wealth levels, including home equity, each dropped significantly during the 2007–9 period. During the 2009–11 period, however, the typical white family's losses slowed to zero, while the typical black family lost an additional 13 percent of its wealth.[8]

Disparate harm also affected poor people generally. The Urban Institute found that people living in communities with high levels of poverty before the Great Recession generally fared worse after in employment, housing, and wealth than people living in communities with less poverty. "Residents of high-poverty neighborhoods were more likely to experience wealth losses [as a result of the recession] and, among those with wealth, a higher percentage loss in family net worth," the institute's researchers reported.[9] These impacts resulted from intentional decisions made possible by the power and influence of money organizers pursuing the interests of their shareholders and investors, as they are supposed to.

The power of organized money plays out most visibly in policy and politics, where many structural and systemic changes take place—new laws, new interpretations of laws, and new practices and ways of organizing money. Money organizers apply power with institutional ego, the expectation that other people should consider their approaches to finance to be as important and correct as they do. In the process, that power transforms the rules we live by and how we live by those rules—our attitudes, behaviors, and culture as well as our duties, requirements, and responsibilities.

The financial services industry spends more on political action than almost every other industry. In the 2016 elections, for instance, financial services topped campaign contributors, investing more than $1.1 billion, almost twice as much as any other single sector.[10] In 2014, a lower-profile election because there was no presidential election, the financial sector's total was only half as much ($527 million) but still twice the next top-spending industry's giving.

Most money organizers prioritize conservative ideas, economic approaches, and policies. In the 2016 presidential elections, including the primaries, 64 percent of all financial sector contributions to candidates and their political committees went to Republicans while 36 percent went to Democrats, according to the Center for Responsive Politics.[11] For Congressional elections in the same cycle, the financial sector gave 54 percent of its political contributions to Republicans and 46 percent to Democrats.[12]

The financial sector is equally aggressive about its investments in lobbying Congress. In 2015, 2016, and 2017, it was the second largest sector (after health care) ranked by lobbying expenses, spending $495 million, $501 million, and $519 million, respectively.[13] For the period 1998–2017 (the complete available public data set), it ranked a close second (again to health care) in spending, totaling $7.9 billion in lobbying money muscle.[14]

As the largest sector in the U.S. economy, financial services has good reason to work for its interests. For the same reasons, policy makers are prudent to listen. In high-stakes politics, with so many billions of dollars in play, elected officials are exposed daily to the power of organized money. Most members of Congress make campaign fundraising calls daily to meet the oppressive financial demands of modern political campaigns.

"Winning isn't easy. Or cheap," Karl Evers-Hillstrom wrote in a four-part analysis of political campaign spending in the 2018 election cycle. "With the 2018 election smashing midterm records and giving way to several record-breaking individual races, the price of a seat—and a vote—is steeper than ever for those entrenched in high-profile contests."[15]

Writing on *OpenSecrets News*, a premier blog on political spending, Evers-Hillstrom explains that the thirty-five successful Senate candidates in 2018 spent $15.7 million, on average, while successful House candidates spent on average more than $2 million.[16] And those figures mask the anonymous outside spending known as dark money, whose donors are almost impossible to trace. According to OpenSecrets.org, using Federal Election Commission data, hundreds of millions in dark money are influencing elections each cycle.[17]

Senator Sheldon Whitehouse, a Democrat representing Rhode Island, is a fierce critic of the many ways money muscle works in politics. He speaks from personal experience. "The internal coordination behind the scenes between the politically active corporate entities, the billionaire funders, the right-wing 'philanthropies,' the front groups, and the lobbying organizations is constant," he writes in *Captured: The Corporate Infiltration of American Democracy*.[18]

> These forces are everywhere, and they are dominant in every area where their influence on government can be brought to bear. They are right now, as a practical matter, our unseen ruling class. When you are running for office, they can quietly back you—or your opponent—with literally unlimited funds, depending on how comfortable they are with how you'll vote. . . .
>
> As a bill moves through Congress, corporate lobbyists exploit procedural opportunities to accomplish the industry's purposes out of view of the public. Once a bill becomes law, relentless industry pressure is brought to bear on the agencies charged with enforcement: appointment of industry-friendly administrators; visible industry "caretaking" of friendly administrators when they depart their posts (and visible "freezes" on those who weren't so friendly); heavy lawyering of the rulemaking and enforcement process, often as simple brute pressure to cause delay and cost; and sometimes direct kickbacks.[19]

*   *   *

There is no real organized progressive counterforce to the mainstream financial sector, although some financial reform organizations like Americans for Financial Reform (AFR), the NCRC, and the Center for Responsible Lending (CRL) lead effective grassroots efforts.[20]

Does money equal power in policy? Mick Mulvaney, former congressman and President Trump's jack-of-all-trades Cabinet member, says it does. He told bankers so who came to Washington, DC, to lobby in April 2018, according to the *New York Times*:

> Mick Mulvaney . . . revealed that, as a congressman, he would meet with lobbyists only if they had contributed to his campaign.
>
> "We had a hierarchy in my office in Congress," Mr. Mulvaney, a former Republican lawmaker from South Carolina, told 1,300 bankers and lending industry officials at an American Bankers Association conference in Washington. "If you're a lobbyist who never gave us money, I didn't talk to you. If you're a lobbyist who gave us money, I might talk to you."[21]

Political money buys access to power; no money, no power. The results? From 2007 through 2017, the financial sector succeeded to a great extent at containing the consequences of Dodd-Frank, preserving its core businesses and business models, and positioning itself to gain in profits and power in the future.

The financial sector regained its financial, political, and legal footing during the Obama presidency. It worked diligently to adapt business models to ensure positive financial results. It supported and developed policy options that aligned with its goals.

The influence of money organizers is shrewdly and strategically bipartisan to exert influence over both sides in Congress, with little room for contrasting voices on issues that are difficult for most of us to understand, let alone argue for or against. This limits discussion and options for financial consumers, workers, advocates, and the general public. Broadening the debates by explaining how financial factors might work for or against an issue—such as eliminating gender bias in compensation—would add new pathways for advocates of liberal and progressive, even centrist, positions.

No surprise that by January 2018 the *New York Times* concluded, in a headline, "Banks Are Big Winners in Tax Plan."[22] And by "banks," the *Times* includes some of the world's largest financial institutions, such as JPMorgan Chase, Citi, and Goldman Sachs, which are market forces in much more than just banking.

The Tax Reform Act of 2017 transformed how money is organized in the United States and around the world, affecting everyone—and no one more than financial services companies that do the organizing. It is a multi-trillion-dollar bundle of incentives for money organizing that changes for years to come how everyone—individuals, organizations, and corporations—will save and invest, where they will live, what they will spend money on, how much they will spend, whether and how much they will give to charities, and most other aspects of their lives. For instance, strict limits on federal deductions for state and local taxes immediately made it more expensive to live in some states and cheaper to live in others. And a change in the standard deduction reduces the tax incentive for low-income and moderate-income wage earners to donate to nonprofits, ranging from their houses of worships to their preferred advocacy organizations. The result is likely to be less support for nonprofits. Of course, Opportunity Zones created a new way for wealthy investors to avoid paying taxes, reducing federal resources particularly for discretionary spending on social programs and other things.

The financial results have started to come in.

"The Four Biggest U.S. Banks Made $2.3 Billion from Tax Law— in One Quarter," read a *Wall Street Journal* headline.[23] The article summarized financial results for the first three months of the first year that the tax provisions took effect. An $8.5 billion investment over ten years returning more than $2 billion in marginal gains in three months sure sounds promising. Many market watchers expect that the tax bill will produce ongoing positive results for financial institutions, at least as long as the economy is stable and strong and possibly even when it is not.

By the third quarter of 2018, several prominent financial institutions (such as Morgan Stanley and Goldman Sachs) reported profits of more than $2 billion each, and the two largest banks reported quarterly profits in excess of $7 billion (Bank of America) and $8 billion (JPMorgan Chase). Despite fluctuations in business line results, taxes were a primary reason for the gains.

The single largest direct benefit to financial institutions is a 40 percent reduction in the corporate tax rate, from 35 percent to 21 percent.[24] And by a decisive margin the 2017 tax reform law benefits wealthy people more than middle- and low-income people, generating more wealth for money organizers to organize, lend, and invest.

The Congressional Joint Committee on Taxation (JCT) found that 44 percent of more than $40 billion in tax savings go to as few as two hundred thousand business owners earning at least $1 million per year.[25] A follow-up analysis by the Democratic staff of the Senate Finance Committee found that 92 percent of the benefits will go to just 24 percent of all small business owners, those making at least $100,000 a year. The 76 percent earning less than that would share in just 8 percent of the $40-plus billion.[26]

An analysis of racial disparities resulting from the 2017 tax law found that 80 percent of the estimated $275 billion in its tax breaks, or $218 billion, will accrue to white households. On average, white households will receive $2,020 in cuts, compared to $970 for Latino households and $840 for black households.[27]

Financial institutions are particularly adept at using their power when changes in laws result in long periods of regulatory implementation at the federal level, that is, as policy makers turn laws into rules. They are particularly good at tying up laws in prolonged rulemaking processes and using the process to advantage.

Rules usually involve complex financial practices that, for the most part, only the financial institutions know intimately—the proverbial devil in the details. The scale and scope of finance makes it difficult, if not impossible, for public interest advocates to follow and understand, let alone work to shape, the corresponding array of complex policy matters. They simply are outspent by orders of magnitude. The complicated mix of financial institution types—insurance companies, banks, hedge funds, etc.—is regulated by an arcane and unmanageable set of government agencies at the federal and state levels. That leaves many cracks for important issues to fall through and encourages "regulatory arbitrage," a high-stakes practice of playing regulators off against one another. Many money organizers then can select the regulator who treats them best.

In addition, financial laws and regulations tend to address past problems than the potential problems in the future. Financial markets and financial institutions change rapidly—at "market speed." Laws and regulations (and lawmakers and regulators) just cannot keep up.

Finally, the close, revolving-door relationships among financial industry executives and financial regulators often align the two sides on issues. It did not start with Donald Regan going from Merrill Lynch to the Reagan administration or with the participants in the 2009 Future of Finance conference. It is a more prevalent and enduring issue in financial services than in many other sectors, such as energy, environment, and transportation, because of the far-ranging yet specialized infrastructure connecting private financial practice and public financial governance. Power, wealth, and influence simply line up more readily around finance. Altogether, the financial sector and its lobbyists yield great power in setting the rules that they will have to live by.

At the grass roots, many people as early as the late 1990s foresaw the slow-moving financial tsunami of predatory mortgage lending that would devastate the low-income communities and communities of colors where they lived and worked. Martin Eakes of the Center for Responsible Lending (CRL) and Self-Help, the nation's largest CDFI, said as early as 2001 that each and every week predatory lenders were taking as much wealth away from low-income homeowners in North Carolina as Self-Help had helped those homeowners build in twenty years.[28] When he warned that eventually the financial sector would experience tens of billions of dollars of losses because of unsound predatory lending, government officials and money organizers all but laughed at him, so the media largely ignored the warnings. Even the late Federal Reserve Board governor Ned Gramlich, a widely regarded progressive economist, was ignored in the early 2000s when he advised then-chairman Alan Greenspan that predatory lending was dangerous and out of control.[29]

In the deep trenches of the Great Recession in 2009 and 2010, progressives trying to transform the financial system lost the war even as they won a few important battles, including Dodd-Frank and the creation of the Consumer Financial Protection Bureau (CFPB). In 2019, the financial system is well on its way back to the structures, systems, products, and procedures that caused the crisis: household credit is high, $869 billion higher at year-end 2018 than the previous high point in 2008 as the economy failed.[30] Lending to subprime borrowers using troubling products and practices is rising.[31] Government rules against discriminatory and predatory lending are getting weaker one big step at a time under the Trump administration.[32] Rules governing financial institutions—especially the largest ones—are softening, and tax policy changes are accelerating the hunt for high-yield investment opportunities. Even worse for progressives, their most distinctive victory—the CFPB—has been overrun by its detractors following Donald Trump's election and seems headed for destruction from within.

There is no doubt that conservatives have won big and are reaping what they sowed. In the decade since the Great Recession, they have used their power to fortify their business models, weaken their critics, restore their profitability, regain their economic dominance, and reassert their world view. Most of the rest of us went along unaware of what was changing around us.

Early warnings could have averted the crisis and the Great Recession. No one listened, however, because there wasn't enough progressive money muscle to counter the conservative narrative. Eakes, NCRC, the AFR, and many others are determined to make sure that doesn't happen when the next financial crisis looms. It is not enough to see the problem, progressives need to be in the rooms to be heard.

Our vision of organized money, the progressive financial system we are working to establish, rests on building progressive money muscle, as well as on innovations in public policy, on the rising tide of social enterprise as a prevalent business model, on a growing number of financial institutions embracing corporate social responsibility (CSR) strategies and on socially responsible investing (SRI, sometimes called social, responsible, and impact investing). We see the makings of a progressive financial network that in the next decade can build enough money muscle to ensure that progressive values are heard and heeded in discussions about finance, the economy, the environment, social equity, global policy, even the future of capitalism.

It doesn't have to be the way it is. Slowly but surely, systemic shifts in how business gets done, what investors expect, and how financial institutions are adapting are creating momentum that makes progressive organized money possible, though surely not yet certain. To build on that momentum, progressives will need to understand the potential of their own money muscle and act together.

5

Progress in Mainstream Money

This is not the first time progressives have seen signs of change in conventional finance, so what's different now?

The ways we do business and finance in the United States have changed for the better in some ways over the past half century, because society as a whole has started to expect at least a measure of concern for the environment, justice, and other social issues. Financial businesses have responded in a range of ways and to various degrees. Corporate social responsibility (CSR) has developed in many companies from its origins as a thin veneer distracting from negative corporate actions to an anchor strategy shaping business strategy, brand marketing, and purpose. Investors seeking social as well as financial returns—as well as a small but growing number of investors willing to concede some financial returns for social returns—have also gone from the fringe of financial markets to the mainstream.

To date, the change has come slowly and incrementally, as a result of public awareness and corporate reputation management, both within businesses as generational changes bring social-concern norms into leadership, and outside them as waves of investors and consumers ask for and demand action. The progress was influenced by the environmental, civil rights, women's, human rights, LGBTQ, and other progressive movements.

We are now past the "proof of concept."

In other ways, of course, business and finance are not better. First, many companies still oppose CSR and social-benefits models. This shows up sharply in wages, which stagnated for decades while greed outweighed basic decency in business. Second, government in general has reduced its efforts to stimulate social outcomes, leaving social fairness and equal opportunity to market forces. There is insufficient capacity among many social benefit advocates to advance their causes, and so conservative money muscle dominates. Third, as we explain in the preface and document in chapter 2, the systemic and structural issues (how things really get done and who makes the rules) are deeply conservative and work to constrain, if not counter, incremental gains.

As a result, we as a nation are in an important time, as we choose whether to go backward or forward. Whether we will keep and advance our gains will depend on the vitality of progressive movements and the power of organized progressive money.

This chapter traces the tensions over the past seventy years between conservative and progressive ideals of business and finance. Progressive influence has gradually led to CSR as a mainstream practice and the influence of socially responsible investment (SRI) as a financial lever pressing companies, especially large public companies owned by stockholders, to tend to their nonfinancial value at the same time as their financial returns. Those shifts have redefined finance and other sectors in ways that lay a foundation for deeper, more transformational change, which points toward the possibility of a new progressive era of commerce.

* * *

Weavers Way Co-op, a small grocery chain in northwest Philadelphia, paid $425,000 on credit card fees in 2018, according to Nor-
man Weiss, the store's purchasing manager. Writing in *The Shuttle*,
the co-op's house publication, he asks if "there is a better method of
offering shoppers a convenient payment method that doesn't send
$425,000 out of the co-op economy to be spent by banks and credit-
card processers on who knows what."[1]

In the same newsletter, Weavers Way general manager Jon Roesser
extols the co-operative ideal. "Sustainable civilizations yield common prosperity," he writes. "As member-owners of Weavers Way,
we are setting the example through our support of a cooperative
enterprise that is forever working toward mutual prosperity."[2]

Weavers Way's credit card fees are part of the billions of dollars
credit card financial institutions and independent processing companies earn annually on transaction fees (apart from annual card
membership fees). Little, if any, of Weavers Way's $425,000 ends up
supporting the co-operative movement.

The co-operative movement is constrained by the short supply
and uneven capacity of a network of value-aligned financial institutions, despite the existence of a $1.44 trillion co-operative credit
union network[3] that is a model for business principles. The problem is that most credit unions are small and offer a limited set of
products, rarely including credit card processing. All but the largest credit unions must rely on banks and other mainstream money
organizers for services, so they give over some of their profit margins. At the same time, the laws, rules, and regulations that define
credit unions limit their ability to grow and operate in ways that
would increase their independence. The power of the co-operative
model to blend profit and purpose and the values of co-operatives
that put member interests before outside investor priorities is
diminished as a result. That is one factor that led Weavers Way to

give a big chunk of business to a friendly and supportive big bank instead of a local credit union when it was expanding its business to a new location recently. The bank offered financing on good terms and worked hard to help the co-op. In addition to the money it will earn from the loan it made to Weaver's Way, the bank is happy to attach its reputation to a much-loved community business.

To reduce its credit card transaction fees, Weavers Way came up with an innovative solution that organized money in a different but beneficial way. It offered its members a 2 percent incentive to pre-pay for purchases through a program it calls EZPay: deposit $100 in EZPay and receive $102 of value.[4] It is cheaper and preferable to pay members 2 percent for use of their money than it is to pay credit card companies more than 2 percent for theirs. In addition, the pre-payments put a small amount of working capital into the business that might even earn a modest return for Weaver's Way. And co-op members who can afford to prepay benefit financially, at least in the 2019 interest rate environment, because they are effectively earning a higher rate on their money than they can earn in savings or checking accounts anywhere. Members who deposited and spent $100 each month in 2018 earned 2 percent per *month* on their money compared to less than 2 percent per *year* in a savings account, or approximately twelve times as much. Consumer co-op members are motivated to use their money to help the co-op, which they own a share of. Larger, conservative companies tend to be motivated primarily by what is going to make them the most profit.

When Jerry Sontag got tired of waiting for the Tesla 3 he had put a deposit on years earlier, he went to a showroom to look at Chevrolet's Bolt electric car instead. He liked it more than he expected and considered buying one. When he scanned the dealer showroom, however, all he saw were Corvettes and trucks. The Bolt seemed to be a good product, but what did it mean to buy a Chevrolet instead of a Tesla? *Did I just want to buy a car?* he asked himself. *Or did I want to support change in the car business?*[5] Was he going to use his money to support Chevrolet, a company that *contributed*, at least on the surface, to lowering carbon production in its product line while working harder to sell vehicles that did not lower carbon output? Or would he choose to support Tesla, a company that demonstrated a commitment to reducing carbon? Would it make a difference?

Sontag is asking the question that millions of others wonder about: how can we support systemic change with our financial choices?

There is mounting interest in and support for business models that combine profit motives with public-benefit goals. While the momentum is not yet sufficient to drive transformation of economic and financial system norms in the United States, it is strong enough to challenge the long-prevailing business model of putting profit above all else.

That's a start.

The conservative business model—predicated on the idea that the sole purpose of a company is to make as much money as possible for its owners—is losing steam in the economic mainstream. No one explained or defended that model better than the brilliant conservative economist Milton Friedman. In his 1962 classic, *Capitalism and Freedom*,[6] he calls social responsibility a "fundamentally subversive doctrine." By that he meant that it is collectivist, either socialist or communist, depending on the language of the time, making the whole of society more important than individuals. The fact that the issue was in dispute nearly sixty years ago, when communism and socialism were at a low point in American civic thought, is evidence both of the enduring demand for businesses to be positive social forces and of the frustrating pace of progress toward that ideal.

In a widely read 1970 article in the *New York Times Magazine*, Friedman argues that any corporation that takes on social responsibilities is committing an egregious violation against its investors.[7] Those ideas went viral following publication in 1980 of *Free to Choose: A Personal Statement*, which Friedman wrote with Rose Friedman, his wife, and the airing of a ten-part TV series that promoted the respectability of profit-at-all-cost economics, making greed a virtue in many eyes during the Reagan era.[8]

Friedman's reasoning won the day and has defined business strategy and financial markets for many formative decades. At the root of his thinking about the purpose of business is the idea that the *only* metric that investors should care about is profit, and therefore the only basis for financial decision making is financial—optimizing self-interest. Wrapped around that premise is the widely held conservative conviction that markets—everywhere and every way things are bought and sold—are infallible, unable to make mistakes. This is known as the efficient-market hypothesis. Because markets unerringly find the "price point" (the price) where willing buyers and sellers agree to buy and sell based on all available information without distortion, they make efficient decisions that are ipso facto correct. So the theory goes. If buyers and sellers cannot agree on a price, there is no "market," and the exchange should not happen. But is a price based solely on profit motive the only way to think about business?

What do we make of Friedman today, when large majorities of people who are polled favor CSR and major corporations, such as Unilever and Bank of America, now fully embrace it? Has our nation and the global business network taken a hard turn to the left? An awful lot of companies now tout the social benefits of their products, their work practices, and their investments. Does it mean that most modern corporations have slipped into collectivism? More than a few conservatives think so.

Friedman's viewpoint deserves better explication than we can provide here, so we strongly recommend that you read his 1970 article. His argument rests on three pillars:

First, investors are seeking only profits, so corporate executives who seek social impacts are misusing investor funds. Second, while people at corporations can pursue socially responsible investing as individuals, corporations are not people.[9] Third, using private investor capital to address social issues is, in Friedman's analysis, private taxation and private fiscal (spending) policy because it uses investor funds in ways contrary to what they intended. Only the state can demand, collect, and spend taxes. This is where Friedman sees CSR as speeding down the slippery slope of collectivism into totalitarianism.

The Friedman business model is organized money that *rejects* social benefits, unless you concede Friedman's central point that wealth creation is the only benefit that matters. If you are a business watcher, you can see that Friedman's model is the template for modern businesses generally, especially for the financial sector that emerged in the last twenty-five years of the twentieth century and thrives today, the one that shed its role as a public service infrastructure and wrapped itself in the robes of market fundamentalism. The sector that helped our nation into the Great Recession and helped itself as we came out of it.

Friedman idealized for-profit corporations, particularly though not solely publicly traded ones (those that are owned by and ultimately accountability to shareholders who buy and sell shares on public stock exchanges). For-profit corporations have proven their ability to make productive use of resources, including money, and to grow with market supply and demand. They "scale"—that is, they can operate sustainably in the marketplace for long periods—and so they can influence how those markets work. They have power, and Friedman favored them using it with few, if any, constraints.

It is not far from Friedman to one of President Ronald Reagan's favorite memes, "That government is best which governs least." In other words, conservative orthodoxy.

In the harsh light of 2019, Friedman's argument is not merely outdated; it misses the point even in retrospect. Investors are demanding that corporations take on social responsibilities ranging from guns to climate change to education to the environment and more.[10] The Friedman doctrine is simplistic at best, and the cornerstone of market fundamentalism at worst.

Friedman's separation of government responsibilities from private companies' responsibilities makes for an unexpected historical point of discussion. In 1970, government's role in social policy was just starting to lose popular and political support, spurred by the grand but overreaching promises of President Lyndon Johnson's Great Society and the end of public trust in government spurred by the Vietnam War. President Nixon's abuse of powers in the Watergate scandal, coupled with the oil crisis of the mid-1970s, eroded public confidence in American leadership, opening the door to conservative icon Ronald Reagan. In turn, Reagan threw open the gates of deregulation, adopting the conservative "self-regulatory" model that we have come to accept widely, from aspects of airplane safety to Opportunity Zones.

As the promises of government social policy sputtered, innovations in public-private partnerships were leading to CSR. They are competitive business imperatives today.

The Friedman corporate model is wrong in theory and in practice. It's wrong for the people who gain the most financially in the short-term, and it's wrong for the people who pay a nonfinancial cost so that others will profit. Even politically prominent conservatives, like the Koch brothers, Charles and David, concede the point in practice, in how they run Koch Industries, even while they oppose it rhetorically for political gain.

Why does it matter that Friedman was wrong? There are three reasons.

First, the idea that only money matters in the "real world" is false. Businesses, in all their corporate forms, are the way our market-centered economy gathers and manages its resources—people and money. No matter the corporate legal structure (limited liability corporation, S corporation, sole proprietorship, etc.), the myth that profit is the only thing that matters misleads even well-intentioned business owners.

Businesses exist to make our lives and our markets work; markets exist to make our society work; and our society exists to foster, among other things, life, liberty, and the pursuit of happiness. Most businesses—big and small—do not chase profit at all costs. Most business owners take their societal responsibilities seriously, whether as a matter of routine or as a brand strategy.

Finance provides critical discipline for qualitative metrics as diverse as justice and environmental protection, just as nonfinancial indicators add a moral, human dimension to money. Neither alone is sufficient. Both together help us keep our social, political, and economic balance. When South Africa set up a Truth and Reconciliation Commission in 1995 after Nelson Mandela was elected president, Mandela cautioned that the truth of apartheid without reconciliation would be unbearably harsh, while reconciliation without truth would be unsustainable. For our nation, and for all capital-centered economies, profit without nonfinancial benefits is socially, politically, and economically corrosive, while societal benefits without profit are unsustainable.

Most of the most successful companies—from microenterprises to multinational corporations—thrive because they aspire to greater purposes than profit alone. Bestselling business advisor Jim Collins learned through research on the performance of more than fourteen thousand companies that the most profitable ones over the long haul succeeded because they focused on maximizing purpose rather than profit. The money followed.[11]

The second reason why Friedman's error matters is that the profit-only myth was made up by those who benefit from it. Proponents of maximizing profit are the ones who shaped the laws, culture, and practices of business and finance, delegitimizing the moral, human dimension along the way. This moral self-deception is at odds with our nation's founding principles and with human nature. The labor movement in the early twentieth century raised wages, improved working conditions, achieved better living options, and otherwise helped working people earn, keep, and build wealth. In fact, that wealth helped grow the financial services industry. In reaction, conservative financial titans helped codify a false narrative into the laws, rules, regulations, and practices that make up the foundation of our money system today.

The third reason is the fact that the conservative business myth has obscured the rich, long history of American commerce and finance built on a foundation of organized money *with* explicit social benefits. Business operates with the consent of society, expressed through government and guided by consumers. To the greatest extent possible, government should help businesses and their owners make profits so that they can continue to operate and provide valuable products and services.

It does not follow, however, that businesses can or should focus *exclusively* on profit. The two of us are all for profit maximization, but never at the expense of society as a whole.

Most money organizers and all corporate board members must meet "fiduciary" standards that require, among other things, that they act in the "best interests" of their clients or the company they serve. Best interests are not the same as maximized profits, however. "There is a common belief that corporate directors have a legal duty to maximize corporate profits and 'shareholder value'—even if this means skirting ethical rules, damaging the environment or harming employees," explains the late Cornell University law professor Lynn Stout, an expert in corporate law. "But this belief is utterly false."[12]

Profit maximization is a legal myth, Stout explains.

So, where did the mistaken idea that directors must maximize shareholder value come from? The notion is especially popular among economists unburdened by knowledge of corporate law. But it has also been embraced by increasingly powerful activist hedge funds that profit from harassing boards into adopting strategies that raise share price in the short term, and by corporate executives driven by "pay for performance" schemes that tie their compensation to each year's shareholder returns.

In other words, it is activist hedge funds and modern executive compensation practices—not corporate law—that drive so many of today's public companies to myopically focus on short-term earnings, cut back on investment and innovation, mistreat their employees, customers and communities, and indulge in reckless, irresponsible, and environmentally destructive behaviors.[13]

That changes everything. It opens up a world of possibilities, because the space between making a profit and maximizing profit is vast, with infinite opportunities.

Friedman was partially right but wrong in the end, as experience and history have shown. It is possible to operate in a for-profit structure, with the advantages Friedman identifies, and also work as a public-purpose company. There is a fast-growing movement of businesses built on that dual-purpose premise, known as Benefit Corporations, or B Corps (see chapter 6). Since Friedman wrote, a small number of large-scale nonprofit companies have succeeded as sustainable growth ventures providing social benefits. In fact, the long history of public-purpose finance shows that for-profit companies organized to provide social benefits also have led to economic growth and financial gains.

More common today, for-profit corporations ranging from Starbucks to Koch Industries to Goldman Sachs have used CSR strategies to increase shareholder value while producing public-purpose goods. CSR is a common, if not yet routine, practice among major corporations. As far back as 2013, more than 90 percent of consumers polled by Carol Cone, the nation's leading purpose-driven brand-marketing expert, rejected the Friedman model in favor of a broad CSR approach. Her research found that "the clear majority expects companies to do more than play a limited role in communities or simply donate time and money."[14]

In an interview, Cone explained that CSR used to describe the *process* of trying to produce positive social impacts but now implies a requirement for clear, measurable *results*. Corporate leaders in CSR tightly link their signature social-impact work with their corporate brands. Disney is focused on stopping child labor around the globe, for example, and Unilever (which owns scores of familiar consumer food, cosmetic, and consumer brands) has set ambitious goals for environmental stewardship. This alignment of profit, practice, and purpose benefits corporations as well as customers, as employees favor companies that create social benefits, often becoming more productive and more likely to stay in their jobs.

Corporate leadership on societal issues is an increasingly important business factor, according to a 2019 survey of employees and the general public. The Edelman 2019 Trust Barometer Survey found that "societal impact" (defined as "the organization's contributions for the betterment of society") is the most effective factor for increasing employee trust of employers, followed by values, vision, and corporate purpose, all ahead of business operations.[15] In general, Edelman found that social responsibility is at the forefront among employee expectations of their companies. Three-quarters of participants in the survey believe that their chief executive officers should lead change rather than respond to government actions. The results around specific issues are compelling—65 percent look to CEOs on equal pay; 64 percent, on prejudice and discrimination; 56 percent, on the environment; and 47 percent, on sexual harassment. The survey included more than 33,000 responses.[16]

"The bottom line: There's more pressure on CEOs than ever to address complicated issues facing society," reported *Axios*, a widely read online news platform, "and those that don't embrace the opportunity could find themselves dealing with frustrated employees and customers."[17]

Starbucks is widely regarded as a leader in corporate social impact. Longtime former chairman and CEO Howard Schultz pledged that the company would always use its "scale for good." Its reputation and impact performance bolstered its brand and so its market value. Its statement of social responsibility has long served as a reference point for other publicly traded companies. Today it is a sign of Starbucks's success that most public companies have independent CSR strategies and Starbucks must compete on CSR as well as financial factors to differentiate itself. Take a look at Starbucks's social impact pledge:

What is the role and responsibility of a for-profit, public company? We have always believed Starbucks can—and should—have a positive impact on the communities we serve. One person, one cup and one neighborhood at a time.

As we have grown to now more than 28,000 stores in over 75 countries, so too has our commitment to create global social impact.

It is our vision that we will help inspire our partners, customers, suppliers and neighbors to create positive change. To be innovators, leaders and contributors to an inclusive society and a healthy environment so that Starbucks and everyone we touch can endure and thrive.

Source Ethically & Sustainably. We are committed to offering high-quality, ethically purchased and responsibly produced products.

Create Opportunities. We are committed to investing in paths to opportunity through education, training and employment.

Lead in Green Retail. We are committed to minimizing our environmental footprint and inspiring others to do the same.

Strengthen Communities. We are committed to offering Starbucks as a place for public conversation and elevating civic engagement through service.

Now take a look at the social-impact pledge made by Koch Industries, whose owners, David and Charles Koch, are leading sponsors and organizers of conservative, far-right-wing, Republican politics and politicians.

Responsibility is our highest priority. For us, creating value goes far beyond economic performance. It means doing the right thing. In the right way. Always. For our customers. For our employees. For our communities. For our environment.

Five steps we take. Every day, we work to create more value, using fewer resources than the day before. We do it by managing our resources in a way that benefits our customers, employees, partners, community members and society with a philosophy of mutual benefit. With more than 300 manufacturing sites across the United States, we're one of America's largest manufacturers. To stay in business for the long term, we must constantly improve and innovate—both in the products we make and how we make them.

> Reducing waste
>
> Saving energy
>
> Recycling resources
>
> Preventing pollution
>
> Community partnerships

To read the Starbucks and Koch Brothers pledges side-by-side is to understand that corporate social responsibility is not a Milton Friedman nightmare but an inevitability. The lack of clear separation *in stated intent* between the two companies, which represent divergent political values, raises questions about the roles that CSR plays. It is necessary for most companies, but is it sufficient? When is it window dressing, greenwashing, or outright deception? When is it transformational? Where is it merely a hedge against contrary forces at a company, and where is it a core principle? How do we know when it's a defensive posture instead of an affirmative strategy?

The decade-long CSR campaign by prominent financial institutions and industry leaders to restore their reputations following the Great Recession offers insights. They were blamed for helping to cause the crisis. They suffered deep reputational gashes that hurt their ability to operate—and so their ability to profit—because the general public distrusted them. As they rebuilt the financial side of their businesses, they set out to regain public trust and retain customers.

Of all the financial institutions that survived the Great Recession, Bank of America may have dug itself the deepest hole, partly because of its 2008 decision to purchase a notorious predatory mortgage lender, Countrywide Mortgage. Bank of America certainly has paid the greatest price, approaching $80 billion in fines, not counting losses related to its business decisions.[18] It slid to the brink of failure, but it is thriving today. Its 2018 profit of $28.15 billion is the largest in the $2.2 trillion bank's history.[19]

Bank of America's chairman and CEO Brian Moynihan rebuilt his company's reputation since the Recession through aggressive CSR, particularly focusing on ESG—environmental, social, and governance—priorities. In 2012, the bank made a noteworthy $125 billion commitment to low-carbon financing strategies and related activities.[20] It backed up its outward-facing pledge by constructing its New York City headquarters building to the highest green standards and pledging in 2016 to operate carbon-neutral by 2020. Most of all, ESG and CSR became a core theme of the bank's public image. It was the first of the largest financial institutions to commit to CSR as a better way to do business than the Friedman way. During the Recession and since, Bank of America became the largest lender to the CDFI industry. The *Wall Street Journal* has labeled Moynihan the "ringleader" of CSR.[21] (The editors were not complimenting him.) The *Journal*'s Sam Walker quoted Moynihan saying, "Our jobs as CEOs now include driving what we think is right. It's not exactly political activism, but it is action on issues beyond business."

To Walker, it *is* political activism, and it needs to stop. "After studying scores of instances of CEO activism, I've noticed one overarching trend. Most business leaders who speak out do so by adopting the moral language of activism. They rarely, if ever, labor to make a business case for their positions."

To the contrary, Bank of America is an active funder of and participant in academic research to document the business case for CSR, a bustling field of research. There is a growing stack of research results suggesting that CSR, especially ESG, make financial institutions perform better financially than those that do not embrace social benefits, but the data are incomplete and, unfortunately, inconsistent in quality and findings.

Moynihan was the undisputed ringleader until Laurence Fink of BlackRock, at $6 trillion the largest financial firm of its type, stated bluntly in January 2018 that companies seeking to receive some of its formidable investment capital need to embrace social responsibilities.[22] This is something new in the financial sector. Fink was promising to use his business, which is a leading force in investing in companies, to leverage social impact in other companies. Fink went further than financial leaders before him, including Moynihan. It's one thing to incorporate CSR into your business, and it's something altogether different to promise to make your business socially responsible at its core.

"To prosper over time," Fink wrote in a strategy letter that made national headlines and was read with disbelief simultaneously in both the financial and social justice worlds, "every company [that BlackRock invests in] must not only deliver financial performance, but also show how it makes a positive contribution to society."[23] There is wiggle room in that statement, but the public promise is significant. Fink's declaration is striking in part because BlackRock is a relative newcomer to CSR, and in larger part because it is the biggest financial company in the United States.

JPMorgan Chase, the largest bank, at more than $2 trillion, is substantially increasing its commitment to CSR, though not yet with the same sense of purpose as BlackRock. JPMorgan's CSR is built around an "inclusive growth" model, meaning a strategy to ensure that economic growth does not discriminate, and it offers SRI products as choices for investment customers. The corporate tone started to change in 2015 when the bank made large investments in the revitalization of Detroit. Investors, customers, the media, the public, and presumably shareholders responded favorably.[24]

In 2018, the company's chairman and CEO, Jamie Dimon, explained that social responsibility is a necessary component of shareholder value—a catchall phrase denoting what the company's owners, who own shares of stock in the company, like about the company. "Building shareholder value is the primary goal of a business," he wrote in the company's 2017 annual report, playing off of Friedman, "but it is simply not possible to do well if a company is not properly treating and serving its customers, training and motivating its employees, and being a good citizen in the community."[25] As encouraging as that sentiment might be, it is artfully incomplete coming from one of the bluntest voices in finance. It is less pointed than that of Fink, who made a blanket pledge. On the other hand, Dimon is known to follow through relentlessly on his commitments.

Goldman Sachs, known for its history of "making markets"—that is, creating new things to trade—has joined the CSR movement as well. A global effort to help women (called 10,000 Women)[26] served as the catalyst for Goldman's reputational restoration following the Great Recession. The company's 10,000 Small Businesses program—pledging some $500 million in grants and concessionary (less expensive and/or more flexible) CDFI financing—is a multiyear effort.[27] It set out to build the business skills of small, growth-oriented businesses (especially those led by entrepreneurs of color) in dozens of U.S. cities, and it made an effort to provide flexible small business financing through CDFIs.[28] The 10,000 Small Businesses program earned lots of positive media coverage for Goldman when it sorely needed it, through a well-run publicity campaign that featured Warren Buffett, a major investor in Goldman (as well as Bank of America and JPMorgan Chase), and former Goldman chairman Lloyd Blankfein schmoozing with local entrepreneurs.

A significant CSR program is a requirement now for major financial institutions. Wells Fargo, which came through the Recession in decent shape but has since suffered repeated self-inflicted reputational injuries that resulted from its customer mistreatment, runs a pioneering Diverse Community Capital program to finance small businesses owned and led by people of color. Aflac, an insurance company, introduced a widely admired toy duck (its logo is a duck) that comforts kids getting treatment for cancer, reinforcing its brand goal of showing that it cares about its customers. Morgan Stanley, another large investment bank, uses its financial expertise to innovate new forms of financing for social impact and the environment.

Lending and, to a lesser extent, investing for CSR, ESG, and charitable purposes is appealing to financial institutions because it is more familiar to them than giving money away. Even when they must make concessions on how much they earn on loans and investments, how the financing is structured, and how much control they have over the use of the money, financing for the public welfare generally works for them. In addition, lending and investing bring a dose of marketlike discipline to public-purpose finance, as long as all parties take seriously the requirement to repay the financing.

Philanthropy, or grant making, is the other significant financial tool for financial institutions interested in public-purpose finance. Philanthropy builds their public images in favorable ways, and it usually creates significant value for recipients and the people they serve, creating a halo effect for the money organizers. It also buys financial institutions new ambassadors—prominent nonprofit organizations that speak out on behalf of their funders.

All told, more than five thousand U.S. banks donated $2.1 billion to charitable causes in 2016, according to the American Bankers Association (ABA).[29] That total increased in 2017 and 2018, and several of the big banks—including JPMorgan Chase and Wells Fargo—made impressively large public commitments. Many of the largest banks and other financial institutions give away more money each year than all but the largest public foundations—the famous ones, like the Gates Foundation, the Ford Foundation, and the John D. and Catherine T. MacArthur Foundation. In 2015, for example, the ten largest banks in the United States donated more than $650 million, much of it to progressive nonprofits.[30] (By 2018, Wells Fargo alone was donating more than $400 million and JP Morgan Chase was keeping pace.) A review of charitable giving by the ten largest U.S. banks over multiple years since the Great Recession found at least as many civil rights, human rights, and other groups with progressive public education or advocacy agendas received grants as did conservative groups, even using a broad definition of *conservative*. In addition, financial executives gave away their own money, often with an eye toward reinforcing the civic brand of the institutions they run.

There are several reasons why financial institutions are among the most influential charitable givers.

First, they've got a lot of money. They earn a lot of profits (most of the time), and are good at organizing money to serve their customers' interests and their own.

Second, financial institutions understand how money can help (or harm) people and communities, and they are generally very good at designing and identifying money-led strategies. Do not lose sight of the fact that most financial institutions use philanthropy to support vital safety net services, such as affordable housing and well-targeted economic development strategies that create jobs. More and more financial institutions—from BlackRock to insurance companies, such as MetLife, to credit rating agencies—are donating in support of financial "wellness" strategies. Due in large part to pioneering work by the nonprofit Financial Health Network (FHN) in Chicago, financial institutions better understand that financial "volatility" makes it hard for a growing number of Americans to manage their money.

Third, banks in particular—banks are the largest and most visible financial industry philanthropists—have a legal obligation to serve their markets broadly (more broadly than they would otherwise if they were simply pursuing profit) under a 1977 law known as the Community Reinvestment Act (CRA). (See chapter 8.)

Fourth, philanthropy is a great tool to address reputational issues. Money—even free money—can't buy love, but billions of dollars of grants *can* win friends. It's a powerful tool that can do a lot of good or a lot of harm. Financial institutions, true to their conservative fiscal outlooks, tend to build and maintain long-term grant relationships most often with established nonprofits who make solid public allies.

And fifth, people and institutions are comfortable giving money to financial institutions for safekeeping. Fidelity Investments, Vanguard, and Charles Schwab—three money organizers known primarily for offering retirement investment products and services—have emerged as some of the nation's largest philanthropic institutions through nonprofit subsidiaries using donor-advised funds.[31] DAFs are repositories for donations by individuals and small groups. Most DAFs let donors contribute money to nonprofit entities set up within financial institutions like Fidelity; they get immediate tax deductions for those contributions, even if the money is not passed on as grants to other nonprofits. In other words, the tax break can be credited when the money is put in, not when it is put to use by a nonprofit. With DAFs, the money can sit for decades. Of course, Fidelity and others are managing the idle funds and getting paid for the service. Fidelity reportedly brings in some $6 billion a year in new donations and has total assets above $21 billion in its DAFs, more than the Ford Foundation's total endowment.[32]

From another, less-than-gauzy angle, philanthropy helps bring lots of profitable business opportunities to financial institutions. Donating money to nonprofits that handle millions, tens of millions, or in some cases billions of dollars each year is "charity with an upside" when those nonprofits hire the business side of the donor institutions to manage the millions and billions. In theory, the philanthropy and the business are completely separate. In practice, not always.

Philanthropy is and will remain a powerful force in American society. In 2017, American individuals and charitable organizations gave more than $400 billion.[33] Individuals are particularly generous, contributing about 75 percent of the total. In addition to large foundations known for many decades of supporting progressive ideas and movements, numerous smaller community foundations, the investment offices of wealthy families, and corporations make large contributions to sustain a wide range of work.

Wealth created as a result of the technology boom since the 1980s is increasingly important in philanthropy. Mark Zuckerberg of Facebook and Priscilla Chan, the physician he married, have become leaders. In 2010, the Chan Zuckerberg Initiative (CZI) gave $100 million for schools in Newark, New Jersey, though the effort was generally considered disappointing.[34] CZI has since pledged $3 billion in donations for science by 2026. Marc Benioff, of Salesforce, and his family have donated many hundreds of millions of dollars for health care in the San Francisco area. Bill and Melinda Gates not only launched a foundation but helped recruit other wealth, in partnership with Warren Buffett. The Gateses and Buffett have already donated more than $70 billion, and they pledge to give away most of the rest of what they own. Their Giving Pledge now has more than 130 commitments from wealthy individuals in twenty-two nations to donate at least half their wealth—at least another several hundred billion dollars.[35]

Philanthropy is an important means of organizing money in service to the public good, yet it has always been a double-edged sword, and new sources and ways of giving have not changed that. More than fifty years ago, noted social critic Lionel Trilling observed, "We must be aware of the dangers which lie in our most generous wishes. Some paradox of our nature leads us, when once we have made our fellow men the objects of our enlightened interest, to go on to make them the objects of our pity, then of our wisdom, ultimately of our coercion."[36] The Rockefeller Foundation, one of the earliest large public foundations, was feared in its day as "another tool of oligarchical control—a 'Trojan horse' in the plot against democracy," according to David Callahan in *The Givers: Wealth, Power, and Philanthropy in a New Gilded Age*.[37]

"Philanthropy is becoming a much stronger power center and, in some areas, is set to surpass government in its ability to shape society's agenda," Callahan cautions. "To put things differently, we face a future in which private donors—who are accountable to no one—may often wield more influence than elected public officials who (in theory, anyway) are accountable to all of us." That should raise the eyebrows of everyone concerned about the level of conservative influence and power over money, including vehicles like donor-advised funds.

Because philanthropy is crucial to the nonprofit economy and nonprofits are important to progressive movements, charitable giving provides important, though perhaps counterintuitive, evidence that it's not always only about the money; it's about how the money is organized. There is no shortage of money, not even "free" money (money that is given away). There is a shortage of organizations ready and able to organize money to seed and sustain enduring progressive changes. (That's what our strategy in chapter 11 is all about; it's why we wrote this book.) As a result, philanthropy meant to make new things possible too often perpetuates the status quo. Among conservative financial institutions and large public foundations, that outcome is common and is generally considered positive.

Critics challenge the assumption that charitable giving is done with good intentions. Anand Giridharadas is a journalist who has challenged how philanthropy is practiced in the United States in his cutting 2018 critique, *Winners Take All: The Elite Charade of Changing the World.*[38]

Writing in the *New Yorker* on the tenth anniversary of the 2008 financial crisis, he details incidents of Wall Street donations that he suggests are meant to forestall more severe costs, such as government regulatory actions and fines.[39] The crisis response of Goldman Sachs and others, he explains, "foretold how finance would, in the coming years, use giving to protect its right to keep taking. Making a difference, when done right, is a great way to protect your opportunity to make a killing—which is why there are so many galas in New York and, at the same time, so much inequality."[40]

No gala gets more attention than the annual gathering of the Robin Hood Foundation. "Robin Hood gathers money from virtually every big name hedge-fund manager," a *Wall Street Journal* preview of the 2018 party explained.[41] It raised well over $100 million from wealthy donors and their guests sitting at tables that cost $10,000 or more (in the form of a contribution) and a performance by Jennifer Lopez. For the very wealthy, Robin Hood is a service that helps them put their philanthropy to work in "small" amounts divided among labor unions, antipoverty organizations, and other New York City–area beneficiaries. Banks have well-staffed philanthropy departments, but hedge fund managers collaborate through the Robin Hood Foundation and other charitable intermediaries.

It is difficult for many progressives to reconcile the sources and uses of money according to their understandings of hedge funds and progressive nonprofits. That's the point. Many progressives are happy to take money from people they oppose and use it against them. "The only problem with 'tainted' money," jokes Elsie Meeks, a prominent Native American leader, "is that there 'tain't' enough of it!"[42] Conservative donors get a small amount of public cover (and a tax break) by demonstrating big-hearted giving. It works well to keep the status quo in place.

In the large space between the work of profit-maximizing companies and nonprofits, there is a growing sector sometimes called social enterprises. They reflect the impulse to restore societal benefits to business and finance. That need to reconcile the extremes of Friedman and the moral urge to care for one another is reflected in longstanding business norms that in practice defy what many business owners preach. All but the greediest business owners readily make accommodations for employees who are sick, customers who are slow to pay bills because of family emergencies, and even suppliers who make mistakes. The reaffirmation of fundamental social norms suggests that we have a chance to organize money to build an economy that balances societal and financial gains.

Commerce is now expressly linked to social responsibility, social policy, and politics. An apolitical, asocial stance is now difficult or impossible to sustain, particularly in finance. In what seems to represent a tectonic shift, in 2018 the annual Survey of Bank Reputations by *American Banker* and the Reputation Institute found, "It is more important than ever for banks to demonstrate a sense of social responsibility and care for their customers. . . . This year, for the first time ever, perceptions of a bank's good citizenship became one of the top three drivers of overall reputation among both customers and noncustomers." Of the top five factors cited for reputational damage, four involved social justice—lower pay for women, unequal opportunities due to racial discrimination, punishing people who reported wrongdoing, and sexual harassment and other inappropriate behavior by management.[43]

According to Brad Hecht of the Reputation Institute, "The more profitable banks became, the higher the expectation and the responsibility on behalf of banks to take that profitability and use it to reinvest in areas of society where they can have a positive impact."[44]

Financial institutions have been affected by and have benefited from socially responsible investing. SRI started in the 1980s when a financial professional named Amy Domini responded to demand for investment products that enabled wealth holders to screen out of their investments objectionable lines of business (known as "sin" businesses such as alcohol, gambling, and tobacco), products (bonds that financed predatory lenders), and even specific businesses that they objected to. SRI today represents as much as $12 trillion in market influence through public and private investments by individuals and institutions, according to US SIF, the industry trade organization.[45] (The group was formerly known as the Social Investment Forum and retains the old initials in its new official name, US SIF: The Forum for Sustainable and Responsible Investment.)

A significant SRI motivation from the start has spurred people and institutions of faith to action—faith-based investors who articulate their spiritual missions through their money. At the Interfaith Center for Corporate Responsibility (ICCR), a New York City nonprofit that pioneered responsible progressive investment, SRI investors have convened for more than forty years to work on dual strategies: how to invest to ensure they're not supporting results they object to, and how to engage in conversations with companies to leverage their holdings into binding agreements about corporate practices and policies. Often they file shareholder resolutions that put company leaders on the record on topics ranging from diversity to carbon to military work. ICCR has been effective. No corporate executive is in a hurry to disagree with a nun, an imam, a rabbi, or any other religious leader in a meeting room full of hundreds or thousands of shareholders.

The volume of money invested through SRI products and investment managers has grown steadily and resolutely, and there is a healthy network of SRI products and investment managers, such as Domini Investments, Trillium Asset Management, and Pax World Funds.

Most of the large, conventional financial institutions have added SRI product lines to the mix because their customers ask for them. SRI products at mainstream financial institutions almost always yield market-rate returns, and there is a small body of research indicating that SRI assets outperform other assets. Demand for SRI products is driving supply. That demand seems to be growing and changing as Baby Boomer wealth transfers through gifts and inheritances to a younger generation.

One result of that generational change is the emerging practice of "impact" investing, a broad array of investment strategies that seek positive options rather than using negative screens, though impact investing and SRI overlap more than a little. Impact investing started with the idea that wealthy individuals and families could make equity investments in private companies that exhibit good practices (e.g., women in senior management positions, health care for foreign workers in supply chains), that are socially responsible (no-waste production systems in which all raw materials are used completely), and that pursue positive societal outcomes (carbon reduction).

A 2010 report prepared by a market research team at JPMorgan Chase estimated that the potential market for impact investments was "vast" because of generational changes affecting investment goals, rising awareness of societal challenges (particularly the environment), and a supportive policy environment.[46] At the time, a growing network of impact investment managers started up and some of the pioneers were later acquired by big financial firms such as Goldman Sachs. Customers wanted the products and services, and the financial intermediaries were responding. Other large money organizers, such as Morgan Stanley, started their own strategies to invest for impact, while progressive foundations, led by the MacArthur Foundation, supported innovative partnerships between mainstream financial institutions and progressive organizations.

The roots of impact investing are in venture capital and private equity on the financial side and philanthropy on the social impact

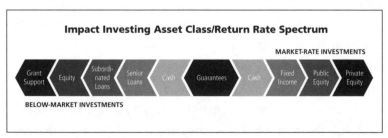

Source: *Impact Investing: A Guide to This Dynamic Market*, Global Impact Investing Network, New York, theginn.org, p. 3.

side. Early efforts focused on private water system infrastructure in developing nations, for example. Impact investors later embraced complex social impact bonds, also known as social performance bonds, with mixed results. Social impact bonds got their start as part of an effort to reduce recidivism among former inmates at a prison in Peterborough, in eastern England.[47] Over time, impact investing has broadened to reflect the full range of social impact financing modes with a range of risk and return possibilities (see below). Initially envisioned as high-yield, high-impact strategies (that is, delivering market-rate returns with philanthropic impact), the field has broadened to include pretty much every type of financing that involves an impact goal. By 2018, the Global Impact Investing Network (GIIN) reported about $228 billion in impact assets under management.[48]

Impact investing has helped fuel a surge in a new form of investment management firms known as family offices. Think of them as investment managers with just one client, usually a wealthy ($100 million or more) person or family. There are more than fifteen thousand family offices around the world according to the accounting firm Ernst & Young (EY).[49] Family offices are likely to be important investors in efforts to capitalize a progressive financial network. Wealth-X, a market research firm focused on very high-net-worth individuals, has estimated that the world's billionaires hold well over $7 trillion. Impact investing looks like a tool that money managers will use to attract the wealthiest families for the foreseeable future.[50]

Beyond impact investing, financial institutions have steadily increased their financing and philanthropy to CDFIs as that industry has grown to almost $150 billion.[51] CDFIs are private financial institutions that focus on benefits for low-income, low-wealth, and other under-resourced people and places. From a quiet start on the fringe of financial markets, CDFIs have emerged as key intermediaries linking mainstream money organizers to emerging domestic markets.

CDFIs are valuable to many kinds of financial institutions—banks, investment banks, insurance companies, and family offices—because they have demonstrated consistent, long-term success at generating good financial *and* impact outcomes. Because the largest form of financial support mainstream institutions provide to CDFIs is debt, the investors are able to offer larger levels of support even when they are making significant concessions on the returns they make on those loans. Bank of America, for example, holds more than $1 billion in CDFI loans.[52]

CDFIs have succeeded at growing to a scale that no one expected when they started, with strong financial performance. Their losses on financing are just slightly higher than those of conventional institutions working in markets assumed to be less risky. As a result, CDFIs have opened doors to market strategies and policies that otherwise would seem untenable.

CDFIs have also created opportunities to make money flow to people and places where it otherwise would not. Due to their success in raising public subsidies, philanthropic grants, faith-based investments, mission-driven SRI money, and flexible bank and investment-bank investments, CDFIs have expanded opportunities for both their local community residents and profit-maximizing financial institutions.

The main stream of the private, for-profit financial sector is not, never was, and never will be filled by companies that put the common good before profit. That stream will not be diverted. It is not primarily in the business of benefits, and there is no evidence to suggest that anything will permanently alter its course. Policy might create more paths to financing *with* social benefits, but financial-systems change has been and will be a result of customer influences, market power, and institutional practices—all defined, of course, by money muscle.

In theory, we see a foundation for a network of organized money *with* social benefits. CDFIs and impact investors have demonstrated the potential for scalable financial intermediaries that produce strong financial and sound results. In practice, it's not as broad or solid as we'd like to believe. The financial institutions we have been involved in personally (Amalgamated Bank in Keith's work and CDFIs in Mark's case) still rely heavily on mainstream financial institutions, because there are too few alternatives. There is a long way to go. Weavers Way, Jerry Sontag, Amalgamated Bank, CDFIs, B Corps, and the robust nonprofit sector are evidence that progressive organized money is possible and sustainable. It's just not clear yet what it will look like.

6

The Public-Purpose Economy

If you want to build a progressive financial system, you need a vision of the purpose it will serve.

The next stage of progress toward a progressive society and economy is an emerging but still hazy vision of a "benefits" economy, in which companies that combine financial incentives and societal good do business routinely with other companies doing the same. It is an effort to build a "public purpose" economy through commerce. The model is coming to life both as an emergent practice led by people who never accepted the separation of financial and social results and as an organized effort to expand the practice by creating a legal and practical structure called Benefit Corporations, or B Corps.

There is significant overlap between the two paths forward, commerce and government. Entrepreneurs are not waiting for the rules to change or for labels to apply to their businesses. B Lab—a nonprofit corporation driving the B Corp idea—is helping them by creating a business category in the law with standards of practice and conduct and a recognizable and respected brand. Both paths are necessary parts of the effort, yet even together they are not sufficient to build a public-purpose economy. At the least they both need to expand by orders of magnitude, build new channels of collaboration into a sustainable business network, and help establish a new financial network, including both mainstream partners and a core group of impact-focused benefit financial institutions. The practitioners must include social entrepreneurs working to grow dual-purpose businesses at a small scale, as well as corporate executives and the subgroup of progressive financiers who want to use their power and influence to foster a benefit economy.

Generations of people who grew up in progressive movements now take their values and skills to work, where they find more and more people doing the same. Many came of age during the fight for civil rights, against the Vietnam War, for environmental sustainability, for women's rights, for gay and lesbian rights, for economic justice and social mobility, for inclusionary policies, and more recently for racial, ethnic, and queer justice—all struggles that took on renewed urgency as a result of the financial crisis of 2008.

Now many of these people are finding an array of values-based options and opportunities in their lives and work. Progressive change is happening even without government leadership. They recognize the limits of government for getting things done (which is different than making it possible for others to get things done). Government is an important lever in making the change happen and last, but it is not the formative lever. And even when government is essential—for example in creating and enforcing voting rights for women and for people of color—it is dependent on progressive money muscle to support and sustain it over time.

B Lab is building a B Corp brand, not for its own sake but to give definition and meaning to the benefit economy it wants to cultivate. In a plain two-story office building on a side street in suburban

Philadelphia, B Lab is working to "end shareholder primacy"—to release Milton Friedman's hold on business. Its leaders believe that the profit motive and general-welfare motive need to be equally important, that greed must not trump the public good.

"The B economy is bigger than B Corps," explains B Lab cofounder Jay Coen Gilbert. "The issue is whether [B Corporations] are part of an economy that is creating a more inclusive and sustainable business world."[1]

B Lab's strategy is to build and organize a network of private forprofit companies on the foundation of parity between profit and purpose. It works toward two central goals:

- To organize a community of B economy leaders and practitioners, and
- To create the legal basis, state by state and nation by nation, for B Corporations that commit irreversibly to the dual roles of business.

In 2006, B Lab set out to "create a better world through business." The impulse is not unique, but the experiences that shaped it are. Friends for more than twenty years, founders Gilbert, Bart Houlahan, and Andrew Kassoy were not starry-eyed ideologues with big ideas. They had started and run a successful business Friedman's way, trusted the model, but didn't like how it turned out. Not at all.

As young, twenty-something entrepreneurs, the trio started, grew, and in 2005 sold a successful global company, And1, which marketed and sold T-shirts and later basketball sneakers and sports gear worldwide. And1 competed and succeeded in a highly competitive business that included Nike, Adidas, Puma, and other iconic sports-gear giants. Who would give that up? And why?

Gilbert and his colleagues did not set out to disrupt the Friedman business model any more than they wanted to sell their company.[2] They sold quality shoes, and they thrived because they had a great brand. And1 made its name on its "street" shoes, countercultural to corporate apparel brands, around the time grunge rock and hip-hop were disrupting mainstream pop music.

"We were experiencing Fortune 500–type growth," Gilbert explains in a glass-walled conference room at the B Lab offices. "We were already a $70 million dollar business," he says. "And literally the next year we were $200 million."

As owners, they gave away 5 percent of their profit, a "couple million bucks" a year, according to Gilbert. They were practicing "two-pocket" philanthropy—organizing their business wealth in one pocket and their spare-change philanthropy in another. And1, like most companies, was not a dual-purpose venture. Five percent is what U.S. tax laws require foundations and other philanthropies to give away annually, and it's a benchmark many wealth holders reference for their giving.

Everything was good for And1 until it wasn't. Two events changed everything.

First, Gilbert says, they realized that there were ten thousand mostly young women in China making their products—shoes and apparel. When they visited the factories, they learned "some pretty difficult things," he says, wincing with his eyes.

"One of my partners went to one of our first factories. He's walking around the factory, and the factory manager—he's looking at lines of young women on the factory lines—says, 'Well, each one of these lines can produce two thousand [pairs of gym] shorts a day, and so we should be able to meet your orders.'"

Gilbert's colleague asked, "What happens if they don't meet the quota?'"

"We beat them," the factory manager answered matter-of-factly. He wasn't kidding.

This was the first troubling experience, but there were other things "like that." The young entrepreneurs had choices to make about their company's operations. "There was, like, avoiding a bad, doing no harm. Then there were other things that were opportunities to do good," Gilbert recalls. "That could be around stock options for everybody in the organization, that could be around creating a great place to work that's fun, with a basketball court in the gym, and kids and dogs in the house."

Another event years later transformed the And1 management team into B Lab social entrepreneurs. It involved profit and purpose.

Six or seven years into the company's fast-growing life, they decided to raise venture capital to expand. It seemed like the right idea at the time. But the VC investments created a "mandatory liquidity event" in the future.

Venture capitalists want to maximize profits in as many companies as possible as quickly as possible; that's how they roll. They look for opportunities to bring new investors into their portfolio companies, often through public sales of the companies on stock exchanges—initial public offerings, or IPOs—which generate substantial profits for the VCs (and other owners).

Purchases of ownership shares are liquidity events—they turn the illiquid ownership shares into liquid (cash) assets. The VCs can take their money, plus profits, and move on. "Mandatory" liquidity events mean that the financial owners—the shareholders—can force the business owners to sell either on a public market or in a private transaction.

"It was a ticking time bomb," Gilbert says. "You know, we were not idiots, but at twenty, I had a basic idea, but I didn't really understand: Wow! This means that we must sell or refinance and go public in five years. . . . So I didn't really know."

So they sold And1. "We did the best we could," Gilbert says, "and the guy we sold to, Jerry Turner, was completely values *not* aligned." Turner had been a sporting goods executive for decades.

It was painful.

"We were, like, a high-priced, premium brand. He had mostly low-end brands, so we were, like, the thing that would help him go public or sell his company for a bigger multiple," says Gilbert. "Total disrespect for the sales and marketing," he continues, mocking Turner's disdain for And1: "'I can make the product for less, and no schmuck is really going to know the difference, and I'll make five extra bucks each shoe because I know the factories.'"

In a sense, B Lab started because of Turner.

Everything changed. In Gilbert's words, "He drove the brand into the ground." He said the founders took away a lesson: "There must be something we could do to make those mission-driven businesses, or that mission, stickier through the inevitable changes in the life cycle of business." He and his partners identified two necessary ingredients for lasting social change. The first is, people need to have the widespread recognition that the system, the Friedman business model, is failing. The second is, you need a viable alternative, one that has the ability to scale.

They drew on their experience, pulled together what they had learned about businesses and benefits, and started B Lab.

Today B Lab reports that more than fifty thousand nonprofit and for-profit companies in at least sixty nations are using its assessment tool to measure progress toward the dual goals of performance and purpose.[3] They include international brands, such as Dannon (yogurt), Patagonia (outdoor clothing and gear), and Eileen Fisher (women's clothing); prominent social enterprises, such as Ben &

Jerry's (ice cream) and Kickstarter (online fundraising); and many more smaller ventures. They also include progressive financial institutions, such as Amalgamated Bank, Virginia Community Capital, and Beneficial State Bank.

Companies can participate in the B Lab world in several ways. The broadest participation comes from using B Lab's assessment tools, which work for both for-profit companies and nonprofits. The goal of the B Impact Assessments is to monitor and document progress on social impact. They emphasize positive factors (work on board diversity, for example) instead of faulting negatives (such as not having a state-of-the-art recycling program). This broadens their appeal and use. The assessments recognize differences among business sectors and account for national, cultural, and other differences in context. That means that a company in Asia might focus on different things than one in Alaska. It also means that financial companies might assess social impact differently than food manufacturers.

The assessment approach is inclusive and affirmative and so operates as an on-ramp to the B Lab community. The B Lab strategy is still forming, and this approach seems to appeal successfully to the broad range of social ventures around the world. B Lab expects its community to expand rapidly.

The strategy is broad, but it also attempts to go deep, by setting rigorous standards that B Lab enforces vigorously. Only for-profit companies can earn B Lab Certification, authentication that they are doing all they can to provide social benefits as well as good financial performance. In addition to completing and meeting the conditions of the B Impact Assessment, companies seeking B Lab certification must make statements in their charters and bylaws that amount to a legally binding commitment to maintaining the B Certification. To do so, they also must operate transparently and work with other B Corps.

B Lab prioritizes for-profit companies because of their role in global markets, explains Dan Osusky, director of standards at B Lab. "Our focus as a mission is to help for-profits be more impactful and differentiated. That's been a core tenet of the certification."[4]

The focus on for-profit companies reflects the organization's history and goals. It can't very well "end shareholder primacy" if it is working with companies that don't have shareholders, such as nonprofits.[5] In fact, a growing number of nonprofit companies do have shareholders through innovative corporate structures, but the difference that B Lab cites is significant. Ownership through capital is different in for-profit companies, and conservative capitalism is the bull's eye in B Lab's target. Whether benefit capitalism is new or only the latest version of an old idea seems less important in the B Lab context than the fact that people around the globe and around the United States are working on it.

The tantalizing prospect of B Lab is its potential to stimulate a business community around its work. Because for-profit corporations dominate and shape global business and, in most places, government policies, B Lab's concentration on them makes sense. In the United States and elsewhere, we organize most of our money with for-profits, and their scale of operations is unsurpassed. When we talk about market scale, we are comparing other things to the size and scope of for-profit businesses operating in that particular market. The scale of finance in the United States is global, meaning it operates in a primary role all over the word. The scale of progressive benefit finance is much, much smaller.

A key for B Lab is connecting its participating companies commercially, socially, and educationally. It convenes B corporations and interested allies around the world in a variety of ways each year. These meetings serve several important purposes—sharing experiences and information, connecting businesses for commercial purposes, and pitching the B Lab vision.

The goal of B Lab is a "B" economy—a system for making, using, buying, and selling things that balances profit and purpose. The concept is still forming, and B Lab seems comfortable letting practitioners and practice define it. It organized a fall 2018 gathering, a Champions Retreat, for conversation about the B economy.[6] It described the B economy as "businesses striving to create a shared and durable prosperity for all" and invited debate about specifics.[7]

B Lab's Anthea Kelsick led the conversation, acknowledging that B economics is a new concept in need of clarity. "Here's my stab at how we might define the benefit economy," she said: "A collaboration of leaders and change makers across all sectors of society, including our B Corps and beyond, to build a more global movement of people, including business as a force for good. The economy works for everyone, and . . . it's made up of people who work for, buy from, invest in, learn, teach, and support those who are trying to creating shared prosperity for all through business."[8]

The result of the patient, perhaps glacial, transformation could be a different type of society, an inclusive prosperity based on one economy, not two—if we can get there. That society will be more inclusive, more just, more environmentally sustainable, and more beneficial for more people in more places. "I hope one day it's not the [benefit] economy, it's just the economy," Kelsick said. "But it's up to us to decide how that definition shifts over time."

B Lab sees itself as organizing a movement to create that economy, organizing influence and power through business. It is one of many U.S. and global efforts seeking to use business as a force for good. As Kim Coupounas of B Lab acknowledged to the participants, the B Corps movement is "part of a much larger global network and movement, and it is filled with people and organizations, many of whom have been at this for many decades, far longer than the B Corps movement."[9] There are many dozens of organizations working to create public-purpose economic systems—some through finance and money, some through policy and government, some through peer groups (such as students and businesspeople), and some through other means and relationships.

B Lab is proving a concept that was decades, if not centuries, in the making and seems likely to emerge further during decades to come: The principles of a public-purpose economy are on-target but still taking shape. The experiment is still in an early stage, and the idea is more convincing than the reality. B Lab's strategy is rooted in an organizational humility that understands that its progress is good but incomplete and that its strategy is necessary but not sufficient, that it is only one part of the solution it is working toward.

Former secretary of state Madeline Albright sees the significance of B Corporations. "I often wonder to what extent business can help society in its goals to alleviate poverty, preserve ecosystems, and build strong communities and institutions. B Lab has proven there is a way."[10]

One thing makes B Lab different: its success at passing benefit corporation statutes in thirty-four states with broad bipartisan support.[11] The laws offer systemic, state-specific ways to set up and run for-profit businesses without favoring investors over all others. B Corporations meet requirements in their legal documents that commit them to producing positive impacts on society, workers, their communities, and the environment. By embedding benefit obligations, they are telling investors, lenders, employees, customers, and others that their responsibility is not solely to produce profits for investors. It seems inevitable that there will be a federal B Corporation law soon. A version of the state statutes is part of Senator Elizabeth Warren's "accountable capitalism" strategy.[12] Other progressives have promoted similar models. While it may be that investor primacy is a myth advanced by market fundamentalists and that the B Corporation option is technically not necessary, it is both pragmatic and positive. It presents an affirmative opportunity for businesses to promote both profit and public good. It is an encouraging foundation for the benefit economy.

7

Pumping Progressive Money Muscle

Is progressive money muscle even a thing?

The potential for an inclusive prosperity based on a public-purpose benefit economy requires a financial system working for and with it as its core purpose, not just as a bundle of interchangeable SRI, CSR, and impact products for eager customers. To foster a benefit economy, new, progressive approaches to private and public enterprises and policies need a comprehensive, inclusive financial system that is much more than our current scattering of socially responsible banks, CDFIs, and impact investing options. To succeed requires more than a well-intended array of mainstream financial intermediaries working at the margins of their core businesses to balance fiduciary obligations to mainstream investors against goals of racial, social, economic, and political empowerment. Those efforts—as important and virtuous as they are—are also necessary but not sufficient.

The best socially responsible efforts by mainstream financial institutions bring both credibility and scale. No matter how conflicted consumers may feel about big banks, Wall Street, and other dominant institutions, most people lean on their expertise, staying power, and money muscle. When BlackRock or Bank of America backs a progressive idea or approach, it becomes a step easier to overcome skepticism from every direction, find ways to collaborate, and reduce costs of progressive finance. In addition, the amount of money the largest financial institutions control and their desire to work at a big scale means that progressive financial institutions can help progressive approaches achieve impacts that they otherwise might not.

We do not expect the entire financial system to turn 180 degrees to commit to progressive finance, or even that those that pledge allegiance to the idea will walk their talk. We would welcome those outcomes, but we do not need them. We intend to use leverage—financial, economic, political, and moral leverage—to make progressive change in the financial system.

The time is right for moral market leadership. "Capitalism needs to be embedded in moral terms and it needs to serve a larger social good," argues David Brooks, a *New York Times* columnist. "Renormalizing and resocializing the market is the great project of the moment. . . . The crucial question is not: How can we have a good economy? It's: How can we have a good society?"[1]

The money muscle of a progressive financial network is a form of moral market leadership that gives progressives leverage on and within the financial system. That progressive money muscle will never be stronger than conservative money muscle—not even close. In an emerging benefits economy, however, in which social impact is an asset in limited supply and progressive financial institutions are leading the way, a progressive financial network must leverage its mainstream counterparts. It can exercise control over what gets done and how—products offered, terms and conditions, markets served, and more. That is not a theory; it's a proven strategy. CDFI leaders call themselves tugboat lenders because they have long prodded the big boats of finance into underserved markets. For that reason, progressive financial institutions must be able to work with—though not for—their conservative business partners.

This is a tension that many progressives have failed to manage well. Socially responsible financial intermediaries of all types rely on conservative institutions, often too much. Even Amalgamated Bank, leading SRI asset managers, and most CDFIs must work closely with and give lots of business to institutions that don't share their values. There is no market alternative yet.

The money muscle of progressive financial institutions comes from their ability to engage with both conservative and progressive leaders that otherwise would be unlikely to sit together other than to disagree. As progressive financial institutions gain expertise and scale, small levers will become money muscle.

The potential for the organized network we are working toward is the ability not only to embrace new, more inclusive and equitable definitions of economic success, but also to bring financial resources and practices, discipline, and policy influence to the efforts to make those successes enduring. To do that we need to lever conservative, not just progressive, money. Organized money can bring organizations and people together in ways that, frankly, nothing else can. For that reason, it represents not only a different business model but a new, restorative hope for constructive economic and fiscal policies across all-too-common divides.

Back in 1985, a radical-left Catholic Worker critic of capitalism, Chuck Matthei, articulated the value of capital-led strategies in a speech that has defined the CDFI industry since. He observed the ability of finance to bridge differences and gaps:

We are forging a kind of new partnership across some very broad divides. It's not a partnership without tensions, but it is a partnership that we should nurture. We are trying to forge a partnership, in some measure, between those who advocate very fundamental social change and those who are calling for the private sector to mend the holes in the social safety net. These are groups that don't normally pass one another's doorways. They don't meet at the office. But they are meeting through the operations of our [CDFIs], and we've got to forge that relationship into an effective alliance, and recognize, over time, its political potential.[2]

The CDFI industry that emerged made significant strides by building bipartisan policy support, introducing new policies for managing organized money, and changing how a still-expanding number of mainstream financial institutions support and work with poor people and communities.

Businesses operating in each other's orbits exert gravitational pull on one another. Decades of growth in socially responsible investing led a few, and then many, conservative financial institutions to accept SRI and later to embrace it. That is the significance of Brian Moynihan's leadership at Bank of America and Larry Fink's promise at BlackRock to incorporate social impact outcomes. Successful financing of affordable housing—producing positive social impact as well as good financial returns—has created a massive market full of investors across political outlooks.

That progress is good but not good enough.

As progressives are rethinking what we need corporations and markets for and what we want them to do, we want to choose for ourselves what works best for our goals. To do that, we need to own financial institutions to leverage assets.

We need to organize a segment of the financial system with progressive ownership, working for progressive goals and outcomes and operating as profitably as the rest of the system *because*—not despite the fact that—it creates societal good. Because the shareholder owners of institutions like Amalgamated Bank are seeking progressive change, Amalgamated is able to resist the pull of its conservative business partners and exert a progressive influence of its own—to act, not to react.

Building and growing a progressive financial network is the means to take full advantage of the shifts in public expectations of businesses and the rise of socially conscious financial products and services. It can and will accelerate change, but more important, it will make changes permanent even when mainstream sentiments pull back. A progressive financial network is not just a way of ensuring that there is a next progressive era; it is a strategy for powering that change and, most important, sustaining it on its own terms.

In this chapter, we describe what that progressive financial network must be and do. In the next chapter, we detail the gains progressive financial institutions have made through U.S. history, and the impacts they have had, to explain that a progressive financial network is viable. Then we show you that there is more than enough progressive wealth to capitalize a progressive financial network, before we put the elements together in our strategy for organized money.

That strategy hinges on building and growing a strong network of progressive financial institutions capable of serving progressive customers—both institutions and individuals, including other progressive financial institutions. The strength of the mainstream financial network is that it works through a system of proven, resilient practices, policies, and relationships—the financial system—that keeps its profits and power for itself. That system makes it easy and cost-efficient to work together. To date, progressive financial institutions have depended on that mainstream system and failed to build their own systems that would enable them to earn profits to build the progressive network instead of depleting it by paying others for work it could do itself. The change will require a clear vision and substantial resources.

Our vision for organized money is a full-service, market-scale network of inclusive institutions within the U.S. financial system.

Full-service means making loans, making and managing investments, holding deposits, processing payments, offering insurance, providing financial advice, and otherwise serving all of the product and service needs of everyone who wants to support an inclusive economy. That requires more than values-based banks and CDFIs; it includes insurance companies, hedge funds, venture capital firms, private equity companies, credit unions, socially responsible investment managers, and other players. Some of those components are operating today, though none are large by financial system standards.

In a full-service system, progressives would pay other progressives, not conservatives, for products and services. The profits it would generate would help finance growth in the progressive sector. An integrated network of inclusive financial institutions increases revenue, decreases costs, and adds to the net worth of its participants. More than that, though, a full-service system would make possible products and services favoring progressive customers in the markets where progressives live and work. For example, a collaborative financial network focused on financing entrepreneurs of color would offer a national capital reach that no single investor could achieve alone. The proceeds would return to the network rather than to more conservative financial institutions. It would be a virtuous circle.

We use the word *network* to refer to both a business model for profitable, sustainable growth over time and an organizing strategy for influence in civic, business, and public life and power in policy and politics. Progressive financial institutions today are too dependent in their business operations on conventional partners to think and act independently and so are constrained by their lack of interdependence with other progressive intermediaries. They need to be organized, systematized, and marketed.

There *are* networks of progressive financial institutions today, but they are narrowly drawn. The CDFI Coalition is a significant policy voice for that segment of the industry; the Community Development Bankers Association (CDBA) works on collaborative business strategies as well as policy; the Global Alliance for Banking on Values (GABV) is an exciting network for information sharing and values promotion; and US SIF (formerly the Social Investment Forum) is an increasingly influential voice for SRI. They are not sufficiently connected and collaborative, however, across institutional types, markets, and products. A new progressive financial network would need to build on and across the existing networks.

The term *market-scale* simply means that the network must be large enough to meet the needs and demands of all organization types and individual preferences in the progressive community and to attract business from moderate and even conservative customers. Scale matters. Right now a large nonprofit has little choice but to bank with one of the ten largest banks, buy insurance from a mainstream global insurance company, and invest its idle money through Wall Street firms. It probably has to borrow from its bank, and if it offers an affinity credit card to its members, it's probably using a credit card issued by—and profiting—a large bank. There are two reasons for this: First, these products are less expensive in large quantities due to economies of scale—making them cheaper to offer when you sell more of them. Second, large nonprofits are complex entities, often with intricate financial needs that only large institutions can meet. The alternative, unfortunately, would be to choose mission-aligned financial partners, who right now make it more expensive for the nonprofit, leaving less money for mission. In addition, smaller institutions generally have fewer products and services, so most progressive financial intermediaries operate with disadvantages compared to larger ones.

A market-scale network would matter to the mainstream financial system and the economy as a whole. Regulators would say it's "systemically important." Accountants might say it is "material." It would be too big to ignore or appease, too influential to marginalize or exclude, and too powerful to take for granted. We believe the progressive financial network must grow to at least $1 trillion in equity ownership shares. To put that in perspective, the entire impact investing industry totals about $218 billion as of late 2018, by the most generous count, and most of that money is not in equity ownership shares in financial institutions. Indeed, very little of it is. Through leverage, $1 trillion would be the foundation for more than $10 trillion in total assets under management dedicated to progressive goals.

It sounds like a lot of money. It is and it isn't. By the time progressives organize that much capital into a system of their own, the U.S. economy may be greater than $200 trillion, so $10 trillion would be enough to matter, to show some money muscle, enough to influence the financial system and the laws that define it, but not enough to dominate the field.

When there is a full-service, market-scale financial segment in operation (we believe progressives can organize it by 2030), the inclusive, purpose-centered movement of businesses and nonprofit organizations will face less financial friction in the marketplace and in public policy. It will benefit from a "positive cycle" of money pooled with other money advancing progressive values and interests. Individuals—whether they have only enough money to make it to their next paycheck or hold billions of dollars in wealth—will be able to support causes they favor with their banking, their savings, their payments, and their investments, not just with their donations. They will have new inclusive financial institutions to choose from, competing for their business, another virtuous cycle that will attract additional customers.

The progressive financial network will be organized around the progressive goals of its customers and clients—institutions and individuals. In contrast to mainstream institutions, however, that base will seek progressive outcomes. The policy and political goals of the progressive financial network will be a product of its customers and their goals. In all aspects—how it raises money, how it runs its businesses, who its customers are, what products it offers, what it uses its profits for, what it does in philanthropy, who it allies with on cultural and civic events, and what it prioritizes in policy—the progressive organized money network can be unique.

The broad expertise that will accrue to this new network will build social capital, intellectual capital, and policy capital. It can and will change conventional conservative thinking. Financial business trends, as well as policy proposals, often are highly technical and reliant on arcane aspects of specialized activities. Socially responsible investors might benefit from network understanding of proposed rules affecting how financial derivatives are traded, for example. The knowledge-sharing potential of a new, full-service network might help those investors by connecting them to derivatives expertise elsewhere in the network. That would increase the capacity of progressive financial institutions to prepare for, shape, and participate in new business opportunities that they otherwise might not know about. In addition, it would enable them and others to respond to policy proposals from powerful advocacy and public education organizations representing conservative outlooks.

Most important, the aggregate money muscle of a progressive financial network would make it easier for its members to always have a seat at the table for important discussions. It would be harder for conservative industry leaders to keep the progressives out, a longstanding problem we have experienced personally and repeatedly. Organized money in a progressive financial network represents a potent new and underutilized source of progressive power. We believe it is more than a game-changer; we believe it is the key to sustainable progressive change.

Through their business ties with others in the inclusive network, progressive money organizers can generate new policies based on their unique expertise with the emerging inclusive economy. In the process, they can expand the playing field for policy makers promoting equitable policies of all sorts in all fields—environment, economy, voting rights, political justice in general, health care, privacy, gender, and so on. Money touches pretty much everything. The progressive financial network has potential to inform and affect fiscal policy (how governments spend money), tax policy (how they raise money), regulatory policy (how they implement policy), and monetary policy (how money is used to stimulate changes in the economy).

The inclusive progressive financial network will generate new business options for participating institutions. Instead of asking mainstream lenders to help them with big loans, they will be able to ask network partners. Insurance companies that manage money for long periods can invest in pools of funds that put 100 percent of their investments into the inclusive economy instead of making smaller allocations. As a model, the Norwegian state pension system has a socially responsible mandate and is a leader in a wide range of progressive investment strategies. According to a 2018 analysis of sustainable investments by McKinsey & Company:

> The management objectives of Norges Bank, which manages Norway's [Government Pension Fund Global], call for the bank to "integrate its responsible management efforts into the management of the GPFG" and note that "a good long-term return is considered dependent on sustainable development in economic, environmental, and social terms, as well as well-functioning, legitimate and efficient markets."[3]

Norway's GPFG is one the world's largest sovereign wealth funds, with more than $1 trillion.

Commitment to SRI varies widely by continent and nation. The commitment is greatest in Europe, followed by Australia and New Zealand combined, according to McKinsey, with more than 50 percent of assets allocated to sustainable investments. Japan, by contrast, is at just 3.4 percent, while the United States is at 21.6 percent.[4]

Inclusive strategies can lower the costs of maintaining a checking account for low-income people, increase lending for affordable housing, make financing available to entrepreneurs outside the conservative mainstream, and help nonprofits working for racial and ethnic justice manage resources better for a lower cost. They can prioritize organizations working to make health care available and affordable for all and increase financing for businesses that pay living family wages. They can increase investments in companies demonstrating good labor practices, including but not limited to pro-union employers.

Through it all, they must make competitive profits, give investors competitive returns, and use their gains, in part, to advocate at the federal level for robust progressive financial policies at the Consumer Financial Protection Bureau, for example, and socially responsible investment rules for retirement funds at the U.S. Department of Labor. They need to increase their clout at the state level to make sure that the Opportunity Zones prioritize benefits for underserved people instead of maximum profits for investors. Also at the state level, they can influence policies affecting insurance companies—including what insurance companies are able to invest in—since most insurance business is regulated by states. Together, they can develop and pursue a financial systems reform agenda that first recognizes and then rewards progressive organized money.

The left has a deeply rooted and sincere distrust of capitalism. The problem is not capitalism, however, but capitalism dominated by greed and market fundamentalism, operated according to Milton Friedman's severe doctrines. That is to say, capitalism in the form most of us know it and experience it is a product of extreme conservative ownership, thought, and purpose. It does not have to be that way unless we let it continue to be.

Capitalism is in need of a new approach. We believe that new approach is within sight and almost within reach. The approach requires financial results as good as conservative money organizers to ensure market disciplines that fuel growth and operational discipline. The progressive model is predicated on the restorative belief that positive social impact is an appreciable and appreciating asset—that it is valuable and adds value. We can capture that value, monetize it, and use it to progressive advantage. A progressive financial network would embrace financial markets but reject market fundamentalism. Operating in a business environment that increasingly expects socially responsible results, it can influence, outdistance, and eventually transform the culture and environment of mainstream finance.

At the same time and in much the same way, this new progressive network approach has demonstrated the ability to change mainstream practices—how the financial system works and whom it works for, how businesses operate and whom they serve, and how government works and whom it works to help. In that sense, just as the financial system has implemented conservative ideas, the progressive network should power the massive array of enterprises, organizations, and people working toward an inclusive, equitable world.

Throughout its long history, the progressive left has had a bad habit of skipping an important step in working for changes. The political left and perhaps the center emphasize organizing people (marches, unions, protests, letter writing, etc.), organizing government (lobbying), and raising donations. Donations are a limited way of organizing money, despite productive crowdfunding models, including ActBlue for political fundraising. To solve problems, progressives too often go from ideas directly to implementation because of the left's over-reliance on government, sometimes resulting in unintended consequences and solutions that don't work. Public housing strategies, starting in the 1960s, met needs in the short term but created many more in the long term. It turned out that government was not good at operating large-scale apartment complexes and scattered-site housing. As an alternative, a series of public-private partnership models emerged, with mixed success. Some of the earliest economic development strategies growing from the civil rights movement put large amounts of funding under the control of people who had never managed that much money with the complexity that government funding creates. Some got through the challenges, but many did not, leaving a mixed performance track record that is still wielded against poor people and people of color today.

Progressives are not alone. Conservatives and moderates also walk down a path littered with ideas that did not work. Trickle-down tax policies, such as President Trump's 2017 tax package, have consistently failed to deliver benefits to working-class and middle-class Americans. Opposition to President Obama's Affordable Care Act (Obamacare) was a policy fiasco and a political disaster for conservatives as millions gained access to health care.

Governments at all levels struggle to implement businesslike solutions with social benefits, and many conventional businesses lack the understanding and incentives to respond in kind. Fortunately, a more mature model for public-private collaboration seems to be on the rise.

"Power increasingly belongs to the problem solvers," Bruce Katz and Jeremy Nowak write in *The New Localism: How Cities Can Thrive in the Age of Populism*, their pioneering 2018 study of innovative public-private efforts around the world.[5] They see a new set of approaches to the creation and use of "public wealth" produced by "new norms of growth, governance, and finance." *The New Localism* points to the promise of pragmatic activism for equity and inclusion in the forms of new business models financed by organized money.

"For generations," they write, "the locus and nature of power seemed settled, reflected in the vertical lines of political authority." They describe the traditional government-centered model of national and state governments "at the apex" and cities and regions "at the bottom, often acting as administrative arms of higher levels of government more than as agents in charge of their own future."[6] In that context, liberals and progressives leaned too heavily on their ability to organize people to shape policy through government. Their excessive reliance on the federal government was the sand castle that Reagan knocked down, the Bushes kicked into the gutter, and Trump washed down the storm drain.

There are inclusive, equitable money organizers in many forms working in the money marketplace. They are the invisible and so-far unassembled foundation stones for a progressive financial network. Pension fund managers, workforce housing funders, financial advisors, socially responsible investors seeking "gender lens" and "labor lens" investments, labor unions, and Amalgamated Bank comprise one part. Environmental activists leveraging credit cards, green bankers, land trusts, impact investors, and philanthropists are another. There is a promising, growing market in green bonds, long-term borrowing structures that make environmental sustainability central to the financing. Women's rights organizations and LGBT advocates also benefit from mission-aligned bank products, such as credit cards, event-based fundraising, and socially screened investment models. Communities of color benefit from minority-owned banks, special-purpose funding strategies, small business financing programs that concentrate on underserved populations, and targeted equity financing. Small business owners and employees, low-income and low-wealth homeowners and renters, students at charter schools, and others take value from the CDFIs at work in rural and urban places in all fifty states and many Native American lands. Entre-preneurs of the new generation—including many in digital centers from Silicon Valley to rural Nebraska—generally start from cultural assumptions based on access, equity, and opportunity for everyone.

These and other financial institutions and strategies are con-strained, however, by two over-riding factors: First, they are small relative to the markets they are working in. In a $100 trillion-plus financial world, even billions of dollars are marginal and lack influence in decision making and market practices. Second, they are not well networked or coordinated. The potential to work together is dramatically unfulfilled, so the potential to network for greater scale is lost.

Progressive financial institutions have more money muscle than they realize. To date, they have lacked the will to organize their power and use it. They need to understand how much they have accomplished to date, what they have yet to achieve, and why they must act now to power the next progressive era.

8

Progressive Finance in the United States

We have a 250-year history of inclusive and progressive finance that is central to our economic and social gains. It is hidden in plain sight. It is surging now.

The distortion of American finance by market fundamentalists has produced a false choice: profit maximization is good, anything else is bad. Or profit maximization works, and nothing else does. Yet over the past 250 years, Americans have created and sustained a wide array of systems that demonstrate the viability of inclusive solutions outside the margins of conventional finance. Mainstream fundamentalist financial thought has argued blindly against them, like a jaded economist who concludes with all the reason of an ideologue, "They sound great in practice, but they will never work in theory."

Progressive finance is about profit but not *just* about profit. There is a limitless number of possible approaches between breaking even and maximizing profit, and through American history that space has filled with innovative, successful financial products and systems. They have included formal ones (banks) and informal ones (lending circles), public and private forms, national and local models, and a wide range of benefits, goals, and outcomes. Today they operate, often hidden in plain sight, at a scale of trillions of dollars. Their promise is greater today than at any other time for two reasons: they have demonstrated success beyond all but the most extreme doubt, and that success has changed the world around them—the economic, social, business, and financial environment they operate in is now providing more than a wisp of wind at their back.

The collective track record of public-purpose finance is proof that it plays a core role in American society and the U.S. economy, and that role is growing. There is a long and deep history of financial institutions that have pushed the limits of profit-centered finance and tested the bounds between philanthropy, policy, and markets. They have ebbed and flowed, however, often because they saw themselves as temporary interventions rather than long-term strategies. Up against the steady growth over time of conventional money muscle, progressive money has won many battles but lost the wars—providing significant benefits to people and society but struggling to sustain their gains.

The history of organized money in the United States is important because it shows what's possible as well as what's problematic. Through this overlooked history is a line running directly from the founding principles of our nation to today's possibilities. That line is intertwined with the history of mainstream finance, sometimes filling gaps in conventional practice and other times challenging it. The path from Alexander Hamilton's late eighteenth-century vision for a national, public-purpose finance system through more than 250 years of creative efforts to 2019 converges in a moment of progressive opportunity—even though progressive trends in business and finance are currently masked by the deeply conservative business model of private gains based on taxpayer risk.

Despite political divisions that threatened to grind the young nation to a halt, Hamilton foresaw the critical need for a financial system that would put the public interest in balance with private interests. He knew it had to be profitable but not profit maximizing. "Hamilton wanted his central bank to be profitable enough to attract private investors while serving the public interest," his biographer Ron Chernow observed.[1] The public interest, to Hamilton, meant robust federal as well as state governments, in addition to healthy commerce. He sought to expand opportunities to a broader public. "In a nation of self-made people, Hamilton became an emblematic figure because he believed that government ought to promote self-fulfillment, self-improvement, and self-reliance," explains Chernow. He structured the bank—particularly its governing board—to those ends.

That was his theory. His experience reinforces the adage that in theory there is no difference between theory and practice, but in practice there is. Politics and competition chipped away at Hamilton's foundation from the start.

The nation after the Revolution was a loose affiliation of states rather than the federal entity that it is today. Americans' primary loyalties were to their states. The essence of Hamilton's idea—that a single, federally mandated financial system would best serve the individual states and the common good—flew forcefully in the face of the prevailing political outlook. Individual states and many of their residents deeply distrusted the federal role and the power of the rich to shape the money system to their own benefit. Hamilton set out to prove them wrong.

Post-Revolution America was controlled almost entirely by wealthy people, mostly landowners like Washington and Jefferson. Hamilton's plan needed to meet their needs first to stand a chance. Their wealth was primarily in real property (land, equipment, and—in the injustice of slavery—slaves), not financial holdings. The money centers of the time were Philadelphia, New York, and Boston. Then, as now, people who owned real property were wary of bankers.

Hamilton's vision was constrained by the world he lived in. The measure of feelings resisting his ideas is best expressed by the fact that they brought together in opposition to his plan three future presidents who rarely agreed on anything—Thomas Jefferson, John Adams, and James Madison. "Among the well-intentioned men who were woefully backward in finance, if forward-looking in politics," writes Chernow, "were Hamilton's three most savage critics of the 1790s: Jefferson, Madison, and Adams. These founders adhered to a static, archaic world view that scorned banks, credit, and stock markets. From this perspective, Hamilton was the progressive figure of the era, his critics the conservatives."[2]

Nevertheless, in 1791, in support of Hamilton's ideas, the federal government started the first of two national banks that operated over the next fifty years, the First and Second Banks of the United States. They created a national economy and financial system, and most people consider them the cornerstone of the nation's remarkable economic history, even as they operated in a constant cloud of distrust and controversy. President Andrew Jackson led the fight that ultimately closed the Second National Bank in 1836, a major moment in the American political transformation known as Jacksonian democracy—in a broad sense challenging governance by and for an elite class of wealthy people and increasing the voice, power, and influence of the citizenry.

Jackson and many others believed the national bank harmed state-chartered banks, which were prevalent. The power of a large, national bank ran contrary to Jackson's view of America as a loose network of interdependent states. Old Hickory also hated paper money, believing only in metal, hard money. After the Second Bank of the United States closed, so many local banks sprouted under state charters that to historians it was "bank mania."[3] In the absence of a national bank and a national currency, the surge in banks—most with their own currencies—required a system of money traders to exchange them all. They were versions of the money traders you find routinely in international airports today. A traveler's home currency might not be accepted in another place without someone to set an exchange rate, say $1.10 in Philadelphia money for each $1.00 from a Boston bank. It was a freewheeling and risky business. It also was the genesis of Wall Street as we know it today—where money gets bought and sold and bets are made on the current and future value of money.

In the 1840s and 1850s, money traders had no easy way of managing the risks of differing values and so erred on the side of caution, which meant discounting currencies from some states more than others.[4] That gave some places financial and economic advantages over others and fostered a measure of disagreement and distrust among the states—a factor that exacerbated the tensions between the young nation's two predominant economies, the agricultural South and the industrial North. Slavery was a defining factor in the former, less visible but not less important indirectly in the latter.

At the same time, the principle that local banks or financiers better understood the people and influences in their markets is a central principle of inclusive finance—and a reminder that the line between inclusion and exclusion is thin. Then, as now, money organizers were more likely than not to support the people they knew and the opportunities they recognized. As a result, many communities organized alternative financial approaches—such as farmers

pooling funds to support one another or groups of immigrants creating lending circles. Those models continue today.

An important prelude to modern progressive finance was the
Freedman's Bank, chartered to provide financial services to freed
slaves and other African Americans, who were excluded from
finance in almost all other ways.[5] President Abraham Lincoln
created the Freedman's Bank on March 3, 1865, in support of the
Freedmen's Bureau, a new federal agency that made land grants and
operated other programs to help former slaves. As a government as
well as a public-purpose institution, it foreshadowed other federal
programs to address inequality, providing financial and economic
aid as well as social standing and support. It is a significant example of how the Civil War and President Lincoln remade the nation
as we know it today, connected in substantial ways by the federal
government.

To finance the Union war effort, Lincoln authorized the sale of
bonds totaling more than $2 billion on favorable terms for inves-
tors but available almost exclusively to wealthy ones.[6] Those terms
included repayment in gold and a guarantee, funded substantially
by a newly established national banking system. "Negotiated, in
effect, between the Lincoln administration and leading Eastern
bankers, a series of laws provided for the granting of federal charters, including the right to issue currency, to banks holding speci-
fied amounts of bonds," explains Eric Foner is his classic study,
Reconstruction: America's Unfinished Revolution.[7] The Civil War
also prompted creation of a national income tax system (taxation
is arguably the most influential money organizer of all) to serve the
public purpose of preserving the Union.[8] "The system both promoted the consolidation of a national capital market essential to
future investment in industry and commerce," Foner concludes,
"and placed its control firmly in the hands of Wall Street."[9]

Headquartered in Washington, DC, at its peak the Freedman's Bank held over $57 million in deposits (adjusted for inflation) from seventy thousand depositors. It operated thirty-seven offices in seventeen states.[10] The Freedman's Bank struggled with its operations, however, losing money due to investment decisions, management issues, and corruption. In 1872 Congress voted to close the Freedmen's Bureau, though the Freedman's Bank lived on. Two years later, Frederick Douglass agreed to run the bank in an unsuccessful effort to rescue it from internal and external Reconstruction-related pressures.

"The [Freedman's Bank] affair ranks as one of the great aspirations, but also genuine racial tragedies, of Reconstruction," observes Douglass's biographer David W. Blight. "The bank could likely have been rescued had the moral and political will existed in the Congress, especially among the freedmen's friends, to underwrite the debts and payments run up by bad management."[11]

Overseen by a board overwhelmingly composed of white men, many of whom failed to show up to do their jobs at board meetings, the bank failed to manage the risks intrinsic to lending. Equally important, it suffered significant losses due to the economic depression of 1873 that led to the failure of many thousands of businesses nationally.[12]

As Blight explains, "The black farmers, washerwomen, ministers, draymen, and general jobbers who had opened their meager accounts and proudly carried passbooks had not made the hapless investments in badly managed construction firms, nor in the hopelessly corrupt Union Pacific or Northern Pacific Railroads. They were the ultimate victims of this debacle when capitalism and racism ground down a jewel of a good idea into dust."[13]

The legacy of the Freedman's Bank, in part, is a network of minority-owned banks working to reduce the financial isolation of people of color. In 1927, the Negro Bankers' Association formed to support banks owned by and serving black people and communities.[14] Today there are twenty-three black-owned banks and a smaller number of U.S. banks owned by members of other minorities. They are small compared to the biggest banks. Founded in 1948, Carver Federal Savings, with almost $700 million, is the largest African American–owned bank in the United States and the only one in New York City. It provides consumer-responsive banking services and reinvests 83 cents of each dollar it takes in from the local community.[15] Native American Bank, the only Native-owned bank in the nation, promotes economic development in Native and other underserved communities. Working throughout much of the United States, it has just under $100 million in assets. It is owned by almost thirty Native American nations and tribes, as well as several public foundations and one large bank.[16] All told, according to the Federal Deposit Insurance Corporation (FDIC), a federal bank regulatory agency, there are 145 minority-owned banks in the United States in all categories (race, ethnicity, gender, nationality, and others). Their combined total assets as of late 2018 were $150 billion.[17]

Credit unions in the United States have about ten times that much in assets—almost $1.5 trillion.[18] Like banks, credit unions accept deposits and so are known as depositories. Credit unions are mutually owned depository financial institutions—that is, they are owned by their members in a cooperative legal structure. Because they have an explicit public purpose of serving their member communities—often by offering better rates, terms, and conditions—they are exempt from federal taxation, a significant benefit. At the same time, however, they are restricted in ways that limit their growth and prevent them from competing in most ways with commercial banks. For example, their small business lending is capped.

There are more than 5,500 credit unions in the United States, serving more than 116 million Americans.[19] Most offer core financial services—savings, investments, payments (checking, digital, or both), and loans, including credit cards. They work on the front lines of alternatives to high-cost payday lenders and check cashers that take advantage of financial consumers with few options.

A subgroup of credit unions—*low-income* credit unions, sometimes called community development credit unions—have played a substantial role in helping minorities and the poor get financial services. More than 2,100 of the 5,500 U.S. credit unions are designated low-income,[20] which means that a majority of their member-owners are low-income (less than 80 percent of the area median income). Low-income credit unions (LICUs), generally smaller than the others, are allowed extra flexibility under some regulations, such as those governing business lending.

The industry regulator, the National Credit Union Administration (NCUA), created the LICU category in 1970 to provide special benefits to institutions serving people with little or no access to conventional financial services. Those benefits include:[21]

- *The right to accept deposits from nonmembers:* Low-income communities often need financial products that are hard to fund without other people's money, because low-income people usually have little money to save.
- *Flexible ways to raise capital, or equity:* which gives them leverage to accept deposits and manage risks. Capital also makes it possible to grow. This helps LICUs to offer more products and create more opportunities.

- *The opportunity to apply for grants from the NCUA:* NCUA runs a special program for smaller credit unions. LICUs also are eligible for special NCUA consulting services. Because they are resource-limited, this program helps them do more for their members.
- *The authority to make more small business loans to members than other credit unions:* In low-income communities, particularly communities of color, small business lending is especially important and usually very hard to come by. It is riskier than many other forms of lending, however, so the NCUA watches it carefully.
- *Fast-track access to federal and some private financing sources:* One of the most significant of these is the Community Development Financial Institutions (CDFI) Fund in the Department of the U.S. Treasury.

From LICUs to the largest, most prosperous credit unions—Navy Federal CU is the largest, with assets totaling more than $55 billion[22]—the legal structure and public responsibilities ensure that they remain public-purpose institutions.

The first modern credit union emerged in Europe in 1850 as a way for farmers to pool resources on a cooperative basis after a crop crisis caused a spike in the cost of loans and other financial products.[23] Drawing on cooperative principles established in England a century earlier around what we now would consider lending circles (see below), credit unions put their profits back into their institutions to benefit their members. Each member has a single vote without regard to how much money they deposit or invest—a direct contrast to equity and stock markets, which tie voting rights to investment amounts. The members elect credit union boards that govern the business; board members often volunteer their services to keep costs down. Credit unions are profitable but not all are profit maximizing.

Every credit union in the United States today has a field of membership—a clearly defined reason for working together cooperatively. The field of membership might be geographic, faith-based, employment-based, or some other organizing idea.

Credit unions came to North America in 1900 as La Caisse Populaire de Lévis in Quebec and in 1909 as St. Mary's Cooperative Credit Association in Manchester, New Hampshire.[24] By the 1920s, the U.S. credit union sector was growing from the opportunity created when banks showed little interest in making small-dollar consumer loans for things like cars and home appliances.

In Massachusetts, retail magnate Edward Filene (best known as the owner of Filene's, a department store) took up the cause of credit unions. "One hundred individuals, saving their money individually, could not provide themselves with much protection," he explained, "But let them organize a credit union and their opportunity to help themselves was multiplied."[25]

With the assistance of a lawyer named Roy Bergengren, workers organized and Massachusetts charted nineteen new credit unions in 1920. They took the organizing effort national. Within five years, twenty-six states had passed laws to charter credit unions, leading to some 1,100 in thirty-two states by 1930. Congress passed and President Franklin Roosevelt signed the National Credit Union Act in 1934, resulting in more than 10,000 credit unions with more than 6 million members in the United States by 1960.[26]

Credit unions anchored a national cooperative movement supported by "systemic" cooperatives (known as wholesale corporate credit unions) instead of big banks, investment banks, and other conventional financial institutions. Credit unions today remain constructively interdependent and work closely with the broader cooperative movement of retailers, manufacturers, distributors, and consumers. The cooperative movement, Filene believed, "is warmly, humanly passionate; and it is demanding day-by-day that there is more real satisfaction and more business success in working together for the common ground."

The financial implosion of 2007 and 2008 hit credit unions— including the wholesale corporate ones—hard. Before the crisis, there were 8,268 credit unions operating, one-third more than today.[27] The U.S. credit union system today, like the banking industry, is much smaller in number of institutions than it used to be.

Credit unions have played a central role in bringing affordable financial products and services to working people when banks and other conventional financial institutions concentrated on wealthier people. They were not alone, however. At the dawn of the twentieth century, a pioneering entrepreneur realized that conventional, mainstream financial institutions were brushing working people aside. Middle- and low-income people were left few loan options but loan sharks.

"It is a very regrettable fact that until very recently the small loan business in this country has been almost entirely and even now is very largely in the hands of discredited and disreputable people," Arthur H. Ham concluded in comments to the Academy of Political Science in 1911.[28] Ham ran the Division of Remedial Loans at the Russell Sage Foundation in New York City. Ham was leading an effort to stop predatory lenders by capping what they could charge for loans. At the same time, he and others were offering affordable alternative loan sources.

"The rapidly rising storm of protest against the evils of usury [unreasonably expensive loans with high interest rates] in this country during the last few years has given an impetus to the remedial loan movement that has taken the form in many cities of competing loan institutions of semi-philanthropic nature," he said. Many of these loans were targeted at specific problems consumers faced, including purchasing supplies for work and covering emergency costs. Most, as a result, were small compared to the markets that mainstream financial institutions served.

Ham and others were frustrated in their campaign for federal legislation setting interest rate caps on small-dollar loans to consumers. "There have been from the beginning," he said, "intimations that a powerful lobby supported by combinations of money-lenders having their headquarters in Washington has been at work to prevent the passage of the bill and that political influence has been enlisted in most unusual and unexpected quarters." Ham was calling out money muscle of the day and objecting to the ability of predatory lenders to block government action.[29]

Ham and his allies wanted policy to emerge from practice by proving that it was possible and sustainable to lend for the same purposes at much better rates for consumers. In 1911, Ham counted twenty-one "remedial loan societies" in twenty cities. They managed $10 million of capital (about $266 million today), enough to earn second glances. In an article explaining the remedial loan funds, "Remedial Loans—a Constructive Program," Ham wrote, "[The remedial loans] are paying a reasonable return on their investment and by their competition are forcing the usurers to reduce their rates or vacate the field."[30] In New York City, he said, the Provident Loan Society, a remedial lender, had driven down interest rates charged by predatory lenders and driven many of them out of business.

New loan products Ham and others planned included small loans secured by mortgages and household furniture. Ham hoped to introduce responsible forms of salary loans—a version of today's payday loans that advance money in exchange for repayment on the next payday. Salary loans were and payday loans are high cost, very tempting for anyone short on cash, and very likely to trap borrowers into a cycle of escalating expenses.

Salary loans were common in New York then, as now. Ham estimated that one out of every twenty residents is "involved with the loan companies, many of whom are every year paying back in interest alone two or three times as much as they ever borrowed."

Congress never acted to protect the working people of New York City or anywhere else from the predatory lending of Ham's era.

What happened instead was improbable and counterintuitive. A group of organized people decided to organize their own money. In 1923, the Amalgamated Clothing Workers of America (ACWA) was starting to organize the hundreds of thousands of clothing workers in places like New York, Chicago, Rochester, and Montreal. The union was made up largely of European immigrants. Twelve years before the passage of the National Labor Relations Act, the union was harnessing the power of organized workers in part by building a community infrastructure that kept the union at the heart of what working people needed desperately but were unable to acquire from traditional means: the union built health clinics, affordable housing, and an insurance company. In 1922, it established the Amalgamated Bank of Chicago and the following year it received a charter from New York State for a sister bank in New York City.

The money to capitalize and start the bank came from the union. The New York bank opened on Union Square in Manhattan, then a social as well as economic, residential, and political center for the labor movement. It offered products tailored for union members, such as the first free savings accounts in the United States and unsecured small loans for working families, a version of the solution that Ham focused on. Well before others, Amalgamated Bank responded to the single greatest financial need that immigrant workers had—the need to send money back to their families in war-ravaged Europe. It introduced a foreign-exchange transfer service that helped its customers send dollars overseas (rather than local currencies). It financed affordable housing for working families. By the 1960s, it was lending nationwide to farmers for water systems infrastructure and other core community development needs. In the 1970s, the bank received regulatory authority to help unions manage the retirement assets of their members.

It started financing cooperative mortgages and lending to striking unions (including National Football League workers in the 1980s) to reduce the cash flow problems that otherwise constrained labor power. And it offered the first totally free checking accounts in New York City, along with other products customized to serve working families. In 2014, the bank was the first institution to extend access to financial services to thousands of immigrant workers when it started accepting New York City's municipal ID as a form of documentation to open bank accounts.

The labor movement played an important role in the mid-twentieth century by financing affordable housing for workers when few others were doing it. Amalgamated Bank played a central role almost a century ago in the union-led Amalgamated Houses, with 1,500 units in Manhattan. The bank also provided high-risk capital to cooperative home owners in the Bronx, lending interested workers up to 50 percent of the down payment amount.[31] In the heyday of labor-managed finance, there were thirty union-owned banks, and labor controlled substantial pension assets and other funds, which it put into progressive ownership models.

Today, labor unions lack both the opportunities and resources to finance workforce housing at scale, even as rental prices make decent housing for working people unaffordable in many places. Union membership and power has declined in part as a result of conservative attacks, notably "right-to-work" laws, which make it harder for unions to organize workers.[32] The decline in labor-affiliated workers resulted in steady decline in money for organized labor to use for everything from organizing to investments.

Use of the type of retirement accounts that labor unions negotiated for their members under the 1947 Taft-Hartley Act[33]—defined-benefit pensions, in particular—also declined with the introduction in the 1970s of individual retirement accounts and the rise in defined-contribution plans, which released employers from making mandatory contributions. Labor's influence over those retirement funds declined as Fidelity Investments and Vanguard took control of the "on-your-own" approach to organizing retirement planning and investment. Amalgamated Bank manages Taft-Hartley pension funds today, but it is a soft business.

While most banks of its size and scope put their advocacy behind traditional bank trade groups, such as the Independent Community Bankers of America or the American Bankers Association, Amalgamated is working with other financial institutions toward common-good outcomes through efforts like the Global Alliance for Banking on Human Values. Amalgamated leaders speak regularly, publicly, and often about issues involving money organizing that works against the average wage earner. Recently, it was the first bank to increase pay for minimum-wage employees. It offers a unique home-loan product to encourage solar panel installations, and it is a leader of the Move Your Money campaign, which encourages depositors to transfer their accounts to banks that align with their values.

After the defeat of the national bank model in 1836, local and demographically defined banks were common. Community-centered bank franchises were the rule, not the exception, through most of the 1800s and well into the 1900s. Federal law, the lack of a single national currency during much of that period, and the inertia of history made it difficult to manage financial institutions across geographies, diverse populations, and different communities.

Today while the nation's ten largest banks hold more than 11 percent of the total financial institution assets in the United States, they comprise less than 0.02 percent of all U.S. banks. Most of the rest are community banks, though the total number of banks (fewer than five thousand) has declined by more than half in the past few decades.[34]

There is renewed interest in creating a network of government-owned community banks, known as public banks, based on the example of the Bank of North Dakota (BND). BND opened in 1919 primarily to meet agricultural credit needs. It was not the first or only public bank, however. As a result of the Second National Bank closing in 1836, seven states created state-owned public banks,[35] and three set up banks with majority state ownership.[36] All eventually closed.

BND operates under a narrow charter. It manages money for the state, provides credit on reasonable terms for state-designated purposes, and supports economic development. At the same time, it is charged with helping and not hindering private banks. According to its founding documents, BND should be "helpful to and to assist in the development of state and national banks and other financial institutions and public corporations within the state and not, in any manner, to destroy or to be harmful to existing financial institutions." With more than $7 billion, including *all* state funds, BND is conservative about risk. That limits what it does with its money and whom it aims to benefit. In addition, it returns all profits to the state.

Advocates for public banking in San Francisco, Los Angeles,

Oakland, Philadelphia, and more than a dozen states are wrestling with the balance of cautious asset management and public-purpose banking. The Public Banking Institute is coordinating legislative campaigns throughout the nation emphasizing public ownership of banks as a hedge against another recession and a countervailing force against Wall Street. However, simply because a bank is publicly owned does not make it necessarily progressive, inclusive, or fair, though it might reduce the risks of greed affecting decisions. The public-bank approach seems more promising in theory than it has yet worked in practice.

Many other financial innovations have started targeting underserved people, some more ethical than others. Check-cashing businesses, for example, provided unbanked individuals a way to cash paychecks, a real value to those who don't use banks. They provide an important service, but many of these storefront businesses are abusively expensive, to benefit the owners at the expense of the customers. Today, a large national network of check cashers works hand-in-hand with banks and other mainstream financial institutions.

In many states, check cashers and even payday lenders get their financing from big banks, so the business is not competing with the banks but making money for them.[37] Some bankers and investors realized that check cashers were an important business complement, because they could make money on check cashers who borrowed from them. At the same time, though no banker likes to admit it, check cashers siphoned away from bank branches the customers who are less profitable to the banks.

More recently, in a similar instance of bank-supported disruption, online lenders rapidly went from curious innovation to credit competition to mainstream financial collaboration. Online lenders, such as Kabbage, focus on small business lending, in part because small businesses often have to make quick decisions in short time windows, and online lending is more convenient than traditional approaches. The laws around small business lending are laxer than for, say, home mortgages, however, and some online lenders charge well over 100 percent interest. In contrast, mortgage loans—which are much less risky—pay less than 5 percent at the time we are writing. Market research suggests that many small business owners, working hard day after day, make snap borrowing decisions. In addition, research among entrepreneurs of color and women entrepreneurs has found them receptive to online lenders because they've had prior negative experiences seeking loans from banks.

JPMorgan Chase and Goldman Sachs have partnered with online lenders (OnDeck and Lending Club, respectively) and slowly siphoned the business into their own corporations. They started by providing investment banking services—helping the online lenders raise funds, for example—and eventually absorbed the online lenders into their business lines.

That's business in financial services. Big, powerful financial institutions "skim the cream," the best from the innovators, and make it their own. The good news is that more customers get access to innovative products. The bad news is that the disruptive potential of public-purpose finance gets lost or discarded as innovators lose control of their products, services, and institutions.

It's a money-muscle thing. Progressive people, organizations, and financial institutions are within reach of it, they know they can succeed, but they have to get to work.

9

The Foundation of a
Progressive Finance Network

In practice, progressive financial institutions have many of the building blocks they need to begin assembling an infrastructure that works for them.

We are approaching the starting line for the next era of progressive, public-purpose finance under market conditions that seem increasingly favorable, with political winds stirring up progressive sentiments, in reach of unprecedented if still insufficient access to power, and leveraging a deep history of experience and expertise. Public-purpose finance today is the product of thousands of innovations over hundreds of years to balance the public good with private interests. They make up the practical foundation of progressive organized money waiting to be organized and leveraged.

Some of these innovations grew as a product of (but not funded directly by) public policy. For example, labor-owned pensions were set up to give working people control over their own retirement funds. Some, such as Amalgamated Bank, arose as institutional responses to market gaps or opportunities. Amalgamated was founded on the need to provide products for working people when most banks did not. Others, such as community banks, grew from the legacy of the U.S. banking system, which started with small, stand-alone banks in individual communities. While community banks today hold modest amounts of assets compared to global banks, they continue to serve as financial anchors in many towns, rural communities, and small cities. That carries a power of its own.

Out of philanthropy over the past fifty years grew program-related investments (PRIs), loans and investments made with charitable program funds that otherwise would be awarded as grants. Public foundations are required by the Internal Revenue Service to give or to lend at low rates on generous terms at least 5 percent of their wealth annually. Mission investors expanded PRIs to include financing using philanthropic endowments (their wealth), as well as program funds (the 5 percent), so that they are fully deployed in support of their missions. These are called MRIs, or mission-related investments. Impact investors are trying to develop models beyond mission investing, using various types of "blended" finance, combining charitable, concessionary, and profit-maximizing funding. Socially responsible investors generally buy shares of large companies as a means of engaging corporate owners in discussions on human rights, labor rights, and community development.

Working across many of these investment models are faith-based institutions, ranging from pastoral pension funds and small pools of capital owned by women religious to faith-affiliated financial companies, such as Thrivent Financial, a multi-billion-dollar non-profit financial fraternal organization. Faith-based intermediaries are often drivers of moral purpose that underlies public purpose finance. The CDFI industry was formed with faith-based money around the dual mandates of morality and fiscal discipline, the keys to its success. From its founding, the industry involved transformational as well as transactional work. Chuck Matthei of the Institute for Community Economics told an early CDFI gathering in 1985, "I think we need to define ourselves as groups that have multiple mission fields. It is our job to address the needs of those who need capital, but it is equally our job to address the people and institutions that invest capital."[1]

That calling remains true. All of these approaches share the central principle of progressive organized money—to serve financial needs, economic goals, *and* societal good. Many share a streak of self-determination: community-owned credit unions, minority-owned banks, and ethnic lending circles, for example, are based on community ownership rights. The benefit of ownership is the right to control how assets are used and what they are used for. Most of the time, owners favor their own interests or rights—as true for mainstream venture capitalists (controlled by fund managers who leverage investor wealth) as it is for community development credit unions (controlled by member-owners). Public-purpose financial institutions, by definition, embrace ownership structures that seek both financial and public benefit results.

The practice of public-purpose finance is wide-ranging today, but the many interrelated strategies routinely operate in isolation from one another, so it can be hard to see the possibility of collaboration. Faith-based investors and CDFIs historically have worked closely together, but public banks and CDFIs have done almost no work together. Community banks are more likely to turn to global banks than to labor pension funds for investments. Impact investors are looking for new investment opportunities, while credit unions look inward at their memberships. When you take in the whole array of strategies, however, you see something important: you see a substantial volume of finance dedicated to good, as well as a long history of financial services serving what the U.S. Constitution calls the "general welfare."

Many of the products, services, and financial institutions were and are profitable but not profit-maximizing, and so fill important functions both for economic markets and social progress. For example, finance circles—informal savings and financing groups often organized within ethnic, racial, and geographic communities—have sustained local economies by investing collaboratively in niche economies (for example, Korean greengrocers, Muslim halal food services, and African arts). Immigrants often brought the approach with them—older than our nation yet on the leading edge of finance in emerging domestic markets. Korean small business lending circles, known as *kye*, date back to the seventeenth century; Chinese lending circles are *hui*; West Indian, *susu*; and Ethiopian, *ekub*. Now a CDFI based in San Francisco, the Mission Asset Fund, is helping to increase the scale and scope of lending circles by developing their systems infrastructure. Hebrew free loan societies—from the Jewish community for the Jewish community—provided small personal and business loans in the early twentieth century and still operate today.

During the 2018–19 government shutdown, when hundreds of thousands of federal employees experienced financial havoc and distress because they were not paid for more than a month, the range of approaches came into play. At one end, mainstream financial institutions showed a willingness to accept late payments and offer loans to affected federal employees. They were egged on by Commerce Secretary Wilbur Ross's public bewilderment that more people were not borrowing money, reflecting his apparent lack of understanding that people working paycheck-to-paycheck might not want to pay the fees and interest on loans to gain access to the money they had already earned. At the other end of the approaches, the Hebrew Free Loan Society of Philadelphia, one of an international network of faith-based lenders, offered free loans without collateral to federal workers, sparking others to do the same. By contrast, many credit unions, community banks, and others added only a dollop of understanding and compassion for customers who thought to ask.

None of the progressive financial institutions or sectors have achieved market scale, however, to match the opportunities and demands of national markets. That is a major challenge; it is hard to sustain power without scale, and purpose without growth. The lack of scale is also an obstacle to an inclusive benefit economy, driving mission-centered customers instead to meet their financing needs using mainstream financial institutions. For example, large public foundations working for climate change need large credit facilities (loans they can use if they need them) for emergencies, and even the largest community banks and CDFIs cannot lend at that scale. So the foundations give that business to major banks. Even large CDFIs (the largest tops $2 billion) bank with mainstream financial institutions because their peer CDFI banks and credit unions do not have the expertise or the financial management capacity to meet their needs. If they had a network that worked for them, they would use it.

The business relationships among financial institutions and progressive advocates are key. Physical and commercial proximity builds trust, advances ideas, opens financial doors, and strengthens participants. There has never been as much proximity among leaders of progressive finance and mainstream financial system executives as there is today. At the same time, the champions of progressive finance are more closely connected than ever to national, state, and local government officials. No small achievement, this access to power represents substantial opportunity to speak for progressive finance and the causes it backs—and substantial risk that business ties to conventional financial institutions could mute the voices of CDFI leaders, progressive activists, and others.

A sense of what is possible and what is at stake is the alliance that developed over the past thirty years between advocates using the Community Reinvestment Act (CRA) and leaders of the CDFI industry, a successful network of private financial institutions. Together they make up a leading edge of progress over the past thirty years even as new approaches leapfrog them. To be clear, neither the CRA nor CDFIs alone in their current forms provide a clear route to the full-service, market-scale progressive financial network we envision. Together, however, they demonstrate in the current political, economic, and social operating environment how community-centered, market-based strategies can achieve public purposes with private capital.

It's a both-and situation.

Until 1977, discrimination in mortgage lending was legal under the National Housing Act of 1934, which resulted in a system of federal provisions for "redlining"—drawing red lines around neighborhoods deemed risky, explicitly blocking loans to neighborhoods where black people lived. Generations of prospective African American homeowners were denied mortgages and thus denied homeownership, which results in significant gains in wealth for millions of white homeowners. Mortgage discrimination was a major factor in what social commentators Melvin Oliver and Thomas Shapiro call "the sedimentation of poverty" in *Black Wealth/White Wealth*.[2] Despite a series of laws to discourage discrimination in housing and other areas of economic life, it took the Community Reinvestment Act of 1977 to outlaw it.[3]

A simple law that requires banks—though not other financial

intermediaries—to serve all people in their "footprint" equally, CRA marked the beginning of the modern era of public-purpose finance. It started as a mandate for banks—in 1977, the core of the financial system—to operate responsibly in relation to racial, income, and wealth differences. The CRA said, in essence, that banks had to serve all the people in the neighborhoods where they took deposits. It required banks (and savings and loans) to serve the "convenience and needs"—with a special mention of credit needs—of the communities where they are chartered to do business. The law instructs that the depositories have a "continuing and affirmative obligation to help meet the credit needs of the local communities in which they are chartered."[4]

CRA has spurred more than $1 trillion in bank financing into low-income communities and is a key driver of success in the modern era of community development finance.[5] It is the most far-reaching antipoverty strategy to date. In addition to driving investments into under-resourced communities and markets, it helped to open conventional financial eyes to opportunities outside mainstream markets. It spurred significant new financing by banks and other institutions, inspired innovation well beyond its original reach, and boosted the CDFI industry into a major role in finance.

The CRA has been particularly important in spurring new financing to African Americans, Latinos, and other racial and ethnic populations. Much of that financing has gone directly from the banks into community businesses, homes, and projects, while a smaller share has passed through CDFIs. CRA has also increased financing to women-owned businesses. Since at least 2005, it has also increasingly supported environmental business and projects. Over time, it has served as the foundation for broader bank corporate social responsibility strategies.

The CRA challenges the private financial marketplace to work the way its champions claim it does.

The CRA goes to the heart of the roles and responsibilities of financial institutions. Its underlying premise challenged Milton Friedman's argument that the only purpose of a corporation is to maximize returns to shareholders. It put the concepts of business and policy in direct conflict—one says the purpose of business is profit *and* the common good while the other holds that the purpose of business is profit alone.

Today the CRA remains effective but limited in scope compared to the expanded roles banking and financial services have taken on. In 1977, very different than today, the main function of banks was to accept deposits. Best estimates are that more than two-thirds of Americans' savings in 1978, when the CRA took effect, were in banks covered by the law; today, the comparable figure is less than 15 percent. As the financial system expanded and non-bank financial institutions introduced new products—starting with the cash management account (CMA) and its descendant array of investment options—Americans moved their savings and investments out of banks and into nonbanks, first to Merrill Lynch but soon to hundreds more nonbank finance firms, such as Charles Schwab, later E-Trade, and most recently online investment platforms such as Personal Capital. As a result, the impact of the CRA diminished proportionally. (Chapter 11 includes a proposal for restoring and expanding its policy value.) Nevertheless, it helped spur socially responsible investing, corporate social responsibility CDFIs, and later impact investing in a ripple of purpose-driven finance well beyond poverty alleviation and nondiscrimination.

The CRA is a totem for inclusive finance. As a result, it is a lightning rod for attacks. Most visibly, CRA opponents blamed it falsely for the mortgage crisis, disingenuously arguing that the law forced banks to make irresponsible home loans. In fact, the vast majority of home loans are made by nonbanks, particularly mortgage companies, which are outside the reach of the CRA.

The CRA is enforced through regular reviews by bank regulators, who assign ratings—outstanding, satisfactory, and unsatisfactory. When banks want to expand, purchase, or merge with another bank, or start certain types of new businesses, the CRA rating is used to assess whether it is meeting its community obligations. If not, the regulator might reject or hold up the proposed transaction while it conducts public hearings or invites public comment. This gives the law—and its supporters—a substantial lever through public opinion and public policy. CRA advocates at the local and national levels often negotiate reinvestment commitments by banks that total billions of dollars.

In its legislative form, the CRA provided the goal but not always the means to expand inclusive financial services to communities where banks would not work. Community advocates pressed banks to do better and do more, often with little success, because there was little risk in inactivity. CDFIs developed to help fill the gaps.

CDFIs are private financial intermediaries that exist to finance things that benefit low-income, low-wealth, and other underserved people and communities. Each type of CDFI provides distinct products and services in local markets, customized to serve customers first and investors second.

More than a thousand CDFIs managing more than $140 billion work today outside the margins of conventional finance to offer responsible financial products and services. They operate in urban, rural, and Native communities in all fifty states. They provide a full array of financial products and services—loans, investments, savings, payments, and more. Like other financial sectors, the CDFI industry includes a small number of very large institutions and a very large number of small institutions.

CDFIs exist in four main forms:

- **Community development credit unions (CDCUs)** are nonprofit depositories (see above). They range in size from small, church-based organizations that provide primarily savings products to multi-billion-dollar, full-service providers. Some, like Suncoast Credit Union in Tampa, Florida, emerged from company-based credit unions; in Suncoast's case, the company was GTE, a multinational telecommunications company that failed in 1982. As a result, many of its former employees became low-income consumers, and the strategic focus of Suncoast shifted to their needs.

  More commonly, CDCUs have emerged from local community organizing efforts. The Lower East Side People's Federal Credit Union in Manhattan was started in 1984 after a series of bank-branch closures in the neighborhood. Today it's a community fixture.

  Low-income credit unions automatically qualify for CDFI Fund certification, and other credit unions can qualify by demonstrating that they are benefiting populations with clear needs using products that address the challenges of their member-customers.[6] There are more than two hundred CDCUs in the United States today, managing more than $60 billion.[7]

- **Community development banks (CDBs)** are for-profit depositories that operate under federal or state bank charters, are governed by all banking laws, and concentrate their products and services on CDFI-eligible populations. The first community development bank was South Shore Bank in Chicago, which was formed in 1973 because other banks were abandoning a community on the South Side of the city as it was becoming majority African American. Shorebank, as it was known, served as the model and advisor for the Southern Development Bank Corporation in Arkansas during the time Bill Clinton was governor there. Secretary Hillary Clinton served on the Southern Bancorp Board, and her law firm provided legal services. When the Clintons moved into the White House, Shorebank and Southern made up half the total of four CDBs in the nation. Today, there are more than eighty, holding more than $35 billion. A growing source of new CDBs are longstanding community banks that have found themselves serving resource-constrained markets with few, if any, other financial institutions in town.

• **Community development venture, or equity, funds** make up a small but important part of the CDFI industry. Established to meet growing needs for growth-oriented small businesses in distressed markets, they provide early-stage risk capital and help entrepreneurs raise investments from more conventional sources.

• **Community development loan funds** are the most common and flexible type of CDFI, in part because they are the easiest to start and fund. They also are not regulated in the ways that banks and credit unions are. That allows them to work more flexibly with their customers. Loan funds finance affordable housing, small businesses, nonprofits, and at times even government programs. Microlenders—financial institutions dedicated to financing self-employed entrepreneurs and very small businesses—usually (but not always) take the form of loan funds.

Most loan funds are nonprofit, though a very few are for-profit businesses. For instance, Clearinghouse CDFI in California is a for-profit loan fund that has financed mortgages for single-family home purchases, multifamily apartment developments in rural communities, and Native-owned businesses in South Dakota. Craft3, a nonprofit CDFI in the Pacific Northwest, pioneered a way for homeowners to borrow for energy efficiency upgrades and pay off the loans directly through their electric utility bills on a monthly basis. The Entrepreneur Fund, based in Duluth, Minnesota, is a prime supplier of financing to microentrepreneurs throughout Northern Minnesota.

In the 1980s, CDFIs struggled to prove their value and their sustainability. They inched along with the support of faith-based investors, PRIs from the Ford and MacArthur foundations, and a nascent group of socially responsible investors. Today they are a force for public-purpose finance widely deployed and respected for their success at combining sound money management and social impact. The role they carved out, straddling the worlds of conventional financial institutions and underserved markets, putting their customers before their investors, is important and instructive to the expansion of a progressive financial network with money muscle.

CDFIs brought a unique—and as it turns out some forty years later, successful—business model that blended public purpose and disciplined financial management to achieve good social, economic, and financial returns. This combination wasn't new, but it resonated for two reasons.

First, because of timing. CDFIs started to get their sea legs as the cash management account (CMA) was pulling the financial system off its moorings, the CRA was gaining momentum, and both financial industry officials and community advocates were in search of ways to bridge the growing cracks in the old financial system. As a result, the CDFI industry has grown more than seventyfold, its financing has increased at least as much, and it has demonstrated the viability and sustainability of purpose-driven finance over time.

Second, because of policy. Newly elected president Bill Clinton had latched on to CDFIs as a signature strategy in 1992. In September 1994 he signed into law the CDFI Fund, a federal program without precedent. The CDFI Fund invested in the financial intermediaries—the CDFIs—rather than individual projects in communities. Like nothing before or since, it reinvented how government can work. And the CDFI Fund has worked well, delivering more than $2 billion in capital to CDFIs while implementing New Markets Tax Credits and other financing opportunities totaling tens of billions of dollars more.

Congress created the CDFI Fund in 1994 with overwhelming bipartisan support and has sustained it through both Democratic and Republican administrations with ongoing broad support.[8] In fiscal 2018, for example, amid widespread funding cuts in Congress for discretionary programs and despite the Trump administration's effort to eliminate the fund, Congress increased its allocation. That appeal across party lines is evidence of an approach with promise.

The CDFI Fund is unlike every other federal program and its success suggests it can advance many fiscal policy solutions. Created to strengthen and expand a network of private financial institutions, it makes equity investments (for nonprofit CDFIs, they take the form of equity grants) on a competitive basis. All other federal programs (with the exception of the Troubled Asset Relief Program, or TARP, which Congress created to rescue financial institutions during the crisis of 2008) invest in specific, designated projects. The CDFI Fund invests more like conventional business investors. It provides capital based on each CDFI's market strategy, its financial strength and capacity, and its management and governance. It's a results-based approach that requires clear goals—measured both in financial and social metrics—like the ones mainstream investors require in their portfolios.

For that reason, the CDFI Fund strategy places a premium on CDFI performance. A clear benefit of the CDFI Fund's equity investing model is that it is more likely to increase the independence of CDFIs rather than create dependence, which often happens when governments provide money for operations rather than capital.

During the Great Recession, CDFIs faced serious challenges. Some experienced substantial losses due to loans gone bad, and a few of them failed or were taken over. Their borrowers were struggling, like most people and businesses in the nation, and needed patience and sometimes adjustments to their loans. Early in the recession, CDFI industry leaders openly discussed the possibility that the industry, which always prided itself on working in markets that others would not risk going into—might not survive the economic downturn. In fact, at some point in 2008 or 2009, everyone involved in the financial system thought, that they might not survive.

The CDFI Fund provided additional financing on a one-time basis. In addition, the Treasury Department created a special program to bolster the equity, or capital, base for depository CDFIs, the Community Development Capital Initiative (CDCI), and it helped many CDFIs to weather the storm.

The CDFI Fund has also become a well-regarded home for other programs favored by both Republicans and Democrats. When Congress created the New Markets Tax Credit program in late 2000, it housed it at the CDFI Fund. Strategies to strengthen Indian

Country, including sovereign Native Reservations, led to a network of Native CDFIs. In response to the housing crisis that occurred during the recession, Congress created the Capital Magnet Fund at the CDFI Fund—a special program, financed by Fannie Mae and Freddie Mac, quasi-governmental agencies at the heart of the housing finance business.

Even in the final year of the Obama administration, when partisan tensions were extremely high, high-ranking officials came together in support of the CDFI industry. "There are very few things that Republicans and Democrats can agree on in this town," Senator John Boozman, a Republican from Arkansas and chairman of the committee responsible for CDFI Fund funding, said privately to a small group of CDFIs, "and you are one." Later that day, a top Obama administration official delivered the same affirmative message directly to one of us (Pinsky).

Mainstream financial institutions came to embrace CDFIs as business partners in social impact strategies. Bank support of CDFIs was not a lark. It was an indirect result of the CRA.[9] In no small part as a result of the Great Recession, when banks found it hard to lend to anyone other than their strongest customers, many financial institutions turned to CDFIs, lending to them so they, in turn, could lend to their communities. That led a growing number of mainstream financial institutions to see the CDFI industry no longer as a CRA strategy but instead as a set of prudent business partners.

In the early 1990s, JPMorgan Chase chairman Jamie Dimon told one of the authors (Pinsky) that CDFIs were one of the worst ideas he had ever heard of.[10] But in 2018, his bank enthusiastically claimed credit for its support of CDFIs in Detroit, Chicago, Philadelphia, and elsewhere. When Wall Street titan Goldman Sachs introduced its 10,000 Small Businesses initiative in 2010, working with Warren Buffett of Berkshire Hathaway and Michael

Bloomberg, another billionaire and former New York City mayor, it structured it around CDFIs financing small businesses.[11] Prudential Insurance has long operated a social investment fund in collaboration with CDFIs. Wells Fargo designed its Diverse Community Capital program to increase CDFI financing so as to increase lending to businesses owned by people of color. MetLife, one of the largest insurance companies in the United States, works with CDFIs and others to help financial consumers navigate the complex and confusing world of organized money.

One consequence of the growing collaboration is that CDFI executives and other progressive financiers found themselves seated at important tables within many of the most powerful institutions. Bank of America's National Community Advisory Council is predominantly populated with CDFI and CRA advocacy CEOs, alongside a smaller group of environmental, civil rights, and social justice leaders. It met regularly with bank chairman Brian Moynihan and other top executives.[12] Goldman Sachs's advisory board for its 10,000 Small Businesses initiative seated the CDFI industry's leadership next to Warren Buffett, Goldman's then-chairman Lloyd Blankfein, Michael Bloomberg, and National Urban League president Marc Morial. Morgan Stanley brought its CEO into a room with a council of CDFIs and other progressive champions, like Prosperity Now's Andrea Levere. JPMorgan Chase's Dimon started meeting regularly with CDFI and other community partners and opened other bank convenings to progressive finance partners, including Amalgamated Bank.

The shared affinity for finance brought the mainstream bankers and CDFI executives together in pursuit of collaborative efforts and, most of the time, shared goals. Progressive finance leaders won respect and support, and most conversations were sincere, productive, and honest. The bilateral transfer of solutions reflected notable gains in power by progressive finance leaders.

In the federal government, progressive finance executives moved closer to power than had seemed possible even a decade earlier. Impact investors, CDFI heads, CRA advocates, and other champions of public-purpose finance met with presidents, Cabinet secretaries, senior officials, senators, members of Congress, and other powerful people. The success of the CDFI Fund—embraced across the political spectrum—made a real difference. Impact investors gained standing in the Obama administration and grew to a position of international influence, leveraging the CDFI track record to demonstrate broader potential.

The extraordinary access to power that progressive financial institutions enjoy today is still, however, an underused resource. The potential is there, but even the aggregate worth of their work is still a sideshow in a hundred-trillion-dollar-plus systems. For business as well as policy reasons, building a progressive financial network depends on growth, which requires a level of investment in and ownership of the progressive end of the financial system that is so far just a dream.

Which raises the question, where is the money going to come from?

10

Whose Wealth Is It Anyway?

Progressives have more wealth than most people know.
Where is it? What is it doing?

Americans as a group, including the majority who comprise the political left and center, are wealthier than you might think, even though the political right is wealthier still. That's no good reason for the imbalance in influence and power, however. The conservative right has organized its wealth for power much better than the left. That means that conservatives are better at organizing money and using it to achieve things, not that they have the right priorities or goals for the nation.

Americans hold more than $100 trillion in "household" wealth, according to the Federal Reserve System, or about half the total household wealth in the world. Most of that is tied up in the costs of living. The question at the heart of this book is whether a small amount of that wealth—1 percent, or $1 trillion—can be organized as ownership stakes in a full-service, market-scale network of financial institutions that share a primary goal of increasing financial inclusion, environmental sustainability, social justice, and fair economic opportunity. That's $1 trillion to leverage another $9 trillion or more to counter the historical financial services conservative bias. And every dollar aligned with you is also a dollar that is no longer aligned against you, so it's like a "twofer."

The potential to create progressive economic, social, cultural, and political influence and power to counter the conservative right is as great as the influence and power that now exists on the conservative side. Aligning financial services with the majority views and values of the American people would transform more than organized money, because organized money is how we get things done. Progressive individuals and organizations have articulated their goals, ranging from family-wage employment to the Green New Deal to voting rights and beyond. They will define the next progressive era; we want to ensure that that era is backed by a financial system that delivers the resources to succeed and sustain itself.

We believe it will get done. In fact, we are sure it can happen, for several reasons.

First, there is plenty of wealth to achieve what we plan to do. It just is not organized in line with the values and vision of the people who earned it.

Against the backdrop of the financial system, let alone the whole U.S. economy, $1 trillion is not actually that much money—1 percent of American household wealth, 8 percent of socially responsible investment funds under management, and two-and-a-half times the amount of money donated by Americans annually. Those numbers tell you it's not a crazy idea. They also suggest that it's not a simple one.

Second, in the segments of the financial system the two of us have worked in, we have helped organize about $150 billion (or 15 percent of our $1 trillion goal) under tougher conditions—specifically, investment opportunities that required wealth holders to make

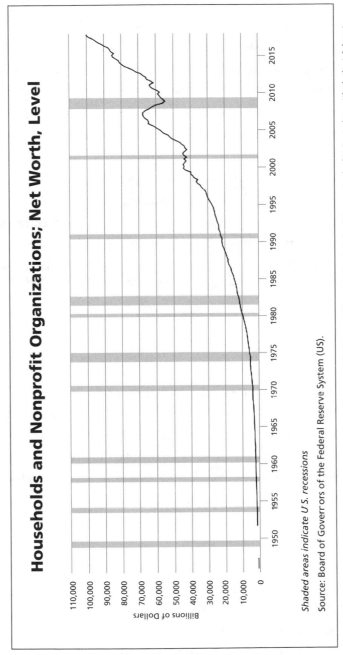

Households and Nonprofit Organizations; Net Worth, Level

Billions of Dollars

110,000
100,000
90,000
80,000
70,000
60,000
50,000
40,000
30,000
20,000
10,000
0

1950 1955 1960 1965 1970 1975 1980 1985 1990 1995 2000 2005 2010 2015

Shaded areas indicate U.S. recessions

Source: Board of Governors of the Federal Reserve System (US).

Source: "Balance Sheet of Households and Nonprofit Organizations," FRED (Federal Reserve Economic Data), Federal Reserve Bank of St. Louis, https://fred.stlouisfed.org/series/TNWBSHNO.

financial concessions on their returns and the risks they took on. That happened due to a mix of strong financial performance, product innovation, public policy, public awareness and branding, good marketing, and—most of all—pragmatic solutions that met needs. The $1 trillion we are focused on would be market-rate, liquid (to ensure investors all the flexibility they routinely expect and need), and market-size (investors would gain comfort from the number of other investors required).

Third, the progressive opportunities that we are aligned with—environmental, racial and ethnic emerging markets, labor, women, and others—are significant growth markets for investors. In fact, they dominate the top-ten lists of investment opportunities. These opportunities that once seemed extraneous to financial markets have become core to a growing number of investors' strategies.

All the more important, aligning money and markets with advocacy and action amplifies the power and influence of both, just as it has for the alliance of conservative finance with advocacy and action on conservative goals.

In addition, the profound shift slowly happening in corporate structure (from the push of B Lab to the pull of investor expectations) and strategy (from the brand-burnishing of corporate social responsibility to the business imperative of customer experience) is a world-changing force. There will be slow gains as well as setbacks. The combination of expanding impact evaluation via big data with the changing norms of a new generation are now undeniable realities in business and finance.

Fourth, there is substantial experience in both the financial practice and the public policy that amounts to proof of concept. We have more than enough evidence that there is demand for capital seeking progressive outcomes. We can count more than $12 trillion invested in aligned purposes through socially responsible investors, mission-related investors, community investors, philanthropy, and impact investors. The shift to capitalizing public-purpose financial institutions should be an incremental step with transformational impact.

Since its beginnings in the mid-1980s, socially responsible investing has grown from a niche in the financial marketplace to a nuisance for conventional money organizers to a market seeking investors to a new asset class. Today, according to the US SIF (formerly the Social Investment Forum), SRI represents more than $12 trillion of assets, an undeniable factor for investors. A *Wall Street Journal* market analysis in the spring of 2018 concluded that ideas that would have sounded like extreme Occupy Wall Street rhetoric a decade ago now are routine in Wall Street marketing materials. "Civic society is calling on the financial-services industry to advance sustainable development goals," JPMorgan Chase reported.[1]

That growth reflects surging interest in the issues that challenge conventional, conservative money organizing: environmental sustainability most of all, as well as global conflicts and human rights, community investing in the United States, concerns about excessive executive pay, equality for women in the workforce, racial and ethnic equity, and broader corporate governance issues.

On the policy front, a focus on social-benefit financial institutions—in contrast to direct project support—has given rise to a new industry with substantial upside potential. This financial intermediary approach of fiscal policy—delivering programs through financing via CDFIs and other types of intermediaries—is increasingly popular at the federal, state, and local levels because it is an effective and proven way of leveraging public resources beyond what they can otherwise achieve. It is a promising example for organized money. In addition to federal use of public-purpose intermediaries, many states have corresponding CDFI and/or tax credit statutes that utilize them.

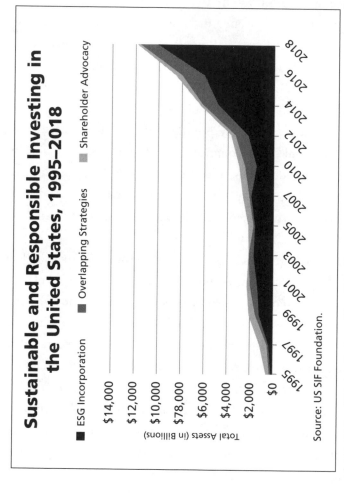

Sustainable and Responsible Investing in the United States, 1995–2018

- ■ ESG Incorporation
- ■ Overlapping Strategies
- ■ Shareholder Advocacy

Total Assets (in Billions)

$14,000
$12,000
$10,000
$78,000
$6,000
$4,000
$2,000
$0

1995 1997 1999 2001 2003 2005 2007 2010 2012 2014 2016 2018

Source: US SIF Foundation.

Source: *Report on US Sustainable, Responsible and Impact Investing Trends 2018* (Washington, DC: US SIF), executive summary, p. 1.

Fifth, close to 50 percent of the wealth holders in America lean left, even if 50 percent of the wealth does not. We do not take it for granted that American wealth is disproportionately held by people with conservative values, even though it disproportionately is controlled by people with conservative values. (That is the heart of the matter we are addressing.) We do not believe—at odds with conventional thinking—that people on the political right are wealthier on average than people on the left.

Each year, autumn is prize season. The Rhodes Trust announces its Rhodes Scholars, elite young adults selected for elite educational opportunities and elite life opportunities. The John D. and Catherine T. MacArthur Foundation announces the MacArthur Fellows, exceptional achievers in a wide range of important but usually arcane and underappreciated pursuits. MacArthur Fellows receive substantial multiyear grants that carry no restrictions for use. The idea is to allow geniuses the financial freedom to do what they think is most important by giving them financial equity of their own to work with.

Perhaps the most titillating fall announcement is the designation of America's wealthiest person and the release of the "Forbes 400: The Definitive Ranking of the Wealthiest Americans." There's just something about extreme wealth. "Seemingly as inevitable as death and taxes, the rich once again have grown richer," Forbes reported in October 2018.

The total net worth of the 2018 Forbes 400 hit $2.9 trillion, reflecting the increasing concentration of wealth among this wealthiest sliver of Americans, $7.2 billion on average. Overall that's a 7 percent increase over 2017, although those figures are distorted a bit by the $78.5 billion gains of number 1, Jeff Bezos of Amazon. Bezos is a new number 1, by the way, with $160 billion, replacing Bill

Gates ($97 billion), who held the position for twenty-two consecu-
tive years. Warren Buffett held steady at number 3 ($88.3 billion).
They are all wealthy primarily because the value of their ownership shares have gone up.

It's worth noting that numbers 1 to 3, with combined net assets
of $345.3 billion—or more than 10 percent of the total worth of the
400—are *not* conservatives, judging by their public statements and
philanthropic choices. (Add number 4, Mark Zuckerberg, and his
$61 billion before you get to more conservative billionaires, such
as Larry Ellison—number 5, with $58.4 billion—and then much
more conservative players, such as the Koch Brothers, Charles and
David—tied for number 7, each with $53.5 billion).

By the way, the biggest "loser"—more accurately, the person
whose net assets dropped the most from 2017 to 2018—was liberal
George Soros, who declined steeply from $23 billion to $8.3 billion.
But he'll be okay; the drop is entirely due to his $18 billion gift to his
charities, the Open Society Foundations.

And the biggest gainer—Jack Dorsey of Twitter—outgained
by percentage even Bezos. His net assets increased 186 percent to
$6.3 billion. It is not the case, though, that he is the beneficiary of
President Trump's Twitter fetish; most of his gains come from his
other big business, Square, a financial company.

Whatever admiration, jealousy, anger, or aspirations the *Forbes*
400 might unleash in you, we want you to focus on one point: There
is a *lot* of money in play, and it is held by progressives, moderates, and liberals as well as by market fundamentalists and other
conservatives.

That's how we know that the big challenge we all face is not the
amount of money we need but who controls it. Financial control
is primarily a question of what we ask our net assets, or equity, to

do—whether we use our equity for self-interest, the common good, or both.

Forbes wants to help us think about that question, too.

The 2018 *Forbes* 400 incorporates two features that seem to reflect the expanding idea that wealth has responsibilities and, by extension, that businesses do, too. The first feature is a Philanthropy Score, which tries to measure each billionaire's generosity. The methodology is intriguing, but the data are, based on our experience, problematic.

On the intriguing side, *Forbes* sets a high financial standard: "Only 29 of America's 400 richest were given the highest possible score," it says. "To get to that recognition, a person had to give away at least $1 billion and/or 20% of their total net worth." It also incorporates qualitative factors, such as major charitable pledges and commitments to give away most of their wealth over time, that are hard to measure consistently.

On the problematic side, however, it appears to skew in an unbalanced way toward progressive philanthropy, such as gifts for education (Zuckerberg) and global health (Gates) and appears to undercount conservative philanthropy, such as the Koch Brothers support for right-wing think tanks, like the Heritage Foundation and the Cato Institute, and issue-specific giving. That seems to misrepresent and underestimate conservative philanthropy, which is both unfair and misleading.

For philanthropic context, the $2.9 trillion in total assets held by the *Forbes* 400 is roughly three times the total assets of *all* the public foundations in the United States, according to the most recent figures from the Foundation Center. There are two interesting thought experiments you can do with these data.

For one, public foundations are required by law to give away (or invest at favorable rates and terms) at least 5 percent of their assets each year. If you applied that 5 percent rule to the *Forbes* 400, you would project charitable contributions of about $14.5 billion. Soros alone gave away $18 billion, by giving it to his network of philanthropies, while public foundations gave away almost $63 billion in the last year reported by the Foundation Center.

Or you can, as a thought experiment, think about the wealth as the financial base for a public-purpose investment strategy. Suppose you treat the $2.9 trillion as net assets that you could borrow against (the way a down payment can earn you access to a loan), as a financial institution would. If you could borrow $10 for every $1 of net assets, you would have $29 trillion to work with to invest in the benefit economy. By comparison, if public foundations leveraged their $900 billion in net assets to $9 trillion, that would be a game changer, too. In other words, you can think of net assets as investment capital and begin to envision what progressive organized money could become. Imagine CDFIs and impact investing at a much larger scale.

Forbes also introduced a set of profiles of Billionaires Building Change, or impact investors. Impact investing is a broad term meant to sweep an array of well-intended financing strategies into a common toolkit. Since the idea came into use eleven years ago, according to the Global Impact Investing Network (GIIN), at least $228 billion is "at work."

The original idea was that impact investors could "do good and do well"—make market-rate returns and finance systemic change. The field has evolved substantially and quickly to include a range of impact financing strategies, from traditional philanthropy (grant making) to concessionary financing (low-cost or other nonmarket terms and conditions) to experimental structures (such as social impact bonds, or SIBs) to market-rate investing. The $228 billion figure includes all of this. Impact investing is a useful term that offers more utility in its descriptive breadth than in its financial depth.

The GIIN doesn't yet count the $330 billion that CERES, the Coalition for Environmentally Responsible Economies, reports were invested in clean energy businesses in 2017. CERES's outlook is that there is real demand for $1 trillion in market-rate private investments in the environmental sector through 2030—a cause for confidence and hope. Stand that up against Bank of America's estimate that the global need for impact capital—what it calls blended capital—is $90 trillion, and you get a sense of the scale of the challenge. Public purpose finance alone is necessary but not sufficient; real progress requires a progressive financial system that can alter the course of the bigger mainstream financial marketplace.

Contrast the $330 billion that CERES counts to the $1.9 trillion that thirty-three global banks invested in the fossil fuel industry around the world from 2016 through 2018, according to Rainforest Action Network, Banktrack, Sierra Club, and other environmental advocates.[2] Even $330 billion is vital and necessary but not sufficient.

Forbes editors featured twenty-four billionaires "leading the way" on impact investing. They included Melinda and Bill Gates, of course, and spotlighted their investments in biotech firms. They reported on Priscilla Chan and Mark Zuckerberg's support for a training program in Africa for software developers, on financing by Pierre Omidyar of eBay for solar-power lighting, and on James Coulter (TPG, a private equity firm) and his multi-billion-dollar The Rise Fund making private equity impact investments in underdeveloped economies. The efforts are important, and fact that *Forbes* put so much emphasis on the practice is significant. This is not Milton Friedman's economy. And this is not the conservative society that it used to be.

A January 2018 Gallup poll found that the difference between the percentage of Americans who identify as "conservative" compared to those who identify as "liberal" is smaller than it has been since Gallup started measuring in 1992. The difference is 9 percent.

More significant from our perspective, 61 percent do not identify as conservative—26 percent liberal plus 35 percent moderate. Dig a little deeper into the Gallup data and you find out that two-thirds (67 percent) of political Independents are either ideologically moderate (43 percent) or liberal (24 percent)—not conservative.

Yet nearly 100 percent of people bank in support of conservative goals.

On *economic*—rather than social—issues, roughly 60 percent of all U.S. adults take a conservative view (economic issues are not the same as financial issues, but still), while about 40 percent take a liberal view, for a "net-conservative" rate of 21 percent. The partisan divide is stark, with a 62 percent net-conservative difference among Republicans (more than 80 percent conservative and less than 20 percent liberal) and a net-conservative score of –15 among Democrats (more than 40 percent conservative and slightly less than 60 percent liberal).

Gallup did not include moderate economic views, so the results are pushed to the binary extremes of conservative and liberal. The conservative preference is clear but it is a trend, not a shutdown fact.

On *social* issues, Gallup found just 34 percent of U.S. adults say they are conservative (30 percent say they are liberal and apparently another 36 percent are moderate), against a backdrop of overwhelmingly conservative use of organized money by financial institutions as a whole.

It seems that the share of American adults supporting nonconservative positions on economic and social issues is much greater than the share of American wealth dedicated to nonconservative uses. There is a lot of room to improve and to loosen the hold that

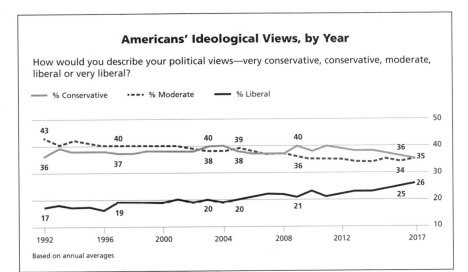

Americans' Ideological Views, by Year

How would you describe your political views—very conservative, conservative, moderate, liberal or very liberal?

───── % Conservative   ▪▪▪▪ % Moderate   ▬▬ % Liberal

Based on annual averages

Source: Lydia Saad, "Conservative Lead in U.S. Ideology Is Down to Single Digits," Gallup, Washington, DC, January 11, 2018.

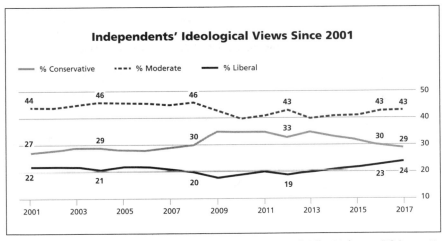

Independents' Ideological Views Since 2001

───── % Conservative   ▪▪▪▪ % Moderate   ▬▬ % Liberal

Source: Lydia Saad, "Conservative Lead in U.S. Ideology Is Down to Single Digits," Gallup, Washington, DC, January 11, 2018.

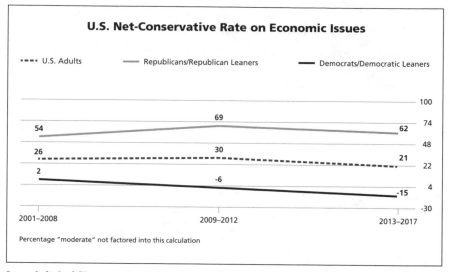

U.S. Net-Conservative Rate on Economic Issues

---- U.S. Adults   ——— Republicans/Republican Leaners   ——— Democrats/Democratic Leaners

69

54   62

26   30   21

2

-6

-15

| 2001–2008 | 2009–2012 | 2013–2017 |

Percentage "moderate" not factored into this calculation

Source: Lydia Saad, "Democrats Growing More Economically Liberal," Gallup, Washington, DC, August 11, 2017.

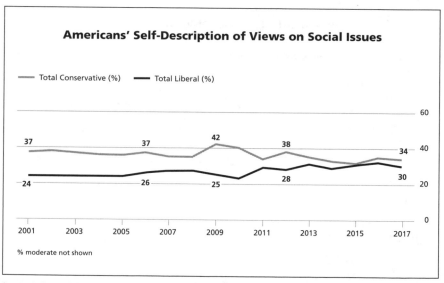

Americans' Self-Description of Views on Social Issues

——— Total Conservative (%)   ——— Total Liberal (%)

37   37   42   38   34

24   26   25   28   30

2001   2003   2005   2007   2009   2011   2013   2015   2017

% moderate not shown

Source: Lydia Saad, "Social Liberals Nearly Tie Social Conservatives in U.S.," Gallup, Washington, DC, July 28, 2017.

conservative finance has on the use of nonconservative money. And there is good reason to think that nonconservatives will act based on good information.

American distrust for financial institutions is pronounced, amplified by their actions before, during, and since the Great Recession. How many times have you heard someone object that no financial executive went to prison for what happened? Still, most Americans find their way to trusting financial institutions—either on their own or because they entrust financial regulators (the government)—enough to keep their money in them. While the Move Your Money slogan generated social media activity, there is no evidence that it produced significant changes in where we store our savings.

Public opinion polls show consistently low ratings on confidence in banks, for example, but the rating numbers and trends for banks over the past few decades are generally consistent with those of other powerful systems, ranging from big business to Congress to news organizations. There's a lot of distrust.

At times, the amount of money organized in precious metals and commodities has increased, indicating a move out of modern financial products, but the ebb and flow has been small and at the margins of markets. Not surprisingly, with historically low interest rates for more than a decade leading into 2019 and massive tax cuts to the wealthy, stock markets have surged. Asset managers, investment managers, investment advisors, investment banks, and other mainstream financial players have thrived, aided by the harried pace of Baby Boomers recovering from the recession on the way to retirement.

As wealth changes generational hands, the rise of impact investing has accelerated. Impact investing is primarily a result of money managers adapting to retain customers who place greater emphasis on social impact, and that is important. The generational transfer of wealth that is already underway—estimates are that as much as $30 trillion will transfer from Baby Boomers to their heirs—is resetting expectations. It appears that younger generations, born since Earth Day (1970) are more likely to think about the societal impact of their money. The more recent their birth dates, the more societal-impact questions they grew up with, in no small part because of the supply of new digital sources of data and information. Reddit chats about finance are nothing like the investment advisory experiences Baby Boomers had or expect to have.

Money managers need to provide social-impact products to next-generation wealth holders. Banks need to provide great mobile banking applications to digital natives. Investment banks need to be socially responsible—authentically so—to earn credibility with younger asset managers, companies, and others. The competition for customers and their dollars is around a bundle of financial and societal benefits.

Over the next decade, that competition will affect not only organized money but also government. In fact, one analysis of the sharp swings in Congress and the presidency is that we are in a moment of significant transformational change—like the 1960s, sure, but also like the 1920s, and like the Civil War era, when we not only redefined what it means to be the United States but also lost one political party (the Whigs) and gained another (the Republicans). Periods of transformation are volatile, disruptive, and tend to make everyone wonder why nothing works the way they thought it did.

That is one explanation of the growing sense among younger Americans that capitalism and democracy as they have experienced them are unacceptable. "It is no surprise that younger Americans have lost faith in a system that no longer seems to deliver on its promise—and yet, the degree of their disillusionment is stunning," Yoni Appelbaum warned in *The Atlantic* in November 2017. "Nearly three-quarters of Americans born before the Second World War assign the highest value—10 out of 10—to living in a democracy; less than a third of those born since 1980 do the same. A quarter of the latter group say it's unimportant to choose leaders in free elections; just shy of a third think civil rights are needed to protect people's liberties."

Michelle Goldberg, a *New York Times* columnist, went further in her December 2017 column, "No Wonder Millennials Hate Capitalism." Citing tax cuts for private schools for the ultrawealthy coupled with spending cuts for public education as well as "smash-and-grab legislative looting, which violates all principles of economic prudence," Goldberg lances conservative Republicans like senators Chuck Grassley of Iowa and Orrin Hatch of Utah.

"After the fall of Communism, capitalism came to seem like the modern world's natural state," Goldberg writes, "like the absence of ideology rather than an ideology itself." Instead, a younger generation of adults who came of age in the hot zone of a fiscal crisis experienced it as "the raw exercise of power by a tiny unaccountable minority that believes in its own superiority." You wonder why young adults trust Twitter but not Congress or the financial system?

"You don't have to want to abolish capitalism to understand why the prospect is tempting to a generation that's being robbed," Goldberg concludes. President Trump's aggressive attack on socialism in his February 2019 State of the Union speech seems all but certain to keep the question of capitalism—specifically what form of capitalism—in public discussion.

We have seen two additional factors that have changed the dynamic of money, wealth, and life.

The first is that the rising generation of adults—which is starting to play a leadership role in business, politics, and society—is unlikely to accept incomplete answers. The pressure for change is strong, real, and progressive, and it is not going away without accountability and answers.

The second is that this generation operates in a different financing paradigm than the one before it, the one older generations take for granted. Baby Boomers grew up in a world rooted in a public-purpose banking system, the one that emerged from the 1930s. It embraced tight regulation in exchange for steady growth and prosperity—albeit primarily for white men, as it silently assaulted the financial well-being of people of color and women. It marketed thirty-year, fixed-rate mortgages and government-backed student loans. It eventually led to responses like socially responsible investing and CDFIs. It is closely tied to the "work hard and get ahead" philosophy that has failed to produce results for Americans whose wages have stagnated, whose corporate benefits have evaporated, whose government has abdicated responsibility for many social programs, and whose leaders belittle them for lack of trust in the American dream.

The next generation—the *current* generation—knows the world through the lens of venture capital and other forms of high-risk, high-return financing. This is a norm rooted in bust-and-boom economics, the promise of financial unicorns (billion-dollar valuations), the short-term results of initial public offerings (IPOs), and the "only you are responsible for you" gig economy. It produces solutions like impact investing and Opportunity Zones. It is no better or worse than more traditional financing models. Jobs are just as hard, or harder; health care and other benefits are expensive and unexpected; home ownership carries the taint of failure; and government in 2019 is not fake news but just fake.

Yet there is wealth and there is money, and it is going to get organized. The old models are necessary but insufficient; mobile banking with incredible artificial intelligence features is cool, but it will soon be a commodity that every bank offers. The threat to banking that pervasive apps like Facebook seemed to pose a few years ago has crumbled as fast as the belief that software is secure. Better to trust an old bank that keeps your money safe. The potential is there for cryptocurrencies as a new way of organizing money, but it is far from proven and that system remains full of flaws.

The motivations and intentions of the people with money are changing, and the financial system must change with them. That means making a financial system suited for an economy built around inclusion and diversity, social justice and opportunity for all, environmental sustainability, and the basic American principle of equity across three dimensions:

- *Financial equity*—the money that people and organizations own.
- *Social and political equity*—fair and equal opportunities without prejudice by race, gender, sexual identity, ethnicity, or other factors.
- *Economic equity*—fairness in the way we organize and use our money leading to greater fairness in the distribution of wealth in the United States and the world.

11

Organizing Progressive Money for Power and Influence

Progressives have never lacked ideas and vision. Organizing progressive money is an unprecedented strategy to power progressive gains.

This book is an organizing guide for an unprecedented strategy to organize progressives' money for power to influence social, environmental, economic, and political change. We are setting out to involve many others to organize $1 trillion over the next ten years in ownership stakes in financial institutions that would comprise a new, progressive financial network—because a vision without resources is a hallucination.

Our strategy is ambitious but realistic, for reasons we have explained: The Great Recession peeled back the lid on the black box of market fundamentalism. The conservative corporate business model is evolving for external and internal reasons. A new business model that incorporates financial and social benefits has sprouted deep roots and broad branches. The nation's long history of public-purpose finance has proved the concept, while a more recent generation has compiled a track record in support of inclusive prosperity. Socially motivated investors have built a multi-trillion-dollar investment platform and are creating new models while progressive wealth is growing. Moreover, progressive political winds are rising for three reasons: conservative political extremism represented by President Trump and the Tea Party, the transfer of economic and financial risk spurred initially by President Reagan to the working majority and away from the wealthy, and the burden placed on taxpayers by market fundamentalists who crafted the private gain-public risk model for American finance.

We want progressives to organize ideas, people, government, *and money*. Each type of organizing has distinct demands, builds on the others, and requires persistence and patience. There are short-term gains, short-term objectives, and long-term goals, all aligned according to a clear purpose. Our purpose is to power the next progressive era to end the long history of near successes by progressive leaders and causes. As Clara Miller, president emeritus of the innovative F.B. Heron Foundation, has said, "I'm tired of being right. I want to win."

Our main goal is to help progressive financial leaders build and grow a network of financial institutions working for progressive causes. At sufficient scope and scale, that network will have the power to influence how the rest of the financial system works, creating a progressive ripple through the financial sector, government, and society. This approach has worked in small ways. Amalgamated Bank helped spur more consumer banking for working people. Socially responsible investing has responded to the goals of public-purpose investors. Black-owned and women-owned banks are driving product and service customization for underserved markets. CDFIs are introducing new models of public policy–enhanced financing. Now our goal is to bring together the many strands of progress to a market scale.

To that end, we aim to organize $1 trillion or more in progressive wealth to own and control the financial institutions in a progressive financial network. We think of that work as "organizing" rather "raising" funds because we believe the money is there already, but it is being used for other purposes. One of our commitments is to make the case to investors so that a wide range of financial entrepreneurs can organize the funds for their institutions. It is our goal to build a strong, broad foundation for a sustainable financial business network. Past efforts to organize progressive financial systems stumbled, in part, due to the limited scope of values-aligned business partners, leaving progressive financial efforts dependent on mainstream and conservative counterparties. That is why we envision a network bringing together the existing efforts, to expand them together and spur innovation of others. As it grows in reach and size, that network would be a more influential part of the mainstream financial system. Again, the power of leverage is key. Even a small progressive financial network offering products that a growing number of customers seek, with expertise to manage growth and the political clout to make itself heard, can disrupt the global financial system.

We cannot raise $1 trillion unless we can promise a constructive use for it. We need progressive financial institutions to invest in and progressive causes to support. The existing array of impact investors, family offices,[1] socially responsible investment managers, CDFIs, values-centered banks, racially and ethnically centered investment funds, and other institutions is more substantial than it seems because they are fragmented, independent, and unorganized. We intend our strategy to spur efforts to work together. We need to make visible the path from a small bank deposit or a modest investment through a values-aligned network to a progressive purpose and then back through financial and social returns to the depositor or investor. That will require efforts to organize institutions, for business reasons, and government, through policy creation and change. Later in this chapter, we summarize examples of the policy opportunities we see today. We expect that a motivated alliance of progressive financial institutions would generate others.

There are more opportunities to collaborate today than most people, including the progressive financial practitioners, utilize. We expect that bringing progressive institutions together, developing with them a common vision emerging from a renewed, systemic commitment to a progressive finance network, creating new pathways to organize the money they need to grow and succeed, engaging them in creative conversations, and encouraging innovative business models will generate substantial and transformational opportunities.

Our network must be grounded in the strength of the progressive community, which comprises tens of thousands of organizations and businesses as well as millions of people. Finance can create competition, but it also can power collaboration. For at least the last fifty years, progressive policy advocacy has been programmatic more than systemic. Organizations have focused on increasing the flows of funding without going upstream to change the hands on the spigots or the policies that have impeded the flow. A community development leader told his peers in the early 1990s that if the political right wanted to immobilize the political left, it would have created the community development movement as it existed—focused downstream, where progressive advocates ended up competing with one another.

To organize practicing financial institutions, which operate every day under the pressing demands of running and growing their businesses, we need to define, articulate, and quantify the real demand for a progressive financial network organized around the goals of progressive causes. Today those data are scattered.

We plan to organize demand around three data-proven insights: First, we'll show that progressive finance is more substantial and consequential than conventional wisdom might suggest. Second, we'll bring into the discussion the many millions of individuals and small organizations committed to progress yet frustrated by history. Third, we'll challenge the conventional belief that the United States has been advancing capitalism in the best way possible. We know there's a better way.

The mythology of "free" markets is false. In fact, it's proof of the problem we need to solve. For the left, widespread resignation to and rejection of capitalism amounts to internalization of extreme market fundamentalism.

This book is a call to action against market fundamentalism and the resulting financial system political bias against progressive causes and values. Conservatives have won and held power because they excel at organizing money as well as people and government. Progressives have lost and struggled because they have ceded the financial system, the most powerful system in the world today, to conservatives. For that reason, our nearest-term goal is to help progressives understand the financial system. We know that this foundational work will take years, if not decades.

Progressives need to align their resources with their aspirations to revive the spirit of public-purpose finance, the lifeblood of the American narrative. It is a pursuit of a form of restorative capitalism that balances the public good with private gain. To achieve it, the left must first see the problem, that its resources are being used against it. Progressives must see the potential of a market-scale, full-service financial network that works for progress instead of against it.

We believe the time is right for this effort because money is available to organize and the progressive movement is resurgent. If we are right, a new progressive finance network can power the next progressive era by finding, gathering, and distributing the financial resources progressive leaders will need to succeed and to sustain gains. The political left does not lack good ideas, but it suffers for its lack of control over its own money.

A topical instance is the push for action on climate change. Only the most cynical people deny that climate change is a crisis and reject the need for aggressive actions by governments and the private sector. Progressive organized money should be, but is not, at the table formulating solutions.

On February 7, 2019, Senator Ed Markey (D-MA), Representative Alexandria Ocasio-Cortez (D-NY), and a Democratic congressional coalition introduced the Green New Deal, a set of ambitious environmental and economic goals. If Opportunity Zones (see chapter 3) epitomize conservative social policy, the Green New Deal embodies progressive ambitions, linking a sustainable environment to a just and sustainable economy. It is not the last progressive moon shot of the 2020 election cycle, to be sure, but it is a defining statement of priorities.

As presented in legislative form, the Green New Deal is precise about the risks in both the short term and the longer term—more than $500 billion in lost economic output, more than 350 million more people exposed worldwide to dangerous heat levels, and $1 trillion in damage to public infrastructure and coastal lands. That clarity reflects the careful analyses of climate change scientists and activists over the last sixty years. It is similarly specific about social and economic justice costs facing Americans—a wealth divide between white and black families of twenty to one, as well as "a gender earnings gap that results in women earning approximately 80 percent as much as men, at the median."

Its goals are similarly clear: net-zero greenhouse gas emissions, millions of "good, high-wage jobs," with "prosperity and economic security for all people of the United States," investments in infrastructure and industry, environmental and health improvements, and other less defined outcomes.

It comes up short on finances, however, leaning heavily, habitually, but vaguely on government funding and leaving out the role of private finance. Urging a "10-year national mobilization" modeled after the New Deal of the 1930s and economic surge due to World War II, the Green New Deal envisions a massive government-led effort that even in summary runs to fourteen points, all good. Not only does it leave out private spending that could be, however, but also it makes no mention of private financing that already is working on climate change in 2019.

Instead it focuses on "providing and leveraging, in a way that ensures that the public receives appropriate ownership stakes and returns on investment, adequate capital (including through community grants, public banks, and other public financing), technical expertise, supporting policies, and other forms of assistance to communities, organizations, Federal, State, and local government agencies, and businesses working on the Green New Deal mobilization." In what seems to be a rebuff of profit-only financial behavior, it excludes the multi-trillion-dollar pool of private financial resources that is already looking to help. We favor another, better way. The problem, we think, is not with the authors of the Green New Deal but with the invisibility of organized money as a strategy for the left. It is of no use if no one knows it exists.

Here, then, is our five-step plan.

Step 1: Talk to People
About Organized Money

The most common response to a new idea is no. We both have plenty of experience listening and responding to doubters. "It sounds great in theory, but it will never work in practice." Nevertheless, we have plenty of evidence that our approach is not only plausible but effective.

We hope this book is the starting point for a national financial systems literacy education effort to increase awareness of the power of financial intermediaries. This previously unrecognized type of literacy can help people make financial systems work for them and their values. The intermediaries are a fact of life, and not just for individual savers or investors. Government cannot function without a robust network of private financial intermediaries.

Organized money is a means to make both Opportunity Zones and the Green New Deal more successful, supporting entrepreneurs of color starting new businesses and community land trusts ensuring housing affordability. It works with one foot in the essential world of public goods and the other in the powerful land of private finance. As a result, it has the potential to attract a large and diverse constituency, ranging from the political left to the moderate right, from people living paycheck-to-paycheck to those with billions of dollars, from activists to actuaries, from working people to corporations, from governments to anarchists, and from finance-averse to financially literate people. Because it cuts across professions, populations, and companies, it touches millions of people in their everyday lives, in their jobs at nonprofit organizations and for-profit corporations, doing their work at CDFIs or global investment banks, studying business at colleges or implementing policy in municipal governments, and living in rural, urban, and Native places.

None of that will matter, though, unless we put the examples, experiences, and expertise in this book and many more into the hands and minds of a critical mass of people working for progressive change. We are planning a sustained public education effort in several phases: first, financial systems literacy; second, progressive financial practice; third, public policy for progressive finance, identifying barriers and opportunities; and fourth, access to progressive financial solutions. We intend to create a public education campaign with discussion guides, ongoing analysis building on this book, a blog for tracking news about progressive organized money, as well as a podcast exploring key issues with experts. It will provide information resources to progressive financial practitioners and their customers to connect them to a broader business strategy for change. We plan to share educational materials by us and others and to provide support to discussion groups of neighbors, activists, organizations, and money professionals. Every successful organizing campaign requires broad, generative conversations to stimulate innovative products, ideas, and approaches. We want to create ways to collect and share creative ideas from individuals, advocates, and financial leaders.

Perhaps the hardest step is the first, making our case for financial systems literacy. Leaders of the mainstream financial system, policy makers, and economists generally are comfortable with the fact that you don't understand financial systems. More than comfortable, they are capitalizing on the fact.

A 2019 presentation prepared by Fidelity Investments for investment advisors focuses on how mainstream money managers can take advantage of investor uncertainty to sell more to anxious customers.[2] Investors "are willing to pay more for many higher-level services an advisor could provide," Fidelity counsels. Based on the 2018 Fidelity Millionaire Outlook Study completed in spring 2018, Fidelity's presentation observed that the participants in the study had the highest outlook ever about current conditions but the lowest outlook in the last decade when asked about the future. Fidelity walks advisors through sales points that will encourage customers to spend more on their financial advisors, including a category called "Reasons for paying more" for a financial advisor. It is hard to miss that point.

Fidelity is not alone or out of line with other money managers. That might be what you need to understand to realize that what you don't know about financial systems could be working against you.

We are not setting out to convince everyone who expresses interest or objections. We want to help organizations and people who see potential in our recommendations to work with one another and introduce collaborations across divides—for example, between private equity managers and voting rights activists. Over the coming years, we expect to engage with thousands of financial, advocacy, nonprofit, and other organizations, with families, and with communities to learn about the effects the financial system has on them and their values and to discuss options for better alignment.

There is an array of programs that train professionals and students for business careers. Some are offered through vocational, undergraduate, and graduate schools, and many are taught on the job. Introducing the organized-money strategy into those channels is key. Organizations like NetImpact, a global network of students and young professionals committed to social, economic, and environmental justice, are vital parts of our proposed progressive finance network, as are professional trade networks like the Global Alliance for Banking on Values and US SIF. Impact-investing events, prime breeding grounds for impact strategies, often bring together philanthropic investors, family offices, mainstream financial institutions, and policy makers. Graduate business schools are fertile ground, as social and environmental justice has become part of the core curriculum at a growing number of them and the students there now are the decision makers of the next few decades. Bringing the financial networks together with advocacy groups, like the National Urban League and UnidosUS, are also part of this organizing effort. The global network of social enterprises—particularly the B Lab network, with tens of thousands of engaged companies—is essential for organizing.

The first two or three years of our organizing effort will involve identifying allies, answering a lot of questions, and fending off skeptics. It will also require listening to all comers, because the challenge is new. No matter how well organized money has worked at the scale of Amalgamated Bank, CDFIs, and impact investing, expanding to market scale is something else altogether. In addition, our vision for organized money through a network of progressive financial institutions is based on the creation of new financial businesses, and there are many people who know better than we do what that will involve. We also expect that there are innovative social entrepreneurs who can introduce us to promising models of business collaborations.

We think people will work with us for at least seven reasons:

First, the political environment has produced a vacuum without practical, sensible ideas. We are not focused primarily on big-P Politics—electing people and that sort of thing. We are talking about the politics that people live every day—the cost of food, wages and benefits on the job, where and how people get the news, who people live near and work with, and whether and where they worship. Money and finance seems to slice through all of that at the speed of light. We have experienced countless instances of people with strong disagreements and businesses with competing interests checking their opposition at the door of a good deal. The result often is greater understanding, if not respect for differences. At a fair price, biases and differences tend to fall by the wayside.

Second, most people interact with financial institutions all the time and so seem likely to want to know more about how they work, particularly people who harbor even a nugget of concern or distrust about them. Inaction about our money organizers, however common, is not the same thing as indifference; just below the surface of most consumers is a set of goals, aspirations, and frustrations.

Third, according to the Financial Health Network (FHN) and others, close to half of all Americans live in a constant state of financial volatility that undercuts their financial health. Many of them must wonder why the financial system isn't working better for them. The fact is that financial institutions—especially consumer financial intermediaries like banks and credit unions—are complex and regulated institutions that operate in a rigid, standardized way. Many try hard to make customer experiences good, but products favor those whose financial lives fit the conventional customer model, and large institutions are sometimes slow and reluctant to adapt. Income or expense volatility, uneven ebbs and flows in money in (freelance work, for example) or expenses (car or home repairs), is a huge factor for lots of people; most financial institutions are not set up for that. They are set up to work for regular, consistent payroll deposits, long-term mortgages, and other conventional products and services. The tension between customers and institutions reflects significant currents of change, and that produces a willingness to consider alternatives.

Fourth, as a nation we are skeptical of business as usual, especially in the long shadow of the Great Recession. The enduring stability of marble buildings and imposing façades reassures only a shrinking minority of our population, having little effect on those who think a bank lives inside their smartphones. Old ways may be necessary, but new ways are alluring, particularly when we think the old ways did not serve us well.

At the same time, a growing number of people are exploring new financial technologies, such as online banking and digital investment management. Efforts by FHN and others to take advantage of digital disruption of financial services to produce more inclusive systems are promising. Particularly important are intergenerational and cultural shifts in how people relate to financial institutions. Large financial institutions are investing deeply in mobile solutions because young adults and generations after them will require them. In addition, some new Americans come from societies where finance is reliant on mobile devices, in part because the old financial system was limited or exclusionary.

Fifth, as a nation, on a bipartisan basis, we are fed up with small, elite groups with outsize power over our lives, like the market fundamentalists. Government and finance score at comparably dismal levels in public confidence polls. The Tea Party's anti-government rhetoric sounds much like the "hippie left" of fifty years ago. The conservative right's judgments about people without money mirror the liberal left's disdain for the people with most of it—despite the fact that many conservatives are without money and liberals populate the *Forbes* 400 list of billionaires. There is potential for new ideas and messages to bridge longstanding differences.

Most people do not know about the power of financial leverage that we described in chapter 1, that a small group of people with a lot of money have extraordinary leverage over the money of a large group of people, most of them with modest or small amounts of money. Those with a vague sense that some "rich" people are "too powerful" seldom know how organized money works. Or how it could work for them.

Sixth, whose money is it anyway? Most progressive don't

recognize the power they could wield. Shareholder engagement efforts by the investors of the Interfaith Center for Corporate Responsibility (ICCR) drive change through proxy fights, but there is untapped power in the stock holdings of progressives themselves. Who wouldn't be frustrated if they thought their money were being used against them? Isn't that what conservatives are fired up about when they attack government? The right responded by bending government to its ends. How come people on the left and center stop short of returning the criticism of conservative financial institutions? It seems imperative to us—not just appropriate—that progressives now use the power of the financial system to turn the financial system toward *their* ends. With organized money, we add a powerful tool to our efforts to influence policy and financial institution practices.

Seventh, we seem to be nearing a point of inflection for corporations in general and for financial institutions in particular. Progressives had a shot to repurpose finance at its core after the financial crisis, but they missed. More than a cautionary tale of opportunity lost, the near miss shows the vulnerability of the old guard. The diminution of the Milton Friedman corporate ideal and the rise of social enterprises, benefit corporations, and public-purpose financial institutions make for a generational chance to make the finance system work better for the left. If we let it pass without collecting our dues, we are throwing in the towel on the next forty years or more, as more and more people seem to realize.

Step 2: Bring People Together

The progressive financial network will require four overlapping and sequential efforts to organize key groups of people—progressive activists; progressive finance professionals, activists, and finance professionals together; and each of the two activist groups with sympathetic mainstream finance professionals. Busy people tend to stay in their respective lanes and associate with people they know and trust. Organized progressive money will require some of those people to step outside their familiar grounds in a steady series of interactions.

From the start, we will need to bring together the full range of progressive activists. A progressive financial network must rest on the public purposes it seeks to serve, not the wants and needs of investors. Proponents need to demonstrate that there is a substantial amount of money interested in what they are doing.

Then public-purpose financial institution leaders will need to convene representatives from all groups in the network to create new business channels for collaboration and mutual benefit, as well as a policy agenda in support of progressive finance. It will be a big step for these groups to make commitments to this effort, for two reasons: first, they are necessarily focused on very specific outcomes, and, second, they are already spending a lot of time seeking capital and they need to be convinced that this approach will be productive.

Advocates and progressive financial institutions are already organized around money, in a sense. They have received investments and funding with expectations that they will do certain things, such as advocate for wage equity for women or finance affordable housing. Their investors and funders need to be brought into this conversation.

These two communities—progressive advocates and progressive financial institutions—must also work together at the national level to agree on goals for a benefit or impact economy that they can embrace. (This is the third organizing effort.) Organizations like B Lab and some national trade organizations provide the platform for starting this work. Fourth, the progressive advocates and financial institutions need to leverage the power of their collaboration by inviting mainstream financial institutions and investors to *their* progressive table. The point of organizing is to change the power relationships to their advantage, and each alone will already have a seat at the mainstream table. Giving mainstream money a reason to sit at the progressive table for discussions, planning, and partnerships will be a key marker of progress in demonstrating progressive power and generating influence.

Many of the organizations and people we seek to bring into the discussions are already addressing facets of progressive organized money, usually without thinking much about the big picture or asking, What if we had financial partners amplifying our work? Whether they are managing investments (for-profit companies) or funding grants (nonprofits) or both, they must meet legal standards for how they manage their money. For instance, large, mature nonprofit organizations have policies about who can and cannot manage their funds and whether they are required, or even permitted, to invest in SRI financial instruments. Their backers have a right to know about those policies before providing money, and they can ask for documentation at any time. Individuals often think about how much they are paying the companies handling their retirement accounts, and they might think as much about the social justice record of the bank where they deposit their payroll.

Few progressives are talking about this network strategically with each other in organized ways. Part of organizing the participants is organizing the conversation. Initially, the conversation will just get people thinking about progressive money and, say, green business strategies. This should happen at sectoral professional meetings, good places for finding common ground.

We won't need new ways of gathering people for several years. We expect to work within the nonstop world of issue-specific and sector-specific convenings that others host for financial, environmental, political, social justice, labor, advocacy, political, and other goals. Because organized money connects people across professions, interests, and issues, we hope to include topics related to organized money as regular content in these conversations and help the conveners take ownership of the topic. Progressive organized money will not go far beyond pleasant discussions, however, if it's driven by outsiders. When environmental, racial justice, and economic development groups all initiate efforts to link their causes to progressive financing, the movement will take on a life of its own.

Over time, the conversation must switch to building the business networks of progressive finance and seeking beneficial legislation and regulations. The current system of laws, cultural norms, and systemic practices is set up to favor and protect the market fundamentalism approach. Most policy exceptions are discrete and unique, such as the CDFI Fund, which works at a modest scale in one part of the benefit economy. Even broader policies, such as the Community Reinvestment Act, which reaches across three regulatory agencies and the entire banking system, are limited to just a part of the financial sector.

For those reasons, this effort will require much more than talk. It will require new modes of organizing, new ways of building and using power, and new, decentralized vectors for action. The sooner our organizing leads to actions, the better our chances to succeed.

Step 3: Innovate

Several things need to happen when people come together to discuss progressive money. The conversations should be rooted in experiences—good and bad—working to align finance with progressive outcomes. In differing settings, the conversations might take different paths. For example, a conversation at an LGBTQ event might focus on products of value to gay people, while a discussion at a major SRI event might focus instead on the need to increase the number of green investment options or ways to help impact investors work with CDFIs. Some innovations will drive business among progressives and their financial partners, and some will influence policy in ways that make it work better for the progressive financial network.

Over time, as the organizing process matures, more effort will go into finding, building, and implementing the components of the full-service, market-scale financial network. For the first four to six years, however, there will be many opportunities to share innovations and collaborate on bringing them to scale. For example, the Calvert Foundation developed a small-investor product decades ago and worked first with CDFIs and later with impact investors to expand its offerings to socially motivated investors.[3] Amalgamated Bank completed an innovative, mission-centered IPO in 2018 that might adapt well to other growth-oriented B Corporations—both financial and nonfinancial—seeking new ways to attract investors.[4] Vancity, which began as a credit union in Vancouver and is now one of the leading public-purpose financial institutions in the world, started a bank as part of its business model so that it could offer mission-aligned credit cards and other products. Vancity's approach would benefit progressive financial institutions of all types that pay fees to conservative credit card banks. Such business adaptations are essential to growth, both because they attract investment capital and because they generate revenues to support the next cycles of work.

Changes last when they come from well-tested innovations. There is broad experience with proven policies that increase fairness and opportunities for people who otherwise would be excluded from the financial system. Our focus is on structural solutions—long-term transformative changes that create lasting differences in how finance works and whom it works for. Structural solutions involve changes in laws and regulations. Systemic solutions are changes in how systems work, not necessarily involving changes in laws or regulations. No financial product of the last fifty years was more systemically transformative than the cash management account, which Merrill Lynch introduced in 1976 (see page 33). Over time, it caused many structural changes. As a rule, financial products and policies based on practice in real life are more likely to avoid unintended (and sometimes intended) consequences. Most—but not all—transformative innovations are complex and expensive and require years of testing and development or policy advocacy.

Some are prime opportunities to introduce change. Opportunity Zones, which we spotlighted in chapter 3, is a game-changing conservative law. It seems to us likely to mislead progressive investors interested in place-based investments and also potentially to clear-cut a much wider swath of privatization through public policy. But we think Opportunity Zones might also be an extraordinary reverse-course opportunity in 2021 for a new president to transform a conservative tax giveaway into a model progressive approach. In fact, it could lay the foundation for the progressive financial network we envision.

As drafted, the Treasury Department regulations for Opportunity Zones set a very low bar for the public-purpose use of funds, allowing just about anyone or any organization to raise an Opportunity Fund. That is a weak link, but we know how to make it a strong one. A progressive president could rewrite the regulations to raise the bar, drawing on the CDFI Fund's much tougher standards. The result would be to require that Opportunity Fund managers demonstrate a history of public-purpose financing, expertise to do it well, and a clear and compelling plan to use the money to benefit disadvantaged residents of the zones. The CDFI Fund's requirements are a useful model but are too narrow as written. CDFIs should be eligible to manage Opportunity Zones, but the scale and scope of OZ financing needs require a much broader range of participants, opening the door to a new generation of progressive financial intermediaries. Using the CDFI Fund model and pairing it with a refined version of the B Lab standards for financial institutions, for example, might get closer to effective, viable public-purpose Opportunity Zones.

With this approach, the potential expanded use of the capital gains tax break fueling Opportunity Zones would carry with it a progressive-friendly set of standards for fund managers. Public-purpose finance guardrails would help ensure that the model would expand progressive outcomes in return for tax-advantaged private investments. Those standards would also attract support for public-purpose finance in other government and private approaches, just as CDFI Fund standards created a tool that is now widely used by state and local governments as well as private investors to include CDFIs in their strategies, expanding the roles and increasing the power of CDFIs.

The idea of adapting the CDFI Fund's unique intermediary-focused model to leverage public funding is an innovation that could expand to other government investments. It is already being tried. Fannie Mae (the Federal National Mortgage Association, FNMA) and Freddie Mac (the Federal Home Loan Mortgage Corporation, FHLMC) are taxpayer-backed, government-sponsored lenders that are important to the housing market. Through the Capital Magnet Fund, which Congress approved in 2008, they fund CDFIs and housing developers through the CDFI Fund. In the last years of the Obama administration, the White House and the Office of Management and Budget pursued several additional ways to apply CDFI-like intermediary-focused strategies throughout the federal government. Done well, these policy changes could serve the expansion of privatization through the discipline of progressive, public-purpose financial intermediaries.

Another policy change for ensuring true public-purpose financing in Opportunity Zones and beyond would be to create a private-sector set of standards based on outcomes, similar to the way LEED (Leadership in Energy and Environmental Design) standards measure environmental sustainability for buildings. Because they are widely recognized and used by lenders and investors, and widely regarded by environmentalists, LEED standards are valued highly by private companies and public policy makers. Complementary standards on other issues—for example, gender equality standards for corporations and inclusive-housing goals for mixed-income housing—could also create progressive boundaries around private investments made possible by public funding.

Other ways to build on successful policy track records would include significantly increasing funding for the CDFI Fund even while the model is adopted by other agencies. Since the fund was created in 1994, its annual funding has increased sevenfold, even though the CDFI industry, with strong performance, has increased in asset size almost seventy-five-fold. The unique success of the CDFI Fund—spurring private-sector financing growth and innovation, and expanding the role of CDFIs in Native and other underserved markets—has resulted in severe constraints in available resources to continue the success, relative to the scale of the industry. Because we are focused on growing the scale of the progressive financial network, which includes CDFIs, an increase in the CDFI Fund from $250 million to $1 billion annually would be a jolt for growth in private progressive finance. CDFIs play a central role in expanding the array of financing and consumer products (such as systems for transferring money from U.S. residents to relatives in other nations) and so can play a catalytic role in creating opportunities for the progressive finance network.

The progressive rallying cry "Move your money"—from institutions we don't want to support to those we do—has fizzled. In part that is because current laws make it almost impossible to move your account data with your money. A customer who wanted to move her account from a big bank that finances fracking (an environmentally harmful way of extracting natural gas) to a local credit union or to a B Corporation bank would lose her history of payments and transactions. That makes it harder to manage her money and creates a high hurdle (reentering her data) to moving it. Online banking—especially for bill payments—is one of the "stickiest" products in finance, meaning that customers who use it tend to stay at their financial institution for a long time. As a result, people don't move their money because it's hard (and unnecessary) work to set up a new online account. Large mainstream banks have substantial advantages because they have the most sophisticated online and mobile banking systems. Progressive depositories would benefit if the United States adopted an expanded version of a European Union rule that would make some, though not all, bank online data portable. If you decide to move your money under the EU rules when they are in place, the financial institution you are exiting must provide your new bank with your historical data. Like the U.S. government's requirement for mobile phones in the 1990s that customers could take their phone number with them when they changed carriers, bank account portability would reduce monopoly control over customer accounts by very large banks and make other financial institutions more competitive for customers. For our purposes, portability would make it easier for financial customers to choose the institutions that best reflect their values and goals.

Among policy possibilities with track records, the Consumer

Financial Protection Bureau (CFPB), which Congress created in 2010, is being stripped of its authority and value by the Trump administration. The CFPB quickly proved its worth when it was established, generating billions of dollars in restitution for consumers victimized by deceptive financial institutions. Simply restoring Obama-era rules for payday lenders, which Trump has negated, would put the CFPB back on track. On that path, it could return to efforts to improve consumer protections in many areas, including online small business lending.

The Obama administration also had enacted an important rule for retirement accounts that, as with benefit corporations, permitted investors to seek both financial and social returns. The Trump administration reversed the rule. With the corporate business model changing and CSR on the rise, and with a majority of states now supporting B Corporation statutes while a federal B Corporation law seems likely, simply reinstating the Obama rule would facilitate investments in public-purpose financial intermediaries.

Finally, a complementary transformational progressive finance policy change would involve the most far-reaching law of its kind, the CRA, or Community Reinvestment Act. CRA needs modernization to bring it in line with the changes that have reshaped financial services. In 1977, when Congress approved the CRA, the basic business of banking was taking deposits from local residents; that is no longer true. Instead, banks operate a stunningly wide array of business lines on a national and often global scale. The CRA needs to be expanded in kind.

Though proponents and opponents of the CRA as it exists worry about opening the law to changes, both the financial system and the laws that govern it are so different than they were in 1976 that there is little reason not to pursue a progressive strategy for the law's modernization. Because the cash management account caused American savers to leave the conventional banking system in favor of the private investment market, the reach of CRA has shrunk. Moreover, the most far-reaching lesson of the financial collapse of 2007–8 is that no financial sector—not banking, insurance, private equity, pensions, brokerages, stock markets, or any other sector—can operate reliably and sustainably without making taxpayers absorb a share of the financial institutions' losses. Therefore CRA coverage should reasonably extend now to all financial institutions, and to all other businesses that operate with taxpayer subsidy. Because we learned how completely the financial sector depends on the public safety net, there is no remaining justification not to require a commensurate commitment to the public good in return. The "private gain at public risk" model that drove the financial industry to fight for its life in 2008 and 2009 needs rebalancing, and modernizing CRA is central to that effort.

This CRA expansion—in the spirit of the 1977 law making it an affirmative obligation of all financial institutions to invest in and serve their markets without discrimination—would vastly expand the private resources available to serve the public interest. Over its life cycle, CRA grew into a powerful source of financing, both for public-purpose activism and public-purpose finance, through community organizations and CDFIs, respectively. A modern, progressive CRA would level the playing field for financial institutions. Those not subject to CRA now (the majority) enjoy an unfair advantage over CRA institutions. The updated law would drive decades of public and private innovation as many additional financial regulatory agencies (beyond the bank regulators) would develop new ways of enforcing the obligation, including through progressive financial institutions.

The potential of these (and other not-yet-identified) changes is not just trillions of dollars of new investments through policies for social, economic, environmental, and political justice. The real potential is the rise of a progressive financial network with the resources, influence, and power to reshape the financial system and bend it toward justice.

Step 4: Organize Money

Efforts to organize progressive wealth are expanding, driven by demand for new financing solutions to address environmental, racial, and other issues and injustices and, on the other end of the capital pipeline, by demand from investors for impact-investment options. The groundwork is in place for growth: the surge in family offices incorporating impact investing, innovative philanthropic models using blended finance (market-rate, discount, and philanthropic), the Amalgamated Bank IPO model for public offerings, social impact bonds, and other structures. They are carrying the momentum of more than thirty years of accelerating success by socially responsible investors, CDFIs, public foundations, philanthropists, and impact investors. The promise of policy could change everything for progressive finance and so for progressive causes. It would mean unprecedented product development and innovation, business model expansion, governance change, technology integration, and policy exploration. It would mean a tidal surge at a time when years of effort are cresting.

The parts remain disconcertingly disconnected and incomplete, however, despite efforts to bring them together. Developing and implementing new ways to organize money at market scale is the biggest and most complex challenge for us, because it is where progressive financial institutions lean most heavily on the big conservative ones. The organizing part of this strategy is a focus on bringing together a wide range of financial practitioners for progressive power and influence. Without a shared vision of a progressive financial network powering a progressive agenda, current progressive leaders will have no real incentive to commit resources and attention away from growing their own institutions. (In other words, if this book does not at least get others in our world thinking about the need to join together for mutual benefit, we have an even bigger problem.) One of the toughest challenges of organized money is building a shared commitment to a future that is more than the sum of its financial parts. It is also an effort to sustain the business of progressive finance by expanding the working relationships among financial professionals so that they are less reliant on financial counterparties that are working at cross purposes. The solutions will come from progressive finance practitioners working together, not from the conservatives or from the two of us.

The potential for market-scale capitalization of inclusive, just, and sustainable financial institutions has never been greater. Much of the $1 trillion goal is possible through combinations of known investment approaches and tools by leveraging experience and taking advantage of policy openings. Organizing money requires giving socially responsible investors good investment choices to build a progressive financial network with financial results as good as or better than their current choices. This approach will not reach market scale if investors cannot earn competitive returns. We must engage impact investors in a strategy that balances short-term impact with long-term transformation. The urgency of greed demands maximum profits *now*, quarter by quarter. There is ample evidence that short-termism (or, as it has been called, now-nowism) is shortsighted, because patient, long-term investors do better financially most of the time. Progressive finance means changing public policies and also changing the ways that mainstream conservative financial institutions relate to progressive ones. Progressive financial institutions should be able to expect public respect for their work, but they too easily settle for background roles in a conservative environment. In fact, progressive financiers should have what Martin Paul Trimble, a legendary CDFI industry leader, called institutional ego, the expectation that others will think that their work is as important as they do.[5] Most important, progressive finance requires its supporters to build a large-scale popular base of the most important keepers of progressive wealth—individuals.

A truism of mainstream finance, stated in various forms by former Citibank chairman Walter Wriston, is that "capital goes where it's wanted and stays where it's well-treated."[6] By that standard, the progressive financial network is far from ready today to satisfy investors. It lacks diversity in investment choices, a full range of financial sectors, sophisticated offerings to suit investor tastes, financial management systems to meet investor needs and regulatory requirements, and other essentials. It would be challenging just to piece together in day-to-day business interactions the products, services, and systems within the progressive network. As a result, there is a pressing opportunity for a coordinated and well-planned innovation effort to build out the components of such a network while negotiating partnerships with mainstream institutions, some of which will be more motivated than others to support this new infrastructure. It's a matter of organizing current efforts at innovation across the progressive financial spectrum and seeding new ones.

Technology is already creating promising new ways of scaling solutions. FHN has brought together fintech (financial technology) companies in pursuit of better outcomes for consumers—what it terms financial wellness. FHN-supported companies tend to cross institutional boundaries and change ideas about what is possible. Sixup is a startup tech company focused on low-income students that reaches across industries to align college choices with student loan options through an outcome-based lifetime lens to support social and economic mobility. It is the kind of tool that could work across a progressive network for credit unions, banks, financial planners, and others. Petal is another FHN company that is using behavioral economics models to bring access to small loans to people without credit histories, often new Americans. Fintech needs to be a big factor in progressive money; we just don't yet know how. Aspiration is a new, online-only financial institution that promises adherence to the socially responsible standard "Do well. Do good." It wants your business, so it lets the customer decide how much to pay for some products—as little as nothing. "We trust you'll pay us a fair fee if we do a good job," Aspiration says. In addition, it promises to give 10 percent of its earnings to charity. Moreover, it promises fair products for everyone, "not just the richest few." As a financial advisory firm in partnership with a small bank, it is betting, well, the bank on its disruptive strategy. If successful, it could open doors for others.

Regardless of good intentions and ambitious goals, it is unlikely that any small progressive financial institutions will develop, introduce, and own the next great innovation—this generation's cash management account. The mainstream financial industry is skilled at keeping its hands on innovative and disruptive products and services and holding them close. They have the money, the policy power, and the market influence to stay in front.

To organize money at the scale they need, progressive financial institutions need to organize themselves.

Step 5: Build Business Networks

A well-organized financial network is the best hope to build power and influence in support of progressive outcomes. That network needs to connect through interdependent business relationships that operate efficiently and build trust. In contrast to conventional finance, which emerged from the large corporate trusts of the late nineteenth and early twentieth centuries, the potential power of progressive money will come from "new" power—decentralized, networked, fast-paced, dynamic, and egalitarian (the opposite of hierarchical). In the early 1990s, the CDFI industry turned its weakness (no visibility, influence, or power in federal policy making or within the banking system) into its strength by positioning itself as an "outside the Beltway" and "community-up" industry working in places no one considered viable markets. It succeeded.

A progressive money network is a distinct means to an unfamiliar end—to build enough power to influence both policy and practice. The end is structural and systemic changes for sustainable and equitable good in financial systems, and in public policies affecting your money and the U.S. economy.

The purpose of the network is to help its member institutions reduce their dependence on business partners who don't share progressive goals. The network cannot and should not aspire to be separate from major financial institutions, regardless of their goals. Quite the opposite: its members need to remain engaged with the people, institutions, and practices they want to affect. They should be thoughtful and strategic about whom they partner with and how. As the progressive network grows, it will see increasing interest and attention from mainstream partners. The potential business of a growing network of financial institutions will override whatever concerns mainstream institutions might have about working against their own interests. Besides, they will consider the progressive financial network too small to exert real power, at least at present.

We believe that the growing importance of progressive issues as part of corporate social responsibility, plus the evidence that the Milton Friedman corporate model has lost favor among the nation's leading financial institutions, will add to the momentum for change among mainstream partners. As social impact grows more important to their investors, their progressive customers, and to their corporate reputations, they will likely find that the progressive financial network (as sketched below) will become more important to their business. Those business interests will affect other decisions they make, including policy decisions, and the influence of the progressive financial network can increase. The progressive financial network alone will have modest influence on them, but the combined effect of customers, investors, and business partners will change the course of mainstream finance toward more progressive practices and results.

At this stage, the limited scale of the progressive financial network compared to the mainstream works to the smaller network's advantage. The progressive financial network's influence will be bigger than its capitalization. In addition, it needs less capital from investors to grow, giving it a measure of agility. In this way, our progressive financial network is well positioned to disrupt classical, conservative finance.

Our version of organized money is not the first or only effort of its kind, and it will succeed only if it dovetails with ongoing efforts and spawns follow-on calls to action. But the circumstances matter; progressive organized money is no longer audacious; it is within reach.

Organizing is a grind. Organizing money is a complicated grind, but to us it's not that hard—really!—based on our professional colleagues' track records of organizing money with social benefits at scale. You might say that the first $150 billion is the hardest. In our eyes, the next decade will be a good era for what we expect to achieve—organizing $1 trillion in progressive ownership stakes in public-purpose financial institutions.

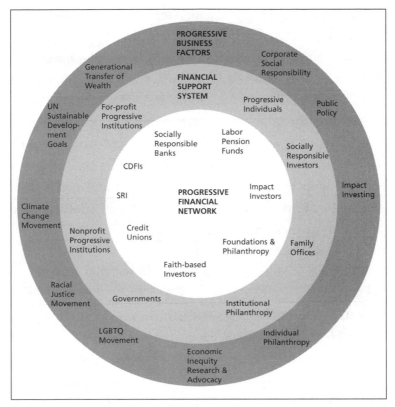

Source: Authors.

We will see.

In 1978, in their book *The North Will Rise Again: Pensions, Politics, and Power in the 1980s,* Jeremy Rifkin and Randy Barber offered a pointed economic analysis of capitalism, which seemed to them to be on shaky, if not its last, legs.[7] "Capitalism, the driving force of the Industrial Revolution for these past two centuries, is casting its final mark on the unfinished business of civilization," they argued. "Capitalism is not likely to exist anywhere in the world a hundred years from now." Perhaps. Rifkin and Barber made a compelling case that pension capital—the retirement savings of union workers—created political potential "as an opening wedge in the development of basic economic alternatives within the United States."[8]

"With pension-fund capital, the American economy has entered a new stage," they promised. They counted more than $200 billion at the time in pension-fund capital comprising the retirement savings of more than 19 million union members and members of public employee investment funds. "American workers are now a major new ownership class. Whether control over their pension capital and, ultimately, over the American economy is transferred to them will depend on many factors, including which initiatives organized labor and the industrial states [in the Northeast and Midwest] choose to take."

Decades after it was published, *The North Will Rise Again* is cautionary in two ways.

First, as it turns out forty years later, 1978 was a turning point for labor in the United States, but not the way labor leaders wanted it to be. It's possible that we, in turn, are misreading the corporate, financial, and political winds in 2019. There is a saying that an optimist thinks these are the best times and that things couldn't get any better, and a pessimist is sure of it. In 1976, the hopeful promise of President Jimmy Carter's election had not yet been enveloped in the national malaise created by persistent high energy costs and the Iranian hostage crisis. The left did not anticipate the political vise grip that President Ronald Reagan would bring to national policy, which led to the firing of striking air traffic controllers, a blow to the labor movement from which it has not recovered.

The second caution that comes from reading *The North Will Rise Again* forty years after its publication is the risk that a new effort will try to fix an old problem. We are not advocating socialism, statism, collectivism, labor control of capital, or the demise of capitalism. The opposite: we are arguing not only for change but also against outdated ideas of change. If Donald Trump is the cutting edge of a new wave of greed rather than an aberrant last gasp of market fundamentalism, the role of a progressive financial network might be a resistance movement more than an economic insurgency.

Market fundamentalism is capitalism done wrong; progressive organized money is an effort to do capitalism right, as a restorative force that carries forward both public and private interests, as our nation's founders intended (and as we explain in the next chapter). Restorative capitalism will be part of a national debate about economic philosophy and financial practices that will take center stage in the 2020 election cycle and influence the nation— and the world—for a generation.

The debate has started with, in a representative sense, Opportunity Zones on one side and the Green New Deal on the other. It is possible, perhaps likely, that a generation from now no one will remember either big idea, but they will live in the world that emerged from this debate. That world will function in part according to laws, rules, products, and practices that will take shape as a result of the decisions we make as a nation about the financial system, the most powerful force in our world, like it or not.

Those decisions will be shaped by the voices and actions of progressive activists and the practices of progressive financial institutions. The progressive voice seems strong in 2019. The progressive finance position needs to get stronger. That will require three things: steady reliance on experience gained as far back as Alexander Hamilton, innovative expansion of current progressive financial systems, and determined collaboration to create new ways of working.

CONCLUSION:
TAKE A SHOT!

We need to create the financial system Alexander Hamilton intended.

We wrote *Organized Money* to challenge the financial system at its core. We also wrote this book to explain to progressives and liberals that they need to understand how the financial system is working counter to their ambitions and values so that they will act to change it. We write from the perspective of financial system practitioners who are, by our values and outlooks, misfits. Our intent is to share what we have learned so that others will work with us to make the system better—that is, to make it respect equally the financial and societal impacts it produces and respond accordingly in balance.

This is not a radical new idea. It is an old idea born in the visions of our nation's founders and based on the burst of ideas and scientific advances in Edinburgh that became known as the Scottish Enlightenment. In particular, it comes from the observations and teachings of Adam Smith, the Scottish moral philosopher whose writings comprise the ideological cornerstone of capitalism. Smith did not believe or say what his self-identified followers—today's market fundamentalists—claim he did.

In 1776, Smith published his most famous work, *The Wealth of Nations*, the first real economic treatise. In it, Smith described a mythical "invisible hand" that alchemically stirred individual acts motivated by self-interest into societal benefits. Over centuries, that idea came to represent the meaning of the work, which was distilled in the 1980s by the fictional character Gordon Gekko in the movie *Wall Street* as, "Greed is good." Many people before and since Gordon Gekko have paraphrased Smith this way, incorrectly, to justify their greed.

The "invisible hand" that Smith imagined stirring countless acts of self-interest into a stew of good outcomes is enticing but empty. Michael Lewis is not the first financial writer to argue that market fundamentalists should read more than just *The Wealth of Nations*, but he makes the case powerfully. "At first blush," Lewis explains, "Smith's classic is a simple paean to the benefits of commerce: between neighbors, between town and country, between nations. The Adam Smith of the early chapters of *The Wealth of Nations* appears to believe that anything that interferes with this commerce—taxes, subsidies—does more harm than good." But there is another Adam Smith, Lewis continues,

> who believes that self-interest is not the sole basis of human behavior, and who leans toward the need for some visible hand to take hold of the market and improve it. This is the Adam Smith who wrote in *The Theory of Moral Sentiments* of the importance of man's natural sympathy for the fellow man to regulate his selfish instincts. This Adam Smith gets less attention than the other mainly, I think, because people see in Adam Smith what they want to, but also because *The Wealth of Nations* is a very long book that most readers put down after they get what they take to be the general idea of it. The passage about the pin factory

[that is the source of the idea of self-interest] comes on page 2 of the original text, which helps account for its fame. Somewhere around page 826 of that edition, Smith offers up a gloomier version of his pin factory, as a soul-destroying enterprise calling for government interference.[1]

In a word, the foundational principle of conservative economic practice is wrong. Greed is not good, though self-interest has its place in the framework of Smith's lifelong work on morality. Smith's study of the pin factory was completed in service of his inquiry into human nature. The context for *The Wealth of Nations* was Smith's *The Theory of Moral Sentiments*, which he published in 1759 and continued to revise until his death in 1790. It begins, "How selfish soever man may be supposed, there are evidently some principles in his nature, which interest him in the fortune of others, and render their happiness necessary to him, though he derives nothing from it, except the pleasure of seeing it."

To Smith, self-interest is part of the equation, not an end unto itself. The key variable is interest in the fortune of others. Economic self-interest works only in the context of and counterbalanced by caring for the greater human good. In *The Wealth of Nations* (book 1, chapter 8), Smith wrote, to the consternation of market fundamentalists, "No society can surely be flourishing and happy, of which the far greater part of the members are poor and miserable." In a period of extreme wealth and income inequalities that are well-documented to follow racial and gender fault lines, we need to pair Smith's analysis with Jamie Dimon's view that the U.S. economy is "fundamentally anti-poor."[2] To conclude that market fundamentalism is anything better than an attack on fairness and equity is to stop reading *The Wealth of Nations* on page 2 and so to miss the point of capitalism. Unfortunately, that is where we are.

The idea that self-interest and the well-being of others must co-exist took root and became distinctly American. In 1776, while Smith was publishing *The Wealth of Nations*, the Continental Congress in Philadelphia was writing and debating the Declaration of Independence. The proximity in time and thought is important, as the Scottish Enlightenment deeply affected American ideas of citizen-rulers and civic responsibility.

In the American experiment of government of, by, and for the people, our founders sought a way of treating each adult white male inhabitant as a citizen, as both a participant in society and as a ruler (one person, one vote). This was a great advance for the time. In rejecting imperial English rule—and imperial rule generally—the Americans lifted individuals from all walks of life to unprecedented heights of authority. For the first time, it mattered what individuals did. From Smith's perspective, that was as true for individuals as economic actors as it was for them as voters. The wealth of nations, in Smith's analysis, was no longer solely a product of royal actions; individual choices, actions, and preferences had consequences and results—even when the individuals were low-status pin-factory workers.

The Americans needed a new word to describe the new concept, to describe what it meant to care both for yourself (self-interest) and the common good. They chose a word that today is at the heart of organized money, if not all finance—responsibility.

Smith died in 1790, but his ideas lived on in the federal financial system that Alexander Hamilton brought to life. With the ink still drying on the U.S. Constitution, three challenges loomed in a national crisis that seemed capable of ending the American experiment when it was barely launched.

The first problem was how to get deeply disaffected Americans, torn by decades of political debates culminating in discordant approval of the Constitution, to work together toward a common purpose. There were words on paper—the Constitution and the Declaration of Independence, in particular—but they were still just words.

Second, where should they site the nation's capital city once and for all? Philadelphia was home to the colonies, New York was the temporary home in 1790, and Congress was deeply divided, North versus South.

Third, how were they going to dig out of the $25 million mountain of debts that the thirteen colonies carried from the Revolution—unequally, some states holding much more debt than others? The wealthiest states, such as Virginia, didn't want to pay for the liabilities that smaller, poorer states carried. Why should they? The more indebted states feared they would fall behind economically and financially, perhaps never to recover.

It took a clever, complicated negotiation—the Great Compromise of 1790—over dinner at the president's home a few hundred yards from Wall Street, at 57 Maiden Lane, to move forward. Alexander Hamilton and Thomas Jefferson, with a nod from President George Washington, advanced a federal system for organizing the nation's money (as the Northerners wanted) in exchange for putting the capital slightly south of the line separating North and South, in the unnamed and unsurveyed land that became Washington, District of Columbia—unoccupied swampland contributed by Maryland and Virginia—as the Southerners wanted.

The new federal government assumed the war debts and in return won the authority to bind the colonies together financially under a national government. The states joined together economically for the first time under a single, national money system. From the nation's start, the financial system stood at the center with great power and influence. The thirteen separately governed, proudly

238   Conclusion

independent colonies were united as a single nation with a common purpose ruled by citizen-leaders. Or at least they would try. We're still trying.

As a financial system and social structure, the United States would advance as a moral society of people responsible both for themselves and for others.

Today money remains at the center of American life. Capitalism as it is practiced now by the financial mainstream is not capitalism at its best. Kevin Phillips, an influential Republican author, characterizes modern financial capitalism with open eyes in his book *Bad Money*: "This is less a market-based Adam Smith brand of triumph than a mercantilist joint venture with U.S. government authority, strategic direction, funding support, and periodic Federal Reserve or U.S. Treasury bailouts of overextended financial institutions."[3]

We live and work in a financialized version of capitalism, where wealth creation is often separate from production, distribution, and consumption of real goods, such as cars, computers, appliances, clothes, and houses. By far the most wealth today is in derivatives—financial products fabricated out of, or *derived* from, other financial products, sometimes several steps removed.

The financial sector—the business of organizing money—is the largest sector of the U.S. economy, accounting for more than 20 percent of gross domestic product, and it is likely to grow.[4] The power of capitalism is not based on who has the most money, however, but rather on who *organizes* the wealth. Who decides where to invest, what to support, how to assess risk, how much to return to investors? Money organizers control vast sums of other people's that affect you and your life in countless ways. Money organizers usually profit in good times and bad; most of the time, money organizers get paid regardless of whether the money owners do well or poorly. And they get paid well.

The people who make and enforce the laws theoretically organize the money organizers in theory. In practice, most of the people who make the laws are dependent on the money organizers. Kevin Phillips noted in 2008, as the financial sector sank, "In 2006, the average member of Congress didn't know a swap contract from an option contract, or a 'conduit' [a vehicle for off-the-books financing] from a clogged suburban drainpipe. In 2008, they knew a lot more."

How did they learn? They asked the money organizers.

Elected officials, financial regulators, central bankers, and others have power and a measure of control over the money organizers. No matter what they choose, however, the money organizers continue to do what they do best—make money by organizing money. And we will not be the first to notice that lots of elected officials, regulators, central bankers, and others overseeing the money organizers are former and future money organizers themselves.

A decade later, the moral dimensions of the financial system are in the spotlight. In May 2018, the Vatican published a remarkable and unprecedented paper critiquing the system and the people who run it. "Economic and financial issues draw our attention today as never before because of the growing influence of financial markets on the material well-being of most of humankind," the authors explain. "The extreme volatility and mobility of capital investments in the financial world permit those who control them to operate smoothly behind every norm that does not aim at an immediate profit, often blackmailing by a position of strength even legitimate political authority."

Like Smith, the Vatican document considers the financial system within a moral framework: "Our contemporary age has shown itself to have a limited version of the human person, as the person is understood individualistically and predominantly as a consumer, whose profit consists above all in the optimization of his or her monetary income. The human person, however, actually possesses a uniquely rational nature and has a sense for the perennial search for gains and well-being that may be more comprehensive, and not reducible to a logic of consumption or to the economic aspects of life."

More people seem to be questioning capitalism today than in a century or more—primarily but not only because it seems to them and others to be unfair in the way it is set up and operated. Exclusive, inequitable, unjust, unsustainable, greedy, immoral—there's certainly room for improvement. But let's not throw out the capitalism with the bathwater. We are confident, with good cause, that a full-service, market-scale system organized by reasonable people in service of widely held values can balance private gains and the common good, that it will be economically positive, socially constructive, culturally rich, and politically sustainable.

Our vision is a restorative financial system. It will not appear through legislation or regulation, though it will not succeed without both. The key to restoring the moral purpose of the financial system is to reinvigorate the moral forces that are working in it already as a fulcrum on which to lever systemic change.

To work, this strategy requires thousands of financial institutions with broad ownership. We count at least $12 trillion in many forms that is seeking inclusive, sustainable, and equitable outcomes by many means. We have set our sights on organizing just $1 trillion, or 8 percent of that $12 trillion in ownership stakes in financial institutions of all types by 2030. That $1 trillion could reasonably leverage an additional $9 trillion of "other people's money" toward our goals. That's a $10 trillion seat at the financial systems table. It's enough to begin to transform how the financial system works and whom it works for. It would demonstrate that enduring changes are achievable.

We believe that progressive people, organizations, and enterprises in the United States cannot hold their own in policy, politics, and civic culture against the conservative and regressive right unless and until they organize their money. One last time, let us put that another way: conservative and regressive people support a financial system that works with and for them; moderate, progressive, and liberal people support a financial system that works for conservative and reactionary people and causes.

We wrote *Organized Money* for a third reason, as well. We believe the system we have for organizing money—the financial system—is a public asset as well as a private business. We want it to work well, fairly, and profitably. We are fighting for an inclusive prosperity built on one fair economy, not two separate and unequal economies. Our nation and our world require a financial system that works for it. Our financial system today is bigger and more powerful than people realize, and it influences almost everything we do and how we do it. The things it does well and those it does poorly often result in outsize consequences.

We believe that a progressive financial network will help us regain our balance as a nation. The intimate but expansive relationships we build with our money bind people together across cultural, social, economic, and political divides. Market fundamentalists celebrate wealth inequality while collectivists abhor it. In between, reasonable people—and that is most of us—join together with understanding and respect for differences and put their money together to get things done.

As a nation, we are still pursuing our foundational principles. We still are defined by our inability to treat all people equally and justly without regard to race, gender, ethnicity, or sexual identity and preferences. We still are charged with the duty to care for the world we live in—the natural world and the world we build. We still hear the lofty call to balance individual freedoms and rights with public safety and the common good. We struggle to make sense of extreme differences in wealth and income in the United States, but then we step back and see the even more severe differences between the wealth of America and the relative poverty of much of the world.

Equity means "fairness and justice," and in financial terms it also signifies ownership. If you buy a house, the share you own is your home equity—the total value of your home (the total asset) less the amount you owe on it (the total liability). When you have financial equity, you have wealth that gives you freedom and options—the independence to decide what is best for you without interference from others. You can relate to the world on your own terms and are not reliant on others to decide what is best for you. Equity equals equity. You can't keep one unless you also hold the other.

The financial system has a responsibility to advance equity equitably, because it plays such a uniquely powerful role. That requires embracing the financial system's public purposes as well as its private benefits. That paradox contains America's greatest hopes and challenges.

We live in a capital-run, money-centered nation because our founders wanted it that way. American democracy and capitalism are indivisible. Held together, they produce tensions that spark creativity, innovation, and opportunities. They also generate risks. Yet to value one without the other is fool's gold. Each seems as if it would make you a winner, but neither alone can. The Revolutionary War–era idea that common people (not just the rich) make important money decisions—that individuals matter to economies—was as progressive then as the idea that every individual (not just imperial rulers) should make policy decisions. More to the point, one will not survive without the other: organized people and organized money, citizen-owners as well as citizen-rulers. The willful and self-serving separation of the two roles is one of the reasons we are struggling as a nation.

More and more people today, on the left and on the right, seem to believe that both experiments may have run their course. We believe that democracy and capitalism—politics and money—offer great opportunities for the more progressive world we and many other Americans aspire to. Bottom line? The only path forward is progress.

Progress requires courage, the same courage that our nation's founders needed to free themselves from the tyranny of unjust governance and to assume responsibility for the American experiment. They were citizen-leaders of a revolutionary approach to self-governance. Progress in 1776 meant empowering white men to act simultaneously as self-interested individuals and public-minded leaders, as citizens serving a greater, common good. We've made progress toward a more inclusive version of the same ideal; now it's time to go the rest of the way.

Progress today means unbinding our ideas and institutions from the financially enhanced vise grip of regressive policies and practices. Conservative money supports diplomacy that seeks to literally and figuratively wall us off from the rest of the world. It gives us economic policies that stoke inequality and home and abroad. It gives us social policies that divide us by race, ethnicity, gender, and sexual identity. It gives us environmental policies that ignore science and deny climate change. It gives us propaganda that spreads lies and calls the truth "fake news." As a result, we suffer self-inflicted wounds from individual and institutional decisions that reward self-interest without regard for the common good, from economic choices that favor the wealthy over everyone else, and—the heart of our message—financial actions that reward harmful regressive priorities.

If the strength of a nation is its ability to disagree productively, we need to agree and disagree not only with our votes and our voices, but also with our money—what we own, what we spend, where we live, and why we save. We live in a financially lopsided world tilting to wealth over well-being; we need to restore our national moral equilibrium. Control of our money is one-sided today in favor of conservative goals and against progressive ones. We need to make the playing field more level, the skill levels more equal, and opportunities to get on the field more just.

Doing so will require a shift in economic and political power that must come in large part through progressive organized money, which is both the means and the end. It is what progressive people and organizations need to do and have so they can control a network of financial institutions in line with progressive values and vision. We are not suggesting that we turn finance on its head by rejecting conservative financial institutions. They have a place. We see progressive finance happening in addition to, alongside, and inside of—not instead of—the existing, dominant conservative financial system. A progressive financial system is diverse. We need both progressive and conservative finance working in creative and constructive tension. We need to stop pretending finance is unbiased and that economics is apolitical.

What's our point?

If you believe, as we do, that everybody to the left of the far right stands in varying degrees for inclusive prosperity, reality-based policies, a healthy working class, equality of opportunity, and a dedication to make America all it was created to be, you are left struggling with one question: what does the right have that the left lacks?

The political right owns and benefits from a global financial system that works *for* it most of the time, not *against* it. The reason for a market-scale, full-service progressive financial network is to harness the power of organized money—for progress. We believe our nation's economy, political system, and culture are ready and receptive.

AUTHORS' NOTE

*O*rganized Money is our best effort to explain what we have learned about money and power as executives in finance and to offer a strategy to make the financial system serve progressive goals, outcomes, and values better than it has in our experiences. It spans subjects that most people, we have learned, do not routinely associate with one another. In an effort to make the book readable for a broad audience, we have made leaps of thought at times. We hope our approach expands the range of people who understand the role of finance and money even if it sometimes flattens out the almost-infinite nuances that the topic presents.

This book is based on facts drawn from research and actions—by others and by us. Any errors in *Organized Money* are our responsibility. We have tried our best to fairly and accurately present facts, opinions, and ideas from all sources and perspectives. The examples of six individuals in chapter 1 to illustrate how people can organize their money and their lives mask private identities and personal information, but their underlying specifics are factual. We rely throughout *Organized Money* on outstanding research and reporting by others across many disciplines, and in many instances on things we have seen, participated in, or observed closely in our work. We recognize that our own perspectives as progressive capitalists might surprise people, and we hope that in the end this book is compelling and correct.

We are grateful to many people who helped us with content, encouraged us, and engaged with us about our ideas. Our thanks go, in particular, to Adina Abramowitz, Nancy Andrews, Nancy Banta, Steve Berkenfeld, Sam Brown, Jano Cohen, Mike Cosack, Alex Crowley, Noel Eisenstat, David Erickson, Mark Finser, Sister Corinne Florek, Lynne Fox, Ginny Flynn, Jay Coen Gilbert, Ron Grzywinkski, John Hamilton, Mary Houghton, Amir Kirkwood, Drew LaBenne, Chuck Muckenfuss, Martin Murrell, Jessica Nowak, Jennifer Paget, Margaret Paget, Mark Pappas, Steve Pastor, Jim Paul, Stephen Perloff, Tina Peterson, Clara Pinsky, Nate Pinsky, Greg Ramm, Alan Reich, Joel Rice, Mary Roger, Jonathan Savrin, Debbie Silodor, Jennifer Tescher, Zach Teutsch, and Martin Paul Trimble. Traci Parks provided invaluable editorial guidance on the manuscript and helped us write for a non-financial audience.

Mark offers deep gratitude to Jeremy Nowak, a friend and mentor like none other right up to his passing in July 2018. His influence on the practice of public purpose finance is greater than words can express. This book is better because of Jeremy's ideas and encouragement and less than it could be because he was gone before he could advise on the manuscript.

We are grateful to the talented and kind team at The New Press. Diane Wachtell, the executive director of The New Press, suggested that we write a book, nurtured our initial thoughts into good ideas, and motivated us to believe we could say something worth saying. Ellen Adler, The New Press's publisher, showed us the support, kindness, and confidence it takes to get to the finished product. Carl Bromley, our editor, gave us plenty of room to explore and guided us firmly and constructively when we needed to make choices. Carl helped us reshape the book until it became the resource we all wanted it to be. Emily Albarillo, our production editor, calmly and gracefully took us through a thicket of details, and Gary Stimeling, our copyeditor, and Laura Starrett, our proofreader, taught us plenty about our own book, pointed out mistakes we otherwise would have made, and helped increase the book's readability. Brian Ulicky and the publicity team at The New Press together with Aileen Boyle of Audere Media and Molly Levinson of The Levinson Group understood why we wrote *Organized Money* and helped us connect to the people who we want to read it.

Finally, we are most grateful to the professionals in finance, particularly those in our world of progressive finance, and the advocates and organizers who make this work worth doing, this book worth writing, and this strategy worth pursuing. The two of us started working together, in part, because we both were determined to help progressive-minded people focus on building a financial system that aligns with their values. For all the reasons we touch on in this book and some we do not, money makes people uncomfortable and sometimes downright scared. Too often it makes progressives feel squeamish. We hope we are starting a process to yoke the power and influence of finance to the causes we are working for.

We both have made it our lives' work to align capital with social, economic, environmental, and political justice. Neither of us started with formal training or experience in finance, and both of us felt drawn and compelled to figure out how to harness the extraordinary power of organized money. Because we have had opportunities to work with remarkable, creative, dedicated people, we hope this book returns the generous inspiration we have benefited from.

We are fortunate to work across vast divides in society and finance—often with one foot in halls of power at the highest levels of government or negotiating with some of the world's wealthiest and most influential people and with the other foot standing

with—and finding ways to finance—people denied basic rights or
living in crumbling homes. Our perspectives reflect the wide range
of our experiences, and all opinions are our own.

ABBREVIATIONS

AFR—Americans for Financial Reform, a progressive advocacy coalition.

B Corp—Benefit Corporation, a company that meets legal fiduciary requirements in thirty-four states as of April 2019, to pursue both financial and non-financial outcomes.

B Lab—A nonprofit corporation based in Pennsylvania and working globally that certifies B Corporations, manages B Impact programs, and advocates for benefit corporations and the laws that enable and support them.

CDB—Community development bank, a chartered bank dedicated to benefiting underserved and under-resourced people and communities.

CDCU—Community development credit union, a chartered credit union dedicated to benefiting underserved and under-resourced people and communities.

CDFI—Community development financial institution, a category of private financial institutions dedicated to benefiting underserved and under-resourced people and communities. CDFIs include community development banks, community development credit unions, community development venture funds, and community development loan funds. In 1994, Congress created a legal definition of a CDFI that is overseen by the CDFI Fund and used by both government and private investors. CDFIs operate both as for-profit or nonprofit corporations.

CDFI Fund—A program in the Department of the U.S. Treasury that invests in and supports CDFIs.

CDLF—Community development loan fund, a revolving loan fund, non-depository financial institution dedicated to benefiting underserved and under-resourced people and communities.

CERES—The Coalition for Environmentally Responsible Economies is an environmental advocacy and research organization.

CFPB—The Consumer Financial Protection Bureau is a federal agency that Congress created to promote fairness and transparency for consumer financial products and services including but not limited to mortgages and credit cards.

CFSI—See FHN.

CMA—The Cash Management Account is a financial product first introduced in 1976 by Merrill Lynch. It disrupted the entire financial system.

CMF—The Capital Magnet Fund is an innovative pool of capital generated by fees on the Federal National Mortgage Association (Fannie Mae) and the Federal Home Loan Mortgage Corporation (Freddie Mac) and used by the CDFI Fund to invest in CDFIs and nonprofit housing developers to increase the supply of affordable housing.

CRA—The Community Reinvestment Act is a law requiring banks to serve their communities without bias, with a particular focus on meeting the credit needs of all residents in their geographies.

CRL—The Center for Responsible Lending is a research and advocacy organization with particular focus on preventing and combatting predatory financial products and services.

CSR—Corporate social responsibility is a business practice of delivering benefits to communities and markets that is a self-regulating way that companies make themselves accountable to their customers, employees, and others.

untitled

DAF—Donor-advised funds are a vehicle for people to organize charitable contributions through financial institutions that operate as charitable entities; DAFs make it possible for donors to give into a holding account, claim tax benefits for that gift, and customize how that money is used for charitable purposes out of the holding account.

ESG—Environmental, social, and governance considerations are grouped as a category of socially responsible investing and corporation social responsibility.

FDIC—The Federal Deposit Insurance Corporation is a federal regulator of banks and manager of an industry-funded, government-backed insurance pool that protects depositors against losses up to a limit set by Congress.

FHLMC—The Federal Home Loan Mortgage Corporation, or Freddie Mac, is one of the leading government-sponsored entities (GSEs) that fund and so influence the offering of mortgages in the United States.

FHN—The Financial Health Network, formerly known as the Center for Financial Services Innovation, or CFSI, works to improve financial health for everyone, particularly people who have little or no access to financial services that enable them to thrive.

FNMA—The Federal National Mortgage Association, or Fannie Mae, is one of the leading government-sponsored entities (GSEs) that fund and so influence the offering of mortgages in the United States.

GIIN—The Global Impact Investing Network is an international association of impact investing advocates, researchers, and practitioners.

GIIRS—The Global Impact Investing Ratings System is an international impact performance system for impact investing.

GSE—Government sponsored enterprises, such as Fannie Mae and Freddie Mac, are private corporations chartered by the federal

government to guide the implementation of federal policy priorities. While they are capitalized by private investors, they enjoy
the advantage of having implicit (and, since the Great Recession,
explicit) federal backing in the event of a financial crisis.

ICCR—The Interfaith Center for Corporate Responsibility is a nonprofit coalition of investors representing faith-based institutions
who use investment to address a wide range of social, economic,
environmental, and political justice issues involving publicly
traded corporations.

IOA—The Investing in Opportunity Act is the statute authorizing
Opportunity Zones.

IRA—Individual retirement accounts are private retirement investment vehicles that make individuals responsible for the selection
and performance of their investments.

IPO—Initial public offerings are the sale of stock ownership in corporations on public markets or exchanges.

LEED—Leadership in Energy and Environmental Design standards are a privately administered set of criteria for building
design and construction; LEED standards are awarded at four
levels—Certified, Silver, Gold, and Platinum—based on points
for green design.

LICU—Low income credit unions are those credit unions in which a
majority of their members are low-income. The LICU designation
is administered by the National Credit Union Administration.

MRI—Mission-related investments are sometimes interchangeable
with impact investments; among philanthropies, mission-
related investments are differentiated from program-related
investments because MRIs are made with the 95 percent of the
money that is not required to be distributed annually while PRIs
are made with the 5 percent of "program" funding that must be
distributed under Internal Revenue Service (IRS) rules.

NCRC—The National Community Reinvestment Coalition is the leading national advocate for the Community Reinvestment Act and for strategies to implement it to benefit underserved and under-resourced people and communities.

NCUA—The National Credit Union Administration is the federal regulator for credit unions.

NMTC—New Markets Tax Credit is an incentive for investors to put money into business real estate and operating businesses on concessionary terms in exchange for tax credits that reduce corporate tax liabilities.

OF—Opportunity funds are vehicles for investing in Opportunity Zones under the Investing in Opportunity Act.

OZ—Opportunity Zones are federally designated geographies that qualify for investment under the Investing in Opportunity Act. There are approximately nine thousand Opportunity Zones as of April 2019.

PE—Private equity is a form of capital investments in businesses that are not made initially through public exchanges or markets.

PRI—Program related investments are philanthropic loans and investments made by foundations for charitable purposes at concessionary rates and/or with concessionary terms. They qualify as distributions to meet the Internal Revenue Service's "5 percent of assets" rules for foundations.

PFN—Progressive financial network is the name this book gives to the market-scale, full-service financial network capitalized and owned by progressive wealth in support of progressive outcomes and to build progressive financial influence and power.

SDG—Sustainable development goals are a set of targets set by the United Nations for inclusive global development, environmental sustainability, and other purposes.

SIB—Social impact bonds are financial vehicles that make financial returns to investors dependent on the social impact performance of the work being financed.

SRI—Socially responsible investing is a $12 trillion practice of investment with the stated goals of producing social benefits, positive societal benefits, and responsible financial systems.

US SIF—US SIF is the leading national advocate for the practice of socially responsible investing.

VC—Venture capital is a form of capital investment to support rapidly growing businesses.

SELECTED RESOURCES

You can find an endless supply of print, digital, and other resources about the financial system but a limited supply of resources that bring a progressive perspective. This short summary of books, organizations, and websites is topical to *Organized Money* and it includes a wide range of views. It is not complete, however. We mean to make it easier for you to learn more about the topics we cover. Our website at organizedmoney.org includes these resources and many more, and we encourage you to visit it for them and for updates on issues related to organized money. In addition, the endnotes in this book will help you identify useful sources of information.

A major topic we care about is how the financial system works—what we call financial systems literacy—told through history and current events. *What They Do with Your Money: How the Financial System Fails Us and How to Fix It* by Stephen Davis, Jon Lukomnik, and David Pitt-Watson breaks down some of the tricks of the trade. *A Financial History of the United States* (all three volumes) by Jerry W. Markham is a useful reference document. Kevin Phillips is a conservative commentator on the financial system, and two of his books in particular—*Bad Money: Reckless Finance, Failed Politics, and the Global Crisis of American Capitalism* and *Wealth and Democracy: How Great Fortunes and Government Created America's Aristocracy*—are persuasive no matter your political leanings.

Money of the Mind: Borrowing and Lending in America from the Civil War to Michael Milken by James Grant is a fascinating critique of moral discipline and laxity in the world of money.

Michael Lewis is a smart chronicler of the cutting edges of the financial system and he does a good job explaining the basics of finance. All of his books on finance are worth reading if you have the time. *The Big Short: Inside the Doomsday Machine* does a better job than any other book for the general reader at making complex financial dealings reasonably simple as it details the financial decisions that caused the Great Recession. (The movie by the same title does the same.) *Flash Boys: A Wall Street Revolt* is important if you want to understand just how far from your daily experience Wall Street trading actually is. In addition, Lewis's compilation of economic classics, *The Real Price of Everything: Rediscovering the Six Classics of Economics*, will teach you more than just about everyone else in the world knows about economics. Even if you don't read the works of Adam Smith and his successors, though, focus on Lewis's commentary. (And take a look in the back of the book where, on a single page, Lewis identifies all the great mainstream economic treatises.) If you can't read them all, Robert L. Heilbroner's masterful summary of economic history through the twentieth century, *The Worldly Philosophers: The Lives, Times, and Ideas of the Great Economic Thinkers*, offers a friendly and insightful summary.

We hope you are driven to go to the original sources so you might form your own opinions—much of what we hear about Adam Smith, in particular, is not accurate. We recommend that you read both of Adam Smith's foundational works, *The Wealth of Nations* (actually *An Inquiry into the Nature and Causes of the Wealth of Nations*) and *The Theory of Moral Sentiments,* and not necessarily in that order. A point of this book is that you cannot accurately understand *The Wealth of Nations* without also reading

The Theory of Moral Sentiments. But both books are thick reading, so go down that road patiently.

We also recommend that you read Milton Friedman's iconic 1970 article in the *New York Times Magazine*, "The Social Responsibility of Business Is to Increase Its Profits." It is hard to understand where American business philosophy came from or how far we have moved without studying that particular stake in the financial ground.

Two books with overlapping titles are useful to understand financial leverage. Supreme Court Justice Louis D. Brandeis's *Other People's Money and How the Bankers Use It* is a critique of finance in another era (the early twentieth century) but its analysis and insight remain foundational today. Sharon Ann Murphy's *Other People's Money: How Banking Worked in the Early American Republic* goes back further into the root causes of the financial system we aim to take on in *Organized Money.*

There is a wave of modern economic thought known as behavioral economics that is fun (we promise), fascinating, and relevant. It is about how we make decisions and why we often make the wrong ones. Related to this book is *Dollars and Sense: How We Mis-think Money and How to Spend Smarter* by Dan Ariely and Jeff Kreisler. It explains and explores common consumer money behavior. *The Financial Diaries: How American Families Cope in a World of Uncertainty* by Jonathan Morduch and Rachel Schneider is a study of real-world financial decision making. It takes you inside the lives of a group of families dealing not just with money but with the shifting political and economic sands around them. Lisa Servon's *The Unbanking of America: How the New Middle Class Survives* takes you on an expertly insightful journey through the financial system beyond banking, a world where more and more people spend their financial lives.

A good way to understand the rise of consumer finance in the modern era is to read Joe Nocera's *A Piece of the Action: How the Middle Class Joined the Money Class*. Not only does it detail the rise of credit card culture and the defined contribution retirement system, it tells the story how the cash management account broke the financial system in 1976 and set off a landslide of systemic changes that are sliding still.

Some of the best analysis of how and why the sands have shifted and often seem to be slipping away under our feet comes from Jacob Hacker's *The Great Risk Shift: The Assault on American Jobs, Families, Health Care, and Retirement—And How You Can Fight Back*. Richard Rothstein documents institutionalized racism in federal policy in *The Color of Law: A Forgotten History of How Our Government Segregated America* and Mehrsa Baradaran breaks down how injustice permeates finance in *How the Other Half Banks: Exclusion, Exploitation, and the Threat to Democracy*.

All the Presidents' Bankers: The Hidden Alliances That Drive American Power by Nomi Prins delivers a cutting analysis of why and how power continues to concentrate at the intersection of the highest levels of politics and finance. *Financial Justice: The People's Campaign to Stop Lender Abuse* by Larry Kirsch and Robert N. Mayer takes you inside the progressive effort to slow predatory lending by creating the Consumer Financial Protection Bureau and provides great insight into why that effort seems always to be rowing against the current.

There are fewer strategies like ours than you might think in the literature and through history aiming to address the structural and systemic challenges that the financial system presents to progressive advocates. A classic is *The North Will Rise Again: Pensions, Politics, and Power in the 1980s* by Jeremy Rifken and Randy Barber. It is thorough and compelling about both the period and the underlying issues that we touch on in this book. More recently, *The Rise of the Working-Class Shareholder: Labor's Last Best Weapon* by David Webber picks up the charge before, the author hopes, it's too late.

There is, however, a network of progressive financial advocacy organizations at work. Americans for Financial Reform (ourfinancialsecurity.org and @realbankreform) is a coalition of many of those organizations. Better Markets (bettermarkets .com and @bettermarkets) focuses on financial fairness through accountability and much of its work involves research and transparency in the financial system. The Center for Responsible Lending (responsiblelending.org and @crlonline) is a research and advocacy effort focused mainly on preventing predatory lending and identifying responsible alternatives. The National Community Reinvestment Coalition, or NCRC (ncrc.org and @ncrc), is the leadership network of community reinvestment act supporters focused on creating an inclusive, just economy. There are many more local efforts that you can locate through these national leaders.

The advocates work closely with networks in related fields. US SIF: The Forum for Sustainable and Responsible Investment (ussif.org and @us_sif) represents the socially responsible investing industry, and the Global Impact Investing Network, or GIIN (thegiin.org and @thegiin), represents the impact investing network. A young global network, the Global Alliance for Banking on Values (gabv.org and @bankingonvalues) is forming an important international effort. In the United States, the CDFI Coalition (cdfi .org and @cdficoalition) works on policy on behalf of the entire CDFI industry. For a summary of the CDFI industry and its role in policy, James Greer and Oscar Gonzalez wrote a useful analysis, *Community Economic Development in the United States: The CDFI Industry and America's Distressed Communities.*

There is also the business of philanthropy and its role in

capitalism. Two recent books give insight into the practice of charity and the directions it seems to be going. David Callahan's *The Givers: Money, Power, and Philanthropy in a New Gilded Age* focuses on the next generation of major philanthropists. *Winners Take All: The Elite Charade of Changing the World* by Anand Giridharadas argues that restoring democratic functions and processes is more important than the money that wealthy people decide to give selectively.

Finally, there is a set of resources waiting for you to tap them. You could do worse than to take this book in to your financial institutions, speak to the most senior person available, and ask them what you want to know about their politics, political giving, policies, board and senior management diversity, and efforts to create inclusive prosperity. Ask them about the things that are important to you.

At the end of the day, organized money is an organizing campaign to bring together $1 trillion in investments to support a progressive financial network. Successful organizing depends on people asking direct questions about the things that matter most to them. On our website (organizedmoney.org) we provide discussion guides, research ideas, and additional resources. We are looking to you and many others who share your progressive values to make the financial system work for you, not against you.

NOTES

Preface: The Problem

1. See, for example, Phillip Swagel, "The Cost of the Financial Crisis: The Impact of the September 2008 Economic Collapse," briefing paper 18, Pew Financial Reform Project, Pew Charitable Trusts, Washington, DC.

2. Barack Obama, "Comments at University of Nevada, Reno," October 25, 2008.

3. Obama, "Comments at Reno."

4. U.S. Congressional Oversight Panel, Special Report on Regulatory Reform, *Modernizing the American Financial Regulatory System: Recommendations for Improving Oversight, Protecting Consumers, and Ensuring Stability* (Washington, DC: U.S. Government Printing Office, February 2009).

5. "The *Wall Street Journal* Future of Finance Initiative," *Wall Street Journal*, March 30, 2009.

6. Heidi N. Moore, "WSJ's Future of Finance Initiative Gets Under Way," *Wall Street Journal*, March 23, 2009.

7. "Participants in the Future of Finance Initiative," *Wall Street Journal*, December 14, 2009.

8. Moore, "WSJ's Future of Finance Initiative Gets Under Way."

9. "*Wall Street Journal* Future of Finance Initiative."

10. "*Wall Street Journal* Future of Finance Initiative."

11. "*Wall Street Journal* Future of Finance Initiative."

12. Author's transcript of *Wall Street Journal* interview with Arthur Levitt during the Future of Finance Initiative.

13. "*Wall Street Journal* Future of Finance Initiative."

14. Joseph E. Stiglitz, "Obama's Ersatz Capitalism," Opinion, *New York Times*, March 31, 2009.

15. At https://www.grantspub.com.

16. James Grant, "The Best Financial Reform? Let the Bankers Fail," Commentary, *Washington Post*, April 23, 2010.

17. Grant, "Best Financial Reform?"

18. Nomi Prins, *All the Presidents' Bankers: The Hidden Alliances That Drive American Power* (New York: Nation Books, 2014).

19. "*Wall Street Journal* Future of Finance Initiative."

20. Robert Kuttner, "The Crash That Failed," *New York Review of Books*, November 22, 2018.

21. Kuttner, "Crash That Failed."

22. Alma Cohen, Moshe Hazan, Roberto Tallarita, and David Weiss, *The Politics of CEOs*, The Project on Corporate Political Spending of the Harvard Law School Program on Corporate Governance, March 2019.

1: You and Your Money

1. Dan Ariely and Jeff Kreisler, *Dollars and Sense: How We Misthink Money and How to Spend Smarter* (New York: Harper, 2017).

2. Thomas Philippon, *Why Has the U.S. Financial Sector Grown So Much? The Role of Corporate Finance*, New York University, National Bureau of Economic Research, and Centre for Economic Policy Research, July 2008.

3. Philippon.

4. Philippon.

5. Jason Zweig, "How Your Brokers Can Make 10 Times More on Your Cash than You Do," *Wall Street Journal*, August 3, 2018.

6. Zweig.

7. Louis D. Brandeis, *Other People's Money and How the Bankers Use It* (New York: Fredcrick A. Stokes, 1914).

8. Stan Choe, "Investing: You May Own Gun Stocks and Not Know It," *USA Today*, October 3, 2017; and Paul R. La Monica, "You May Own Gun Stocks and Not Know It," The Buzz, CNN Business, December 3, 2015. FactSet Research reported in 2015 that Vanguard, Fidelity, and BlackRock, which each have hundreds of mutual funds, are the top three shareholders of Smith & Wesson (SWHC), one of the nation's largest gunmakers.

2: Market Fundamentalism

1. Civil Rights Act of 1968, Pub.L. 90-284, 82 Stat. 73.

2. Consumer Credit Protection Act of 1968, Pub.L. 90-321, 82 Stat. 146.

3. Home Mortgage Disclosure Act of 1975, Pub.L. 94-200, 89 Stat. 1124.

4. Joe Nocera, *A Piece of the Action: How the Middle Class Joined the Money Class*, rev. ed. (New York: Simon & Schuster, 1994, 2013).

5. R. Alton Gilbert, *Requiem for Regulation Q: What It Did and Why It Passed Away*, Federal Reserve Bank of St. Louis, February 1986.

6. Nocera, *Piece of the Action*.

7. Prabal Chakrabarti et al., eds., *Revisiting the CRA: Perspectives on the Future of the Community Reinvestment Act*, Federal Reserve Banks of Boston and San Francisco, February 2009; and Devin Case-Ruchala, "A Next System of Community Investment: Community Reinvestment Act Reform in the 21st Century," Next System Project, Democracy Collaborative, October 31, 2018.

8. William J. Egan, "Merrill Lynch Takes on the Banks," *Washington Post*, July 3, 1977.

9. Riegle-Neal Interstate Banking and Branching Efficiency Act of 1994, Pub.L. 103-328, 108 Stat. 2338.

10. Gramm Leach Bliley Financial Services Modernization Act of 1999, Pub.L. 106-102, 113 Stat. 1338.

11. Dodd Frank Wall Street Reform and Consumer Protection Act, Pub.L. 111-203; and Michelle Price and Pete Schroeder, "After U.S. Dodd-Frank Law Changes, Lobbyists Fight for More, Reuters, May 23, 2018."

12. Luisa Kroll and Kerry A. Dolan, "*Forbes* 400," October 3, 2018. Left money arguably includes the wealth of Jeff Bezos (Amazon), Bill Gates (Microsoft), Warren Buffett (Berkshire Hathaway), Mark Zuckerberg (Facebook), and Michael Bloomberg (Bloomberg). Right money includes Larry Ellison (Oracle) and the Koch brothers, David and Charles. The two others in the top ten, Larry Page and Sergey Brin (Google), are harder to categorize.

13. Author interview with Corinne Florek, March 9, 2018.

14. Mehrsa Baradaran, *How the Other Half Banks: Exclusion, Exploitation, and the Threat to Democracy* (Cambridge, MA: Harvard University Press, 2015).

15. Baradaran.

16. Baradaran.

17. "10 Surprising Findings About the Gender Gap at Financial Institutions," *Women's World Banking*, July 11, 2016, https://www.womensworldbanking.org/insights-and-impact/10-surprising-findings-gender-gap-financial-institutions.

18. Melvin Backman, "The Worsening Problem with Finance Diversity Is About More than Headcounts," *The Atlantic*, January 6, 2016.

19. Backman.

20. Josh Lerner, "Diversifying Investments: A Study on Ownership Diversity and Performance in the Asset Management Industry," Knight Foundation, January 2019.

21. Karen Firestone, "When Will We See More Gender Equality in Investing," *Harvard Business Review*, March 25, 2019.

22. Jason Richardson et al., "Bank Branch Closures from 2008–2016: Unequal Impact in America's Heartland," research memo, National Community Reinvestment Coalition, Washington, DC.

23. Richardson.

24. Aaron Glantz and Emmanuel Martinez, "For People of Color, Banks Are Shutting the Door to Homeownership," Reveal News, Center for Investigative Reporting, Emeryville, CA, February 15, 2018.

25. Richard Rothstein, *The Color of Law: A Forgotten History of How Our Government Segregated America* (New York: Liveright, 2017).

26. Rothstein.

3: Missing the Opportunity

1. An Act to Provide for Reconciliation Pursuant to Titles II and V of the Concurrent Resolution on the Budget for Fiscal Year 2018 (Tax Cuts and Jobs Act), Pub.L. 115-97, 131 Stat. 2054.

2. "Opportunity Zones Resources," Community Development Financial Institutions Fund, U.S. Department of the Treasury; and "Opportunity Zones Frequently Asked Questions," Internal Revenue Service.

3. "Opportunity Zones," IRS FAQ.

4. Jim Tankersley, "Trump to Steer More Money to 'Opportunity Zones,'" *New York Times*, December 12, 2018.

5. Stephen Braun, Jeff Horwitz, and Bernard Condon, "Ivanka, Kushner Could Benefit from Opportunity Zones Tax Break They Pushed," Associated Press, December 12, 2018.

6. Jim Puzzanghera, "A Decade After the Financial Crisis, Many Americans Are Still Struggling to Recover," *Seattle Times*, September 11, 2018.

7. Ann Carrns, "'Opportunity Zones' Offer Tax Breaks and, Maybe, Help for Communities," *New York Times*, February 15, 2019.

8. Carrns.

9. Carrns.

10. "Final Tax Bill Could End Up Costing $2.2 Trillion," Committee for a Responsible Federal Budget, Washington, DC, December 18, 2017.

4: What Is Money Muscle?

1. Kevin Phillips, *Bad Money: Reckless Finance, Failed Politics, and the Global Crisis of American Capitalism* (New York: Viking, 2008).

2. Michael Greenstone and Adam Looney, "The Lasting Effects of the Great Recession: Six Million Missing Workers and a New Economic Normal," Brookings Institution, Washington, DC, September 12, 2013.

3. Bonnie Kavoussi, "Recession Killed 170,000 Small Businesses Between 2008 and 2010: Report," *Huffington Post*, July 25, 2012.

4. William R. Emmons, "The End Is in Sight for the U.S. Foreclosure Crisis," Federal Reserve Bank of St. Louis, 2016.

5. Phillip Swagel, "The Cost of the Financial Crisis: The Impact of the September 2008 Economic Collapse," briefing paper 18, Pew Financial Reform Project, Pew Charitable Trusts, Washington, DC.

6. Kai Ryssdal, "Panic, Fear and Regret," interview of Timothy Geithner, Ben Bernanke, and Henry Paulson, Marketplace, Minnesota Public Radio, Marketplace.Org.

7. Sarah Burd-Sharps and Rebecca Rasch, *Impact of the US Housing Crisis on the Racial Wealth Gap Across Generations* (New York: Social Science Research Council, June 2015).

8. Burd-Sharps and Rasch.

9. Robert I. Lerman and Sisi Zhang, *Coping with the Great Recession: Disparate Impacts on Economic Well-Being in Poor Neighborhoods*, report 6, Opportunity and Ownership Project, Urban Institute, Washington, DC, 2012.

10. "Top Organization Contributors," Center for Responsive Politics, https://www.opensecrets.org/orgs/list.php?cycle=2016. CRP counts as financial services three closely related fields: insurance, financial insti-

tutions, and real estate. Per its website: "Finance, Insurance, and Real Estate: Includes banks, insurance companies, securities and investment firms, the real estate industry, accountants, and a variety of other financial interests. As with past years, this sector ranks first in lobbying expenditures and campaign contributions." Many others also see the three as inseparable under the financial services banner.

11. "Top Organization Contributors."

12. "Top Organization Contributors."

13. Calculations by authors based on the Center for Responsive Politics Data Set.

14. Center for Responsive Politics Data Set.

15. Grace Haley and Karl Evers-Hillstrom, "State of Money in Politics: Female Donors Gaining Influence as 2020 Kicks Off," News, OpenSecrets.org, Center for Responsive Politics, Washington, DC, February 22, 2019.

16. Haley and Evers-Hillstrom.

17. "Dark Money Basics," OpenSecrets.org, Center for Responsive Politics, Washington, DC.

18. Sheldon Whitehouse, *Captured: The Corporate Infiltration of American Democracy* (New York: The New Press, 2017).

19. Whitehouse.

20. The combined lobbying budgets of the three organizations—apparently the largest counterforces to the financial services industry—is negligible. In part, that is because they are nonprofit organizations, which are permitted by law to spend no more than 20 percent of their budgets on lobbying. In addition, none of the three run political action committees or other political giving entities. If political giving is a competition, this one is a rout.

21. Glenn Thrush, "Mulvaney, Watchdog Bureau's Leader, Advises Bankers on Ways to Curtail Agency," *New York Times*, April 24, 2018.

22. Jim Tankersley, "Banks Are Big Winners from Tax Cut," *New York Times*, January 16, 2018.

23. Michael Rapoport, "The Biggest U.S. Banks Made $2.5 Billion from Tax Law—in One Quarter," *Wall Street Journal*, April 17, 2018.

24. Zoë Henry, "The Tax Bill Is Final: Here's What U.S. Businesses Need to Know," *Inc.*, December 20, 2017.

25. *Tables Related to the Federal Tax System as in Effect 2017 Through 2026*, Joint Committee on Taxation, U.S. Congress, April 23, 2018.

26. Naomi Jagoda, "Tax Committee Report: Much of Law's Pass-Through Benefit Goes to the Wealthy," *The Hill*, April 23, 2018.

27. Meg Wiehe et al., "Race, Wealth and Taxes: How the Tax Cuts and Jobs Act Supercharges the Racial Wealth Divide," Institute for Taxation and Economic Policy, Prosperity Now, October 2018.

28. Personal communication to Pinsky.

29. Greg Ip, "Did Greenspan Add to Subprime Woes?" *Wall Street Journal*, June 9, 2007.

30. "Quarterly Report on Household Debt and Credit, 2018: Q4," Center for Microeconomic Data, Federal Reserve Bank of New York, February 2019, newyorkfed.org/microeconomics.

31. "Transunion Industry Insights Report," Chicago, November 2018.

32. Dave Lieber, "Under Trump, Consumer Protection Grows So Weak You Won't Recognize It," *Dallas News*, February 2018, https://www.dallasnews.com/news/watchdog/2018/02/14/trump-consumer-protection-grows-weak-wont-recognize.

5: Progress in Mainstream Money

1. Norman Weiss, "Suggestion Book: Trendspotting with Norman," *Shuttle Online*, Weavers Way Coop, Philadelphia, PA, February 2018.

2. Jon Roesser, "GM's Corner: The Cooperative Revolution Is Overdue," *Shuttle Online*, Weavers Way Coop, Philadelphia, PA, August 2018.

3. "Quarterly Credit Union Data Summary 2018 Q3," National Credit Union Administration, Alexandria, VA, September 30, 2018.

4. "EasyPay Pays You More," Weavers Way Coop, Philadelphia, PA.

5. Conversation with Sontag.

6. Milton Friedman, *Capitalism and Freedom* (Chicago: University of Chicago Press, 1962).

7. Milton Friedman, "The Social Responsibility of Business Is to Increase Its Profits," *New York Times Magazine*, September 30, 1970; and Friedman, *Capitalism and Freedom*.

8. Milton Friedman and Rose Friedman, *Free to Choose: A Personal Statement* (New York: Harcourt Brace Jovanovich, 1980; New York: Mariner Books, 1990); and *Free to Choose: Ideas for Our Time*, 10-part series, Public Broadcasting System, 1980.

9. *Citizens United v. Federal Election Commission*, 558 U.S. 310 (2010). The U.S. Supreme Court has ruled that corporations *are* people for the purposes of making political contributions, holding that money is a form of speech and that limiting political giving would be a constraint on free speech.

10. Friedman allowed for the possibility that investor sentiment could change, but he might never have imagined that it actually would.

11. Jim Collins, *Good to Great: Why Some Companies Make the Leap . . . and Others Don't* (New York: HarperBusiness, 2011).

12. Lynn Stout, "Corporations Don't Have to Maximize Profits," *New York Times*, April 16, 2015.

13. Stout.

14. *Cone Communications/Echo Global CSR Study*, Cone Communications, Boston.

15. Tonia E. Ries et al., *2019 Edelman Trust Barometer Global Report*, Edelman Trust Management, New York.

16. Ries.

17. Sarah Fischer, "CEOs Under More Pressure to Save Society," *Axios*, January 21, 2019.

18. Steve Goldstein, "Here's the Staggering Amount Banks Have Been Fined Since the Financial Crisis," *MarketWatch*, February 24, 2018.

19. Hugh Son, "Bank of America Boosts CEO Brian Moynihan's Pay 15% to $26.5 Million After Record Profit Last Year," *Finance*, CNBC, February 8, 2019.

20. "Bank of America Announces Industry-Leading $125 Billion Environmental Business Initiative," press release, Bank of America, Charlotte, NC, July 27, 2015.

21. Sam Walker, "You're a CEO—Stop Talking like a Political Activist," *Wall Street Journal*, July 27, 2018.

22. Laurence D. Fink, "Larry Fink's Annual Letter to CEOs: A Sense of Purpose," BlackRock, New York, January 16, 2018.

23. Fink.

24. Interview of Joe Bower by Brian Kenny, "Why JPMorgan Chase Is Investing Millions in Detroit," Working Knowledge, Harvard Business School, April 26, 2018.

25. *Annual Report 2017 of J.P. Morgan AG*, JPMorgan, Frankfurt am Main, Germany."

26. Goldman Sachs, 10,000 Women, GoldmanSachs.com.

27. Goldman Sachs, 10,000 Small Businesses, GoldmanSachs.com.

28. In his role as chief executive officer of a CDFI industry organization, Pinsky informally advised on the design of 10,000 Small Businesses and served on the 10,000 Small Businesses Advisory Board. His organization received grant funding from the Goldman Sachs Foundation to implement and operate a program that was affiliated with 10,000 Small Businesses.

29. "How Do America's Banks Help Grow Communities?" American Bankers Association, grow.aba.com.

30. Based on Internal Revenue Support Form 990 tax filings for the banks' foundations.

31. Richard Eisenberg, "There's a Target on Charity's Booming Donor-Advised Funds," *Forbes*, August 2, 2018.

32. Eisenberg.

33. *Giving USA 2018: The Annual Report on Philanthropy for the Year 2017*, Giving USA, Chicago.

34. Greg Toppo, "What Did Zuckerberg's $100 Million Buy in Newark? A Bit of Progress," *USA Today*, October 16, 2017.

35. The Giving Pledge, GivingPledge.org.

36. Michael Knox Beran, "Lionel Trilling and the Social Imagination," *City Journal*, Winter 2011.

37. David Callahan, *The Givers: Wealth, Power, and Philanthropy in a New Gilded Age* (New York: Knopf, 2017).

38. Anand Giridharadas, *Winners Take All: The Elite Charade of Changing the World* (New York: Knopf, 2018).

39. Anand Giridharadas, "After the Financial Crisis, Wall Street Turned to Charity—and Avoided Justice, *New Yorker*, September 15, 2018."

40. Giridharadas, "After the Financial Crisis."

41. Rob Copeland, "Hedge Funds' Favorite Charity Is Funding Their Opponents," *Wall Street Journal*, May 14, 2018.

42. Conversation with Pinsky.

43. Rob Garver, "Bank Reputations Fall for First Time in Five Years: 2018 Survey," *American Banker*, June 28, 2018.

44. Garver.

45. *Report on US Sustainable, Responsible and Impact Investing Trends 2018*, US SIF, Washington, DC.

46. Nick O'Donohoe et al., "Impact Investments: An Emerging Asset Class," Global Impact Investing Network, New York, November 29, 2010.

47. Emma Disley, "Evaluating the World's First Social Impact Bond," RAND Corporation, Santa Monica, CA.

48. Abhilash Mudaliar, Rachel Bass, and Hannah Dithrich, *Annual Impact Investor Survey: 2018*, Global Impact Investing Network, New York, June 2018.

49. Anupreeta Das and Juliet Chung, "New Force on Wall Street: The 'Family Office,'" *Wall Street Journal*, March 10, 2017.

50. Vincent White et al., *World Ultra Wealth Report 2018*, Wealth-X, New York.

51. Community Development Financial Institutions Fund, U.S. Department of the Treasury, CDFIFund.gov.

52. Public statements of Bank of America executives Brian Moynihan and Dan Letendre.

6: The Public-Purpose Economy

1. Interview of Jay Coen Gilbert by Pinsky.

2. Descriptions of AND1 and B Lab are based on Pinsky interview with Jay Coen Gilbert, with some additional information from public sources.

3. Bcorporation.net.

4. Interview of Dan Osusky by Pinsky.

5. Interview of Dan Osusky.

6. See champions-retreat.bcorporation.net.

7. Material presented at the event and distributed after.

8. Anthea Kelsick, recording and transcription of remarks at B Lab 2018 Champions Retreat, New Orleans.

9. Kim Coupounas, recording and transcription of remarks at B Lab 2018 Champions Retreat, New Orleans.

10. "About B Lab," bcorporation.net/about-b-lab.

11. "State by State Status of Legislation," Benefit Corporation, benefitcorp.net/policymakers/state-by-state-status.

12. Rick Newman, "How Elizabeth Warren Wants to Remake Capitalism," Yahoo Finance, January 2, 2019.

7: Pumping Progressive Money Muscle

1. David Brooks, "The Remoralization of the Market: The Right Response to Economic Populism," *New York Times*, January 10, 2019.

2. Chuck Matthei, *Who We Are, What We've Learned, and Where We're Going* (Greenfield, MA: Institute for Community Economics, 1985).

3. Sara Bernow, Bruce Klempner, and Clarisse Magnin, "From 'Why' to 'Why Not': Sustainable Investing as the New Normal," McKinsey & Company.

4. Bernow et al.

5. Bruce J. Katz and Jeremy Nowak, *The New Localism: How Cities Can Thrive in the Age of Populism* (Washington, DC: Brookings Institution Press, 2018).

6. Katz and Nowak.

8: Progressive Finance in the United States

1. Ron Chernow, *Alexander Hamilton* (New York: Penguin, 2005).

2. Chernow.

3. Jerry W. Markham, *A Financial History of the United States: From Enron-Era Scandals to the Great Recession (2004–2009)* (Abingdon, UK: Routledge, 2011), 168.

4. Dan Rottenberg, *The Man Who Made Wall Street: Anthony J. Drexel and the Rise of Modern Finance*, rev. ed. (Philadelphia: University of Pennsylvania Press, 2006).

5. "The Freedman's Savings Bank," FreedmansBank.org

6. Eric Foner, *Reconstruction: America's Unfinished Revolution, 1863–1877*, rev. ed. (New York: Harper Perennial, 2014).

7. Foner.

8. An *Act to Provide Increased Revenue from Imports, 37th Congress, Session 1, Chapter 45, August 5, 1861, 12 Stat. 292.*

9. Foner, *Reconstruction.*

10. "The Freedman's Savings Bank"; and David W. Blight, *Frederick Douglass: Prophet of Freedom* (New York: Simon & Schuster, 2018).

11. Blight.

12. Blight.

13. Blight.

14. "History," National Bankers Association, www.nationalbankers
.org/history.htm.

15. Carver Federal Savings Bank, www.carverbank.com.

16. Native American Bank, www.nabna.com.

17. "FDIC Definition of Minority Depository Institution," Minority
Depository Institutions Program, Federal Deposit Insurance Corporation, www.fdic.gov/regulations/resources/minority/mdi-definition.html.

18. "Quarterly Credit Union Data Summary 2018 Q3," National
Credit Union Administration, Alexandria, VA, September 30, 2018.

19. "Quarterly Credit Union Data Summary."

20. "Low-Income Designation," National Credit Union Administration,   www.ncua.gov/support-services/credit-union-resources-expan
sion/field-membership-expansion/low-income-designation.

21. "Low-Income Designation."

22. "Quarterly Credit Union Data Summary."

23. "Our History," World Council of Credit Unions, www.woccu.org
/about/history.

24. "Our History."

25. Edward Filene, *Speaking of Change: A Selection of Speeches and
Articles* (New York: Published by former Associates of Edward A.
Filene, Collection of the Prelinger Libaary, 1939), 159.

26. "Historical Timeline," National Credit Union Administration,
www.ncua.gov/about-ncua/historical-timeline.

27. National Credit Union Administration, NCUA.gov.

28. Arthur H. Ham, "Remedial Loans—a Constructive Program,"
*Proceedings of the Academy of Political Science in the City of New
York* 2, no. 2, Business and Public Welfare (January 1912): 109–17,
www.jstor.org/stable/1171943.

29. The specifics changed, but ninety years later opponents of predatory lending would again make the same arguments, raise the same
objections, and feel the same frustration about predatory lenders and

their money muscle. Again in the 1990s and 2000s, advocacy efforts targeted predatory lenders. One result was creation of the Consumer Financial Protection Bureau in 2010, ninety-eight years after Ham spoke up.

30. Ham, "Remedial Loans."

31. Erik Forman, "How Unions Can Solve the Housing Crisis," *In These Times*, September 23–October 2018.

32. Forman.

33. Labor Management Relations Act of 1947 (Taft–Hartley Act), 29 U.S.C. §141–97, 80 H.R. 3020, Pub.L. 80–101, 61 Stat. 136, June 23, 1947.

34. "Banking Information," American Bankers Association, www .aba.com/Tools/Economic/Documents/NumberofInstitutionsMer gersandCharters.pdf

35. Alabama, Kentucky, Illinois, Vermont, Georgia, Tennessee, and South Carolina. See Jerry W. Markham, *A Financial History of the United States: From Enron-Era Scandals to the Great Recession (2004–2009)* (Abingdon, UK: Routledge, 2011), 168–80.

36. Missouri, Indiana, and Virginia. Markham, *A Financial History*, 168–80.

37. Pat Garofalo, "How Banks Slid into the Payday Lending Business," TalkPoverty.org, October 18, 2018.

9: The Foundation of a Progressive Finance Network

1. Chuck Matthei, *Who We Are, What We've Learned, and Where We're Going* (Greenfield, MA: Institute for Community Economics, 1985).

2. Melvin Oliver and Thomas M. Shapiro, *Black Wealth/White Wealth*, rev. ed. (Abingdon, UK: Routledge, 2006).

3. Community Reinvestment Act, 91 Stat. 1111, October 12, 1977.

4. Community Reinvestment Act.

5. Josh Silver, "Increasing Community Development Financing

Data a Necessaary Componenet for CRA Reform," NCRC, March 25, 2019, https://ncrc.org/increasing-community-development-financing -data-a-necessary-component-for-cra-reform.

6. CDFI Fund "certification" is a statutory-mandated process of determining that a CDFI's primary purpose is community develop-ment, broadly defined, and that it is principally a financial institution. CDFIs provide supplementary technical assistance and other services to their customers, and to qualify as a CDFI an applicant must dem-onstrate that financing is its primary function. Riegle Community Development and Regulatory Improvement Act of 1994, 12 U.S.C. 4719, Pub.L. 111-203, 124 Stat. 2131.

7. Community Development Financial Institutions Fund, U.S. Department of the Treasury, CDFIFund.gov.

8. Riegle Community Development and Regulatory Improvement Act of 1994, 12 U.S.C. 4719, Pub.L. 111-203, 124 Stat. 2131.

9. Community Reinvestment Act, Pub.L. 95-128, 91 Stat. 1147, title VIII of the Housing and Community Development Act of 1977, *12 U.S.C. $2901* et seq.

10. Jamie Dimon, personal communication to Pinsky.

11. Pinsky was involved in this in his role as CEO of a CDFI industry organization.

12. Co-author Pinsky served on the advisory groups at Bank of America, Goldman Sachs, and Morgan Stanley, as well as advisory boards at Wells Fargo. Co-author Mestrich was included in a gather-ing of key institutions at JPMorgan Chase.

10: Whose Wealth Is It Anyway?

1. Matt Wirz, "Social Investing Has New Message: Bond Managers See It as a Crucial Ingredient of Risk Management," *Wall Street Jour-nal*, June 19, 2018.

2. Rainforest Action Network et al., "Banking on Climate Change:

Fossil Fuel Finance Report Card 2019," March 2019, www.ran.org
/bankingonclimatechange2019.

11: Organizing Progressive Money for Power and Influence

1. Anupreeta Das and Juliet Chung, "New Force on Wall Street:
The 'Family Office,'" *Wall Street Journal*, March 10, 2017. The rapid
increase over the last ten years in the number of family offices and in
the total assets under their management is stressing financial institutions, which are ceding significant control to the family offices, as
well as users of capital, borrowers and investees who are seeing new
and unfamiliar names and approaches in the money marketplace. "For
clans with at least $250 million in assets to invest, family offices have
become the preferred vehicle through which to put their money to
work, because they afford complete control and near-secrecy," Das and
Chung reported in the *Wall Street Journal* in 2017. Family offices are
taking fees away from conventional money organizers. They operate
with lower costs because they are unregulated, and they are invisible
to the markets because they are intensely private. Because they are run
to serve family interests, they tend to be aligned with the family's values. How much money flows through family offices? Jim Burns, of the
investment firm KKR, told the *Journal* that it's an "ocean of wealth." It
could be hundreds of billions of dollars, but that would be a relatively
small ocean. Trillions? Maybe.

2. "Adding Value in an Era of Uncertainty: Divergence in Current
and Future Millionaire Sentiment Accentuates the Importance of
Having an Advisor," Fidelity Investments.

3. Abby Schultz, "Calvert Community Investment Notes: Doing
Good, While Getting a Bond-like Return," *Barron's*, December 2,
2016.

4. Amalgamated Bank IPO, Renaissance Capital, www.renaissan
cecapital.com/Profile/AMAL/Amalgamated-Bank/IPO.

5. Martin Paul Trimble, conversation with Pinsky.

6. Quoted in multiple forms and locations, including Rich Karlgaard, "Capital Goes Where It's Welcome," *Forbes*, May 18, 2009.

7. Jeremy Rifkin and Randy Barber, *The North Will Rise Again: Pension, Politics, and Power in the 1980s* (Boston: Beacon Press, 1978).

8. Rifkin and Barber, 12.

Conclusion

1. Michael Lewis, ed., *The Real Price of Everything: Rediscovering the Six Classics of Economics* (New York: Sterling, 2008).

2. Interview with CNN Business, March 18, 2019, https://www.cnn.com/videos/business/2019/03/18/jamie-dimon-jpmorgan-chase-economy-opioids-orig.cnn-business.

3. Kevin Phillips, *Bad Money* (New York: Viking Penguin, 2008), xiii.

4. Philippon, *Why Has the U.S. Financial Sector Grown So Much?*

INDEX

ABOUT THE AUTHORS

Keith Mestrich is the president and CEO of Amalgamated Bank (AMAL), the nation's leading socially responsible bank. With twenty-five years of experience working in the labor movement and nonprofit organizations, Keith is a leader in the effort to build wealth for a purpose, not just for a profit.

Mark A. Pinsky led the $150 billion community development financial institution (CDFI) industry from 1995 to 2016. With a track record of aligning capital with social, economic, environmental, and political justice, he was the strategic leader for the industry's growth from $2 billion to $140 billion. He is the author and editor of several books and speaks regularly on finance and society. He lives in Philadelphia where he runs Five/Four Advisors, a strategic advisory firm.

PUBLISHING IN THE PUBLIC INTEREST

Thank you for reading this book published by The New Press. The New Press is a nonprofit, public interest publisher. New Press books and authors play a crucial role in sparking conversations about the key political and social issues of our day.

We hope you enjoyed this book and that you will stay in touch with The New Press. Here are a few ways to stay up to date with our books, events, and the issues we cover:

- Sign up at www.thenewpress.com/subscribe to receive updates on New Press authors and issues and to be notified about local events.
- Like us on Facebook: www.facebook.com/newpressbooks.
- Follow us on Twitter: www.twitter.com/thenewpress.

Please consider buying New Press books for yourself; for friends and family; or to donate to schools, libraries, community centers, prison libraries, and other organizations involved with the issues our authors write about.

The New Press is a 501(c)(3) nonprofit organization. You can also support our work with a tax-deductible gift by visiting www.thenewpress.com/donate.